Business School Edition

TOTAL GLOBAL STRATEGY
Managing for Worldwide Competitive Advantage

GEORGE S. YIP

John E. Anderson Graduate
School of Management
University of California, Los Angeles

Prentice Hall, Englewood Cliffs, New Jersey 07632

Library of Congress Cataloging-in-Publication Data

Yip, George S.
   Total global strategy : managing for worldwide competitive
advantage / George S. Yip—Business school ed.
      p.   cm.
   Includes bibliographical references and index.
   ISBN 0–13–124488–4
   1. International business enterprises—Management.   2. Strategic
planning.   I. Title.
HD62.5.Y56   1995
658'.049—dc20   94–17656
                                                               CIP

Acquisitions editor: Natalie Anderson
Editorial assistant: Nancy Proyect
Editorial/production supervision
   and interior design: Linda B. Pawelchak
Cover design: Tom Nery
Production coordinators: Herb Klein/
   Patrice Fraccio

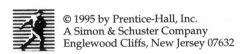 © 1995 by Prentice-Hall, Inc.
A Simon & Schuster Company
Englewood Cliffs, New Jersey 07632

Printed in the United States of America
10 9 8 7 6 5 4 3 2 1

ISBN 0-13-124488-4

Prentice-Hall International (UK) Limited, *London*
Prentice-Hall of Australia Pty. Limited, *Sydney*
Prentice-Hall Canada Inc., *Toronto*
Prentice-Hall Hispanoamericana, S.A., *Mexico*
Prentice-Hall of India Private Limited, *New Delhi*
Prentice-Hall of Japan, Inc., *Tokyo*
Simon & Schuster Asia Pte. Ltd., *Singapore*
Editora Prentice-Hall do Brasil, Ltda., *Rio de Janeiro*

To Andrew and Sarah

Contents

Chapter 6
Creating Global Marketing   123

Chapter 7
Making Global Competitive Moves   150

Chapter 8
Building the Global Organization   161

List of Exhibits

Companies Named in This Book

Preface

This book argues that most multinational companies lack an adequate global strategy. These firms may have learned how to operate in foreign countries by adapting their core business strategy to international environments. But the rapid changes creating more open world markets are rendering that approach inadequate and increasingly obsolete. Companies now need a total global strategy that includes a globalization component. Such a globalization strategy seeks to manage multinational businesses on an integrated, worldwide basis, not as a loosely knit federation of subsidiaries. But the extent of integration needed varies by industry and company situation. A central theme of this book is that almost all industries have global potential in some aspects and not others. So this book provides a systematic framework for evaluating which elements of strategy to globalize and by how much. I do not advocate any one solution, but instead a methodology for arriving at the right solution for a particular company or business. Perhaps most important, this book provides a practical guide on *how* to implement a globalization strategy in order to achieve a successful, total global strategy.

WHO SHOULD READ THIS BOOK

I have written this book for several types of managers (and aspiring managers) as well as for those who teach, study, and research global strategy.

Worldwide Business Managers

This book is addressed first to the manager responsible for the performance of a worldwide business. This responsibility may not be direct, and there may not be a single executive with worldwide responsibility. One of the topics of this book is how to organize that responsibility. Addressed to the worldwide business head, this book is also relevant for those to whom he or she reports and for those who report to or work with him or her.

Corporate Managers

The corporate-level executive will find this book helpful in dealing with the business-level executives who run worldwide businesses, and in understanding what corporate/management can expect and should provide. But because of its focus on businesses this book does not address corporate-level global issues such as raising financing on a global scale or setting corporate objectives in relation to global societal considerations. The book touches on, but does not emphasize, the role of the corporate chief executive in global strategy.[1]

National Managers

The manager in a single country will find this book helpful in better understanding the role of his or her business in the global strategy of the worldwide business. In some ways, this is a book that a national manager will not want to read, but should. The book concerns the new trend that is curtailing the autonomy of national managers. These managers will find that the reduction in autonomy will be greater and more painful without an understanding of its global strategic imperatives. (This book does not cover how to develop a business in a foreign country or how to be a manager of a foreign subsidiary. Many other books exist on those topics.[2])

Managers in Domestic Companies or Businesses

Today very few industries are free from foreign competition or the threat of it. Even when competitors are not foreign, they are often subsidiaries of multinational companies, and their local strategies can be affected by their parents' global strategies. So managers of purely domestic companies or businesses will find it worthwhile to understand the global forces and competitive developments that may come to affect their own prospects.

Suppliers to Multinational Companies

Because a major theme of this book concerns where multinational companies should locate their activities and where they should source their supplies, this book is also highly relevant to managers of their suppliers. Multinational suppliers to multinational companies need to learn how to deal with the new breed of "global customers." And purely local suppliers need to understand the new global strategy also. A local supplier to a local subsidiary of a multinational company can find that its business dries up quickly when the customer's parent company switches to a global sourcing strategy.

Educators of Future Managers

Educators should find useful this book's systematic integration of many ideas on global strategy. The explicit framework of this book readily lends itself to both classroom exposition and support of case discussions. *Total Global Strategy* can be assigned as a supplementary text in courses on international management or as the prime text in conjunction with the type of casebooks that are beginning to be written on the topic of global strategic management.[3] This business school edition includes assignment questions at the end of each chapter and is accompanied by a teacher's manual.

Researchers

The framework presented in this book might be characterized as taking a *contingent and continuum* approach to global strategy. The contingent approach of this book builds on the pioneering work of Michael E. Porter on the role of industry conditions.[4] The main ways in which this book differs from Porter's work is that, first, I spell out in detail the interaction between industry globalization drivers and the appropriate global strategy response, and second, I devote great attention to the implementation of global strategy, an issue largely unexplored by Porter and others. This book also differs from the excellent work of Kenichi Ohmae by providing a more systematic framework to the analysis of global strategy. Compared with the insightful works of Christopher A. Bartlett and Sumantra Ghoshal[5] and C. K. Prahalad and Yves L. Doz,[6] I place much more stress on business-level as opposed to corporate-level global strategy.

RESEARCH, CONSULTING, AND TEACHING BASE
OF THIS BOOK

This book is based on extensive research, consulting, and teaching about global strategy, mostly concentrated over the last five years, as well as on my broader business experience of having worked for ten years in a variety of multinational companies and their service providers.

From 1989 to 1991 I conducted studies of the use of global strategy by American, European, and Japanese companies, sponsored by the Marketing Science Institute.[7] These studies involved my personally visiting the head offices of twenty-three of the world's largest multinational companies and interviewing over fifty senior executives at these companies about the global strategies of over thirty of their worldwide businesses. In total I studied eighteen worldwide businesses belonging to U.S. companies (including Armstrong World Industries, Bausch & Lomb, Citicorp, Chrysler, Colgate-

Palmolive, Eastman Kodak, E. I. du Pont de Nemours, Honeywell, IBM, and McDonnell Douglas); six worldwide businesses belonging to European companies (including Beecham, Nestlé, Royal Dutch/Shell, Thomas Cook, and Volkswagen), and seven worldwide businesses belonging to major Japanese multinational companies. The interviews covered each of the elements in my framework: industry globalization drivers, global strategy levers, and global organization. So the interviews provided mini–case histories of how different businesses rated globalization forces in their industries, how they responded to these forces in terms of the use of global strategy, and how they were organized and managed in regard to being able to implement global strategy. I have included findings from these studies throughout the book, although for reasons of confidentiality, I have not identified individual companies. I have already reported the results of the study on the American companies in a Marketing Science Institute report.[8]

I was also able to test most of the concepts and measures in this book in working with member companies of the Profit Impact of Market Strategy (PIMS) Program from 1987 to 1989.[9] This effort involved extensive, in-depth data collection and analysis, working with a large team of senior executives in each of four worldwide and two Europewide businesses. In each case I was involved with the business for about six months. This work was in the context of a pilot study for setting up a PIMS global strategy program. Working with the Strategic Planning Institute (SPI), I developed a global strategy questionnaire from my frameworks. This questionnaire was structured to collect matching information from the six to eight largest country-subsidiaries in a given multinational business, as well as information about the worldwide business, its markets, and its competitors. Because this was a pilot study and because of a desire to preserve confidentiality, I have not reported any data from these studies. But the insights I learned are used in many parts of this book.

I have consulted to over a dozen major multinational companies in the United States and Europe on issues of global strategy and global organization during the last five years. This consulting experience has greatly helped me to develop and test my ideas. I have also used the frameworks and ideas in this book in several executive education programs both in individual companies (in the United States, Mexico, Europe, and the Pacific Rim) and in programs offered by Georgetown and UCLA. Last, I have tested the concepts with nine sections of three classes of MBA students at Georgetown University.

ACKNOWLEDGMENTS

Many people and organizations have helped me with the development of this book. I first began work on the topic of global strategy in collaborating with Mike Yoshino of Harvard Business School and Pierre Loewe of The

MAC Group. MAC's development budget, directed by Larry Bennigson, supported my early work. The Marketing Science Institute (MSI) has been very generous in supporting my interview studies in the United States, Japan, and Europe, as well as in providing access to its member companies. I am particularly grateful to George Day, Paul Root, and Katherine Jocz at MSI. The Strategic Planning Institute has also been very helpful in setting up the pilot PIMS global strategy program. Of the many SPI and PIMSA staff who helped me I particularly wish to thank Brad Gale as well as Bill Jones, Brian Keidan, Bob Luchs, Keith Roberts, Joel Rosenfeld, Catherine Roy, Don Swire, and Marinus Zyta. Koji Tsubaki of Waseda University has been very generous in both getting me access to Japanese companies as well as helping me at many of the interviews. Bob Fulmer of Columbia University and The College of William and Mary has made it possible for me to test my ideas in executive education programs, as have José de la Torre and Victor Tabbush at UCLA and Wayne Cartwright of the University of Auckland.

But it is to the School of Business Administration at Georgetown University that I owe the greatest thanks, and particularly to Dean Robert Parker and Associate Dean Robert Thomas for their encouragement and support almost from the day I first conceived of this book. Georgetown gave me an intellectual home as I conducted the research for this book and wrote it, as well as financial and research support. Georgetown's commitment to global business provided a very fruitful environment for my efforts. My new home, UCLA's Anderson Graduate School of Management, has supported me in the creation of this business school edition of *Total Global Strategy*.

Many other colleagues have given generously of their time and thinking in helping me develop my ideas and in reading my manuscripts. These include Johny Johansson, Bob Thomas, and Elizabeth Cooper-Martin of Georgetown; Bob Buzzell and John Quelch of Harvard Business School; Ruth Raubitschek of New York University; Charles Baden Fuller of London Business School and the University of Bath; Carol Franko of Harvard Business School Press; George Cressman of DuPont; Will Rodgers of Hamilton Consultants; and Bruce Orr and John Campbell of Union Carbide. Three reviewers provided by Prentice Hall have been very helpful: Alan Cody of Arthur D. Little, Ed Davis of the University of Virginia, and Allen Morrison of the University of Western Ontario. I greatly appreciate their thorough and frank suggestions. I am also grateful to my editors at Prentice Hall— John Willig, Phil Ruppel, Drew Dreeland, and Eve Mossman—for their encouragement, ideas, and support for the 1992 professional edition of this book; and to Natalie Anderson and Frank Lyman for their support of this business school edition.

I wish to thank also all those executives who gave generously of their time for my research. This kind of work would not be possible without the cooperation of companies.

Many research assistants at Georgetown helped me. These include Tapan Bhat, Rodanthe Hanrahan, George Coundouriotis, Manoj Varma, Niels Nielsen, Steve Pearson, Jeff Lander, and David Williams. Lan Nguyen has skillfully and patiently produced the many exhibits in this book. I must also thank the MBA students in my Global Environment of Business course at Georgetown for their enthusiasm and application in working with my concepts and frameworks and also Tom Brewer, with whom I shared the course, for his cooperation.

Last, but most important, I thank my wife Moira and my children, Andrew and Sarah, for their patience, understanding, and forbearance while I was away on my many trips or hidden away in my study.

Center Lovell, Maine,   GEORGE S. YIP
and Santa Ana, California

NOTES

1. For a book focusing on the role of the corporate chief executive in global strategy, see C. K. Prahalad and Yves L. Doz, *The Multinational Mission: Balancing Local Demands and Global Vision* (New York: The Free Press, 1987).

2. See Michael Czinkota, Pietra Rivoli, and Ilkka Ronkainen, *International Business* (Chicago: The Dryden Press, 1989), and Franklin R. Root, *Entry Strategies for International Markets* (Lexington, Mass.: D. C. Heath, 1987), for how to develop a business in a foreign country; and Roderick E. White and Thomas A. Poynter, "Strategies for Foreign-Owned Subsidiaries in Canada," *Business Quarterly*, Summer 1984, pp. 59–69, for the role of international subsidiary managers.

3. See, for example, William H. Davidson and José de la Torre, *Managing the Global Corporation: Case Studies in Strategy and Management* (New York: McGraw-Hill, 1989), and Paul W. Beamish, J. Peter Killing, Donald J. Lecraw, and Harold Crookell, *International Management: Text and Cases* (Homewood, Ill.: Richard D. Irwin, 1991).

4. See Michael E. Porter, "Competition in Global Industries: A Conceptual Framework," in *Competition in Global Industries*, ed. Michael E. Porter (Boston: Harvard Business School Press, 1986), and Michael E. Porter, "Changing Patterns of International Competition," *California Management Review*, Vol. 28, No. 2, Winter 1986, pp. 9–40.

5. Christopher A. Bartlett and Sumantra Ghoshal, *Managing Across Borders: The Transnational Solution* (Boston: Harvard Business School Press, 1989).

6. Prahalad and Doz, *The Multinational Mission*.

7. There have been few studies that actually measure the use of global strategy. Two exceptions are Kendall Roth and Allen J. Morrison, "An Empirical Analysis of the Integration-Responsiveness Framework in Global Industries," *Journal of International Vol. 21, No. 4, Fourth Quarter Business Studies*, 1990, pp. 541–564; and Allen J. Morrison, *Strategies in Global Industries: How U.S. Businesses Compete* (Westport, Conn.: Quorum Books, 1990).

8. See George S. Yip, "Do American Businesses Use Global Strategy?" Working Paper No. 91-101 (Cambridge, Mass.: Marketing Science Institute).

9. The PIMS program of the Strategic Planning Institute is a long-established project by which companies share strategic information. A very large number of research studies have been conducted on the PIMS data bases over the last twenty years. But although PIMS data come from a large number of countries, primarily in North America and in Europe, the data are essentially domestic in nature with no international variables. Furthermore, relationships among subsidiaries in different countries are not identified. See Robert D. Buzzell, and Bradley T. Gale, *The PIMS Principles: Linking Strategy to Performance* (New York: The Free Press, 1987), for a description of the PIMS program, its findings, and a list of published studies using the PIMS data.

About the Author

George S. Yip teaches business strategy and international marketing at the Anderson Graduate School of Management, University of California, Los Angeles, and also taught for seven years at Harvard Business School and Georgetown University. He has been selected by both faculty and students for best teacher awards. Dr. Yip consults and lectures for companies around the world. He also worked for ten years in management positions with major multinational companies and consulting firms. He is the author of *Barriers to Entry* and of articles in the *Columbia Journal of World Business, Harvard Business Review, International Marketing Review, Sloan Management Review*, and *Strategic Management Journal*. He holds B.A. and M.A. degrees in economics from Cambridge University, a master's degree from the Cranfield School of Management, and an M.B.A. and doctorate from Harvard Business School.

Chapter 1

Understanding Global Strategy

Turning a collection of country-businesses into one worldwide business that has an integrated, global strategy presents one of the stiffest challenges for managers today. Because of its difficulties, being able to develop and implement an effective global strategy is the acid test of a well-managed company. Many forces are driving companies around the world to globalize—in the sense of expanding their participation in foreign markets. Companies also need to globalize in another sense—that is, integrating their worldwide strategy. This global integration contrasts with the multinational approach in which companies set up country subsidiaries that design, produce, and market products or services tailored to local needs. This multinational model is now in question and may be considered a "multilocal strategy" in contrast to a truly global strategy.[1]

Many managers are asking if they are in a global industry and whether their business should have a global strategy. The better questions to ask are: How global is their industry and how global should their business strategy be? This is because virtually every industry has aspects that are global or potentially global— some industries have more aspects that are global and more intensely so. Similarly, a strategy can be more or less global in its different elements. An industry is global to the extent that there are intercountry connections. A strategy is global to the extent that it is integrated across countries. Global

1

strategy should not be equated with any one element—standardized products or worldwide market coverage or a global manufacturing network. Global strategy should, instead, be a flexible combination of many elements.

Recent and coming changes make it more likely that in many industries, a global strategy will be more successful than a multilocal one. Indeed, having a sound global strategy may well be the requirement for survival as the changes accelerate. These changes include the growing similarity among countries in what their citizens want to buy, a point argued forcefully by both Theodore Levitt of the Harvard Business School and Kenichi Ohmae of McKinsey & Company.[2] Other changes are the reduction of tariff and nontariff barriers, technology investments that are becoming too expensive to amortize in one market only, and competitors who are changing the nature of rivalry from country-by-country competition to global competition.

Trade barriers are also falling: The 1987 Canada–United States Free Trade Agreement, the North American Free Trade Agreement between the United States, Canada, and Mexico, and the continuing integration of the European Union provide some of the most dramatic examples. Under pressure from its Western trading partners, Japan is also gradually opening up its long barricaded markets. Maturity in domestic markets is driving companies to seek international expansion. This is particularly true for American companies that, nourished by a huge domestic market, have typically lagged behind their European and Japanese rivals in internationalization. The recent surge of foreign acquisitions in the United States has further globalized the nature of competition in many industries. Between 1977 and 1986 the share of U.S. manufacturing assets owned by foreign companies doubled from 6% to 12% and has continued to rise.[3] Increased volatility in exchange rates has helped to spur cycles of acquisitions as companies in countries and temporarily high exchange rates buy assets in countries with temporarily low rates.[4] The rise of the NICs (newly industrializing countries like Hong Kong, Taiwan, South Korea, Singapore, Thailand, Malaysia, Mexico, and Brazil) has also increased the number of viable sites for sophisticated manufacturing operations with low labor costs. Even China and India are beginning to join the industrialized world and the global market economy.

Almost every product or service market in the major world economies has foreign competitors—computers, fast food, medical diagnostic equipment—a nearly endless list that is growing rapidly. Increasing foreign competition is in itself a reason for a business to globalize—in order to gain the size and skills to compete more effectively. But an even greater spur to globalization is the advent of new global competitors who manage and compete on an integrated global basis. *These global competitors have been primarily Japanese!* Their central approach to global competition is one of the factors that has allowed Japanese companies to conquer so many Western markets.[5] While this is not a book about Japanese management, it contains many examples of Japanese successes via the use of global strategy.[6] Indeed, these examples suggest that the use of the kinds of global strategy described in this book has been one of the causes of Japanese companies' success over the last twenty years.

In addition, the communications and information revolution has made it much easier to manage in a globally integrated fashion. Improve-

---

Black & Decker's Switch to Global Strategy[7]

Black & Decker, a $5 billion (in 1990) U.S.-based manufacturer of hand tools, provides an example of a company that switched to a global strategy. In the 1980s, Black & Decker was threatened by external and internal pressures. Externally, it faced a powerful Japanese competitor, Makita. Makita's strategy to produce and market globally standardized products worldwide made it a low-cost producer and enabled it to steadily increase its share in the world market. Internally, Black & Decker's international fiefdoms combined with nationalist chauvinism to stifle coordination in product development and new product introductions, resulting in loss of opportunities.

Responding to increasing competitive pressures, Black & Decker decisively moved toward globalization. It embarked on a major program to coordinate new product development worldwide in order to develop core standardized products that could be marketed globally with minimal modification. The streamlining in R&D also offered scale economies and less duplication of effort—and new products could be introduced more quickly. The company also strategically emphasized design and has become a leader in design management. It consolidated worldwide advertising by using two principal agencies, giving Black & Decker a more consistent image worldwide. Black & Decker also strengthened the functional organization by giving functional managers a larger role in coordinating with country management. Last, Black & Decker purchased General Electric's small appliance business to achieve world-scale economies in manufacturing, distribution, and marketing.

The globalization strategy initially faced skepticism and resistance from country management. The chief executive officer took a visible leadership role and made some management changes to start the company moving toward globalization. These changes in strategy helped Black & Decker increase revenues by almost 30% between 1986 and 1990.

ments in air travel, computers, satellites, and telecommunications also make it easier to communicate with, and control, far-flung operations. The facsimile machine has made one of the most dramatic changes. Its immediacy and completeness of communication have plugged the globe into every executive's desk.

KEYS TO A SUCCESSFUL TOTAL GLOBAL STRATEGY

A total global strategy has three separate components, depicted in Exhibit 1–1:

1. *Developing the core strategy,* which is the basis of sustainable strategic advantage. This is usually, but not necessarily, done for the home country first. Without a sound core strategy on which to build, a worldwide business need not bother about global strategy.
2. *Internationalizing the core strategy,* through international expansion of activities and adaptation of the core strategy. Companies need to have mastered the basics of international business before they can attempt a global strategy (because the latter often involves breaking the rules of international business).
3. *Globalizing the international strategy,* by integrating the strategy across countries.

Multinational companies know the first two steps well. What they know less well is the third step. In addition, globalization runs counter to the accepted wisdom of tailoring for national markets.[8] *This book focuses on the third step in building a total global strategy: global integration.*

EXHIBIT 1–1   Total Global Strategy

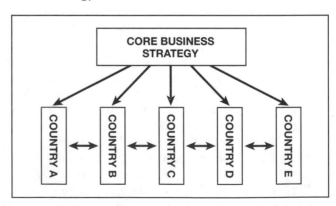

1. Develop Core
   Business Strategy

2. Internationalize
   the Strategy

3. Globalize
   the Strategy

Source: Adapted from Yip (1989).

Developing a Core Business Strategy

Each separable business in a company needs its own core strategy.[9] Defining the business in the first place can be a major task. Major parameters of the definition include the types of customers served and the types of products and services offered. The type of product or service can be split into two separate dimensions—the type of need met and the type of technology used to meet that need.[10] For example, one business may be in the total packaging business, while another may define its business more narrowly as the plastics packaging business.

A core business strategy includes several key elements:

- Type of products or services that the business offers
- Types of customers that the business serves
- Geographic markets served
- Major sources of sustainable competitive advantage
- Functional strategy for each of the most important value-adding activities
- Competitive posture, including the selection of competitors to target
- Investment strategy

Strategy writers have sometimes urged the broadest possible definition of a business and criticize managers who restrictively define their business. But the breadth or narrowness of a business definition is a key element of strategic choice and directly affects sustainable strategic advantage. It is better to devote limited resources to sustaining advantage in a narrowly defined business than to overspread resources so that no advantage is sustained. In recent years the more prominent failures have come from too expansive a business definition. People Express, at one time a highly successful airline in the United States, collapsed when it expanded beyond its East Coast cup-price niche. Saatchi & Saatchi, once the world's largest advertising agency group, had to reverse its expansion into the consulting business. The company had expected, wrongly, to conquer this new business as rapidly as it had conquered its traditional business.

Developing an Internationalization Strategy

When a business expands outside its home market, it needs to internationalize its core business strategy. The first and most important step in internationalizing the core business strategy is to select the geographic markets in which to compete. This choice has much more importance for an international business than for a national business. In the early part of its life, a national business does face issues of geographic market selection as it expands within its domestic market. These issues include identifying market attractiveness, potential competition and ways in which to adapt to local conditions, and ways in which to manage the business across a larger geographic area. For some retail or service businesses, geographic market selection continues to be vital because of the importance of site location. But for most businesses international market selection presents issues that are much more challenging than selection within a domestic market. The sources of this challenge include the role of barriers to trade, such as import tariffs and quotas and foreign ownership rules, as well as differences from the home country in laws, language, tastes, and behavior.[11] Other aspects of internationalization strategy involve how to adapt products and programs to take account of foreign needs, preferences, culture, language, climate, and so on. *But the end result is typically that the company winds up with strategies and approaches that have large differences among countries.* These differences can then weaken the company's worldwide cost position, quality, customer preference, and competitive leverage.

Developing a Globalization Strategy

To overcome the disadvantages created by internationalization, companies need a globalization strategy that integrates and manages for worldwide business leverage and competitive advantage. *What aspects of strategy should be globalized? Managers can answer this question by systematically analyzing industry conditions or "industry globalization drivers," by evaluating the benefits and costs of globalization, and by understanding the different ways in which a globalization strategy can be used through "global strategy levers."*
Exhibit 1–2 shows the framework for diagnosing and developing globalization strategy. Industry globalization drivers are externally determined by industry conditions or by the economics of the business, while global strategy levers are choices available to the worldwide business. *Industry globalization drivers* (underlying market, cost, and other industry conditions) create the potential for a worldwide business to achieve the *benefits* of global strategy. To achieve these benefits, a worldwide business needs to set its *global strategy levers* (e.g., use of globally standardized products) appropriately relative to the industry drivers and relative to the *position and resources* of the business and its parent company. The *organization's ability to implement* the formulated global strategy affects how well the benefits can be achieved. It also affects how ambitious the global strategy should be, and conversely, the desired global strategy affects how the organization should be structured and managed.

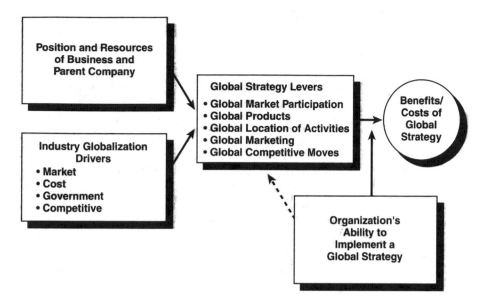

EXHIBIT 1–2 A Framework for Global Strategy

Source: Adapted from Yip (1989)

Another way of viewing the relationship among these different forces and factors is in terms of a globalization triangle. As depicted in Exhibit 1–3, industry globalization drivers, global strategy levers, and global organization factors need to work together to achieve potential globalization benefits.

EXHIBIT 1–3 The Globalization Triangle

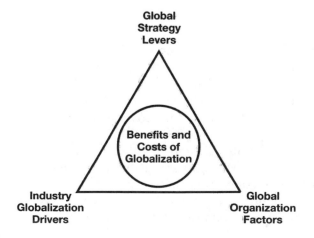

SOME DEFINITIONS AND DISTINCTIONS

Global, etc.

The recent popularity of global strategy has caused overuse of the terms "global" and "globalize." Instead of being used to designate a particular type of international strategy, these terms are being used to replace the term "international." One reason is that "international" has come to represent, particularly in the United States, the now unfashionable distinction between domestic and nondomestic business. Everyone seems to want a global strategy rather than just an international one. As a result of the widespread use of the term "global," we are losing the ability to refer to different types of international strategy. More important, executives will find it easier to delude themselves that they have a global strategy if they are careless as to what they call their worldwide strategy.

The term "worldwide" will be used as a neutral designation. "International" will refer to anything connected with doing business outside the home country. "Multilocal" and "global" will refer to types of worldwide strategy. Much of this book will cover what these types of strategy mean. Briefly, a multilocal strategy treats competition in each country or region on a stand-alone basis, while a global strategy takes an integrated approach across countries and regions. "Multilocal" is preferable to "multinational," as the latter term has come to be associated with a type of company. Indeed, a multinational company can pursue different types of worldwide strategy for each of its different worldwide businesses. For example, as a multinational company, General Electric, Inc., may pursue a global strategy for its turbine engine business but a multilocal strategy for some other business.

Country, etc.

Issues of global strategy apply not just at the worldwide level but at the regionwide level. For example, companies seeking to meet the challenges and exploit the opportunities of "Europe 1992" are, in essence, developing a global strategy at the continental level.[12] The term "regional" will be used to refer to multicountry areas, typically covering all or most of a continent. The term "country" can also be problematic. For example, is Benelux one country or three? Legally it comprises three countries, but many companies manage it as one. Management is the key. Even more ambiguous is the group of Central American countries lying between Mexico and Colombia. The term "country" will be used to refer to single countries or groups of small, contiguous countries that are managed as one country.

Recent Changes in General Globalization Drivers

Although it is not the purpose of this book to examine general changes in globalization drivers, some of these widespread changes include the following:

Market Drivers

- Per capita income converging among industrialized nations (e.g., Japan overtaking the United States, Hong Kong overtaking New Zealand)
- Convergence of lifestyles and tastes (e.g., McDonald's in Paris and Perrier in America)
- Increasing travel creating global consumers
- Organizations beginning to behave as global customers
- Growth of global and regional channels (e.g., agreement in 1989 by three of Europe's largest supermarket chains to cooperate in purchasing and marketing, namely, Casino of France, Ahold of the Netherlands, and Argyll Group of Britain)
- Establishment of world brands (e.g., Coca-Cola, Levi's, Louis Vuitton)
- Push to develop global advertising (e.g., Saatchi & Saatchi's commercials for British Airways)

Cost Drivers

- Continuing push for economies of scale (but offset by flexible manufacturing)
- Accelerating technological innovation
- Advances in transportation (e.g., use of Federal Express to deliver urgent supplies from one continent to another)
- Emergence of newly industrializing countries with productive capability and low labor costs (e.g., Taiwan, Thailand, and China)
- Increasing cost of product development relative to market life

Government Drivers

- Reduction of tariff barriers (e.g., Canada–United States Free Trade Agreement of 1987; the North American Free Trade Agreement)
- Reduction of nontariff barriers (e.g., Japan's gradual opening of its markets)
- Creation of trading blocs (e.g., Europe 1992)
- Decline in role of governments as producers and customers (e.g., denationalization of many industries in Europe)
- Privatization in previously state-dominated economies, particularly in Latin America
- Shift to open market economies from closed communist systems in Eastern Europe
- Increasing participation of China and India in the global economy

Competitive Drivers

- Continuing increase in level of world trade
- More countries becoming key competitive battlegrounds (e.g., rise of Japan to become a "lead" country)
- Increased ownership of corporations by foreign acquirors
- Rise of new competitors intent upon becoming global competitors (e.g., Japanese companies in automotive and electronics industries)
- Growth of global networks making countries interdependent in particular industries (e.g., electronics)
- More companies becoming globally centered rather than nationally centered (e.g., Stanley Works, a traditional U.S. company moving its production offshore; Uniden, a Japanese telecommunications equipment producer that has never manufactured in Japan)
- Increased formation of global strategic alliances

Other Drivers

- Revolution in information and communications (e.g., personal computers and facsimile machines)
- Globalization of financial markets (e.g., listing of corporations on multiple exchanges, global market collapse on Black Monday in 1987)
- Improvements in business travel (e.g., Concorde and rise of international hotel chains)

Worldwide Business

A worldwide business is one that has widespread and significant operations on more than one continent. Furthermore, a worldwide business is defined as one that produces as well as sells in multiple countries (if not continents). Thus a purely export-based business is not a worldwide business by my definition. A worldwide business may also not be recognized as such—the company may view itself merely as a collection of similar businesses operating in different countries. One topic of this book will be how to recognize a worldwide business. Such a business may use multilocal or global strategy or some combination of both.

INDUSTRY GLOBALIZATION DRIVERS

Four groups of "industry globalization drivers"—market, cost, government and competitive—represent the industry conditions that determine the potential and need for competing with a global strategy.[13]

Together, these four sets of drivers cover all the critical industry conditions that affect the potential for globalization. While other groupings are

---

Electrolux's Market-Participation Strategy
in Appliances

The Swedish appliance giant, the Electrolux Group, is pursuing a strategy of building a significant share in major world markets. The company aims to be the first global appliance maker. In 1986, Electrolux took over Zanussi Industries to become the top producer of appliances in Western Europe. Later that year, Electrolux also acquired White Consolidated Industries, the third largest American appliance manufacturer. These market moves have given Electrolux a very strong global position. (Still, Electrolux has had to pay a significant price for its global position. Restructuring following the acquisitions combined with the worldwide recession in 1990–1991 to greatly reduce profits.)

---

possible, these four distinguish among the sources (market or cost, etc.) of the drivers and, therefore, help managers to identify and deal with them more easily. Drivers are primarily uncontrollable by the worldwide business. As illustrated in Exhibit 1–4, each industry has a level of globalization potential that is determined by these external drivers.

EXHIBIT 1–4   Industry Globalization Potential

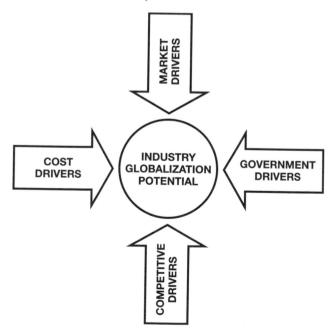

Boeing's Global 737 Model

Aircraft manufacturers have excelled at producing globally standardized products. At the same time, they have been flexible in meeting differing worldwide needs by adapting the standardized core product. In the early 1970s Boeing found sales of its 737 model beginning to level off. Boeing turned to the Third World as an attractive new market but found initially that its product did not fit the new environments. Because of the shortness of Third World runways, their greater softness, and the lesser technical expertise of Third World pilots, Boeing found that its planes tended to bounce a great deal. When the planes bounced on landing, the brakes would fail. To fix this problem, Boeing modified the design of the 737 by adding thrust to the engines, redesigning the wings and landing gear, and installing tires with lower pressure. These adaptations to a standardized core product enabled the 737 to become one of the best-selling planes in history.[14]

Market globalization drivers depend on customer behavior, the structure of distribution channels, and the nature of marketing in the industry. Cost drivers depend on the economics of the business. Government globalization drivers depend on the rules set by national governments. Competitive drivers depend on the actions of competitors. Each group of drivers is different for each industry and can also change over time. Therefore, some industries have more globalization potential than others, and the potential changes too. A common group of changes, increasing the globalization potential of many industries, is spurring the interest of managers in global strategy.

GLOBAL STRATEGY LEVERS

Globalization strategy is multidimensional. Setting strategy for a worldwide business requires choices along a number of strategic dimensions. Some of these dimensions determine whether the strategy lies toward the multilocal end of the continuum or the global end. There are five such dimensions:

- *Market participation* involves the choice of country-markets in which to conduct business and the level of activity, particularly in terms of market share.
- *Products/services* involves the extent to which a worldwide business offers the same or different products in different countries.

Japanese Global Competitive Moves

Japanese companies seem to make more use than American or European companies of global competitive moves.[15] Bridgestone Company, the Japanese tire manufacturer, has tried to integrate its competitive moves in response to global consolidation by its major competitors: Continental AG's acquisition of Gencorp's General Tire and Rubber Company, General Tire's joint venture with two Japanese tire makers, and Sumitomo's acquisition of an interest in Dunlop Tire. These competitive actions forced Bridgestone to establish a presence in the major American market in order to maintain its position in the world tire market. To this end, Bridgestone formed a joint venture to own and manage Firestone Corporation's worldwide tire business. This joint venture also allowed Bridgestone to gain access to Firestone's European plants. Eventually, Bridgestone made a full acquisition of Firestone. Bridgestone has had to be willing to pay the price of its increased global market participation—it has had to contend with major losses at Firestone. In the same industry, Michelin has also suffered recent losses after its 1990 acquisition of Uniroyal boosted its market participation in the United States as well as propelling it past Goodyear to become the global market share leader.

- *Location of value-adding activities* involves the choice of where to locate each of the activities that comprise the entire value-added chain—from research to production to after sales service.[16]
- *Marketing* involves the extent to which a worldwide business uses the same brand names, advertising, and other marketing elements in different countries.
- *Competitive moves* involves the extent to which a worldwide business makes competitive moves in individual countries as part of a global competitive strategy.

For each global strategy dimension or lever, a multilocal strategy seeks to maximize worldwide performance by maximizing local competitive advantage, revenues, or profits, whereas a globalized strategy seeks to maximize worldwide performance through sharing and integration. Intermediate positions are, of course, feasible. A business that has a fully globalized strategy would make maximum use of each of the five global strategy levers and would therefore have fully *global market participation, global products and services, global location of activities, global marketing,* and *global competitive moves.* But, of course, not every business should use such a strategy. An overview of each lever is provided here.

Salomon's Retaliation in Skis

Some European and American companies do successfully integrate their competitive strategy, as U.S.-based Salomon did in the ski equipment industry. Tyrolia, an Austrian ski-binding competitor, attacked Salomon's stronghold position in its biggest market, the United States. Rather than fighting Tyrolia only in America, Salomon retaliated in the countries where Tyrolia generated a large share of its sales and profits—Germany and Austria. Taking a global perspective, Salomon viewed the whole world—not just one country—as its competitive battleground.[17]

Market Participation

In a multilocal market participation strategy, countries are selected on the basis of their stand-alone potential in terms of revenues and profits. In a global market participation strategy, countries need to be selected in terms of their potential contribution to globalization benefits also. This may mean entering a market that is unattractive in its own right, but one that has global strategic significance, such as the home market of a global competitor. Or it may mean concentrating resources on building share in a limited number of key markets rather than more widespread coverage. A pattern of major share in major markets is advocated in the concept of the United States–Europe–Japan "triad."[18] In contrast, under a multilocal strategy no particular pattern of participation is required—the pattern accrues from the pursuit of local advantage.

Products and Services

In a multilocal product strategy, the products and services offered in each country are tailored to local needs. In a global product strategy the ideal is a standardized core product that requires a minimum of local adaptation. Cost reduction is usually the most important benefit of product standardization. Theodore Levitt has made the most extreme case for product standardization.[19] Others stress the need for a broad product portfolio, with many product varieties in order to share technologies and distribution channels, or stress the need for flexibility.[20] In practice, some multinationals have pursued global product standardization to a greater or lesser extent some of the time.[21]

Activity Location

In a multilocal activity strategy, all or most of the value chain is reproduced in every country. In another type of international strategy—exporting—most of the value chain is kept in one country. In a global activity strategy, the value chain is broken up, and each activity may be conducted in a different country. The major benefits lie in cost reduction. One type of value-chain strategy is partial concentration and partial duplication. The key feature of a global position on this strategy dimension is the systematic placement of the value chain around the globe.

Marketing

In a global marketing strategy, a uniform marketing approach is applied around the world, although not all elements of the marketing mix need be identical.[22] Unilever achieved great success with a fabric softener that used a globally common positioning, advertising theme, and symbol (a teddy bear), but a brand name that varied by country. Similarly, a product that serves a common need can be geographically expanded with a uniform marketing program, despite apparent obstacles of differences in marketing environments.

Competitive Moves

In a multilocal competitive strategy, a multinational company fights its competitors one country at a time in separate contests, even though it may face another multinational in many of the same countries. In a global competitive strategy, competitive moves are integrated across countries. The same type of move is made in different countries at the same time or in some systematic sequence, or a competitor is attacked in one country in order to drain its resources for another country, or a competitive attack in one country is countered in a different country. Perhaps the best example is the counterattack in a competitor's home market as a parry to an attack on one's own home market.

What Salomon did illustrates that integration of competitive moves is more than just coordination, such as simultaneous or sequenced price moves. Integration requires a concerted effort to compete on a global, not a country-by-country, basis. Coordination is part of integration. Other parts include identifying and targeting global, regional, and local competitors. Having a global attack and defense plan for each major competitor is crucial. A major objective may be to limit a potential global competitor to its home country. An American company has devised a strategy to contain a

Japanese competitor that has yet to move outside Japan. To prevent this competitor from using joint ventures outside Japan as stepping stones to globalization, the American company makes preemptive joint venture agreements with the Japanese company's potential partners.

BENEFITS OF GLOBAL STRATEGY

Use of global strategy can achieve one or more of four major categories of potential globalization benefits:

- Cost reduction
- Improved quality of products and programs
- Enhanced customer preference
- Increased competitive leverage

Exhibit 1–5 summarizes which lever achieves what benefits, as well as the major drawbacks of global strategy.

Reducing Costs

An integrated global strategy can save worldwide costs in several ways:

- *Economies of scale* can be achieved by pooling production or other activities for two or more countries. For example, production of large volumes of compact disc players can result in economies of scale. Realizing the potential benefit of these economies of scale, Sony Corporation has concentrated its compact disc production in Terre Haute, Indiana, and Salzburg, Austria.
- *Lower factor costs* can be obtained by moving manufacturing or other activities to low-cost countries. This has, of course, been the motivation of the recent surge of offshore manufacturing, particularly by American firms. For example, the Mexican side of the U.S.-Mexico border is now crowded with *maquiladoras*—manufacturing plants set up and run by American companies using Mexican labor.
- *Focused production* means reducing the number of products manufactured, from many local models to a few global ones. Typically, unit costs fall as the number of products made in a factory declines. Such reduction in product variety cuts the costs involved in setup, downtime, extra inventory, and the like.[23]
- *Flexibility* can be exploited by moving production from location to location on a short-term basis to take advantage of the lowest cost at a given time. Dow Chemical takes this approach to minimize the cost of producing chemicals. Dow uses a linear programming model that takes account of cross-country differences in exchange rates, tax rates, transportation, and labor costs. The model comes up with the best mix of production volume by location for each planning period.

| Global Strategy Levers | Benefits | | | | Major Drawbacks |
	Cost Reduction	Improved Quality	Enhanced Customer Preference	Competitive Leverage	All Levels Incur Coordination Costs, Plus
Global Market Participation	Increases volume for economies of scale.	Via exposure to demanding customers and innovative competitors.	Via global availability, global serviceability, and global recognition.	Advantage of early entry. Provides more sites for attack and counterattack, hostage for good behavior.	Earlier or greater commitment to a market than warranted on own merits.
Global Products	Reduces duplication of development efforts. Reduces puРchasing, production, and inventory costs.	Focuses development and management resources.	Allows consumers to use familiar product while abroad. Allows organizations to use same product across country units.	Basis for low-cost invasion of markets. Offsets disadvantage of low market share.	Less responsive to local needs.
Global Location of Activities	Reduces duplication of activities. Helps exploit economies of scale. Exploits differences in country factor costs. Partial concentration allows flexibility versus currency changes and versus bargaining parties.	Focuses effort. Allows more consistent quality control.		Allows maintenance of cost advantage independent of local conditions. Provides flexibility on where to base competitive advantage.	Distances activities from customer. Increases currency risk. Increases risk of creating competitors. More difficult to manage value chain.
Global Marketing	Reduces design and production costs of marketing programs.	Focuses talent and resources. Leverages scarce, good ideas.	Reinforces marketing messages by exposing customer to the same mix in different countries.		Reduces adaptation to local customer behavior and marketing environment.
Global Competitive Moves				Magnifies resources available to any country. Provides more options and leverage in attack and defence.	Local competitiveness may be sacrificed.

EXHIBIT 1–5 How Global Strategy Levers Achieve Globalization Benefits

- *Enhancing bargaining power*, via a strategy that allows for switching production among multiple manufacturing sites in different countries, greatly increases a company's bargaining power with suppliers, workers, and host governments. Labor unions in European countries are now very concerned that the creation of the single European market after 1992 will allow companies to switch production from country to country at will. This integrated production strategy would greatly enhance management's bargaining power at the expense of unions.

Improving Quality of Products and Programs

Focus and concentration on a smaller number of products and programs, rather than many products and programs typical of a multilocal strategy, can improve the quality of both products and programs. Global focus is one of the reasons for the Japanese success in automobiles. Toyota markets a far smaller number of models around the world than does General Motors, even allowing for its unit sales being half that of General Motors. Toyota has concentrated on improving its few models while General Motors has fragmented its development funds. For example, the Toyota Camry is the U.S. version of a basic worldwide model and is the successor to a long line of development efforts.[24] The Camry is consistently rated as among the best in the class of medium-sized cars. In contrast, General Motors' Pontiac Fiero started out in the early 1980s as one of the most successful small sports cars but was withdrawn after only a few years on the market. Industry observers blamed this on a failure to invest development money to overcome minor problems.

Enhancing Customer Preference

Global availability, global serviceability, and global recognition can enhance customer preference through reinforcement. Soft drink and fast food companies are, of course, leading exponents of this strategy. Many suppliers of financial services, such as credit cards, have to provide global presence because of the travel-related nature of their service. Manufacturers of industrial products can also exploit this benefit. A supplier, who can provide a multinational customer with a standard product around the world, gains from the worldwide familiarity within the customer organization. Computer manufacturers have long pursued this strategy.

Increasing Competitive Leverage

A global strategy provides more points to attack and counterattack against competitors. In an effort to prevent the Japanese from becoming a competitive nuisance in disposable syringes, Becton Dickinson, a major American medical products company, decided to enter three markets in

Japan's "backyard." Becton entered the Hong Kong, Singapore, and Philippine markets to prevent further Japanese penetration.[25]

DRAWBACKS OF GLOBAL STRATEGY

Globalization can incur significant management costs through increased coordination, reporting requirements, and even added staff. Globalization can also reduce management effectiveness in individual countries if overcentralization hurts local motivation and morale. In addition, each global strategy lever incurs particular drawbacks.

A global strategy approach to market participation can incur the drawbacks of an earlier or greater commitment to a market than warranted on its own merits. Many American companies, such as Motorola, are struggling with long-term efforts to penetrate Japanese markets, mostly in order to enhance their global competitive position rather than to make money in Japan for its own sake.

Product standardization can result in a product that does not fully satisfy customers anywhere. When companies first internationalize, they often offer the standard domestic product without adapting it for other countries and suffer the consequences. For example, Procter & Gamble stumbled when it introduced Cheer laundry detergent in Japan. P&G used, with minimal change, the U.S. product and marketing message (that the detergent was effective in all temperatures). After experiencing serious losses, P&G discovered two instances of insufficient adaptation. First, the detergent did not suds up as it should because the Japanese use a great deal of fabric softener. Second, the Japanese wash their clothes mostly in either cold tap water or bath water, so that the claim of working in all temperatures was irrelevant. P&G achieved success with Cheer only after reformulation of the product and changing the marketing message.

Concentrating activities distances those activities from customers and can reduce responsiveness and flexibility. It also increases currency risk by incurring costs and revenues in different countries.

Uniform marketing can reduce adaptation to local customer behavior and the marketing environment. For example, the head office of British Airways mandated that every country use the "Manhattan Landing" television commercial developed by its advertising agency, Saatchi & Saatchi. While the commercial won many awards, it has been criticized for using a visual (New York City) that was not widely recognized in many countries.

Integrating competitive moves can mean sacrificing revenues, profits, or competitive position in individual countries. This is particularly true when the subsidiary in one country is asked to attack a global competitor in order to send a signal or to divert that competitor's resources from another country.

FINDING THE BALANCE

The most successful worldwide strategies find a balance between overglob-
alizing and underglobalizing. The ideal strategy matches the level of strategy globalization to the globalization potential of the industry. A business
in an industry with low globalization potential should have a strategy that
is not very global. A business in an industry with high globalization potential should have a generally global strategy. A business suffers *global strategic disadvantage* by using a strategy that is less globalized than the potential
offered by its industry. The business fails to exploit potential global benefits
such as cost savings via product standardization. In contrast, a business
suffers *national strategic disadvantage* by being too globalized relative to the
potential offered by its industry. The business does not tailor its products
and programs as much as it should. While there is no systematic evidence,
comments by executives generally suggest that far more businesses suffer
from not enough globalization than from too much, or at least that their
focus of attention is on increasing their level of globalization. In one of my
research studies, all, except one, of eighteen worldwide businesses had
strategies that were underglobalized relative to the potential of the industries in which they competed.[26]

Managers should avoid viewing industries as global or not global, but
as being more global or not in particular dimensions. For example, an industry may have high globalization potential for globally standardized
products but low globalization potential for centralized manufacturing. The
paint industry satisfies fairly similar needs around the world, particularly
in interior applications where intercountry differences in weather and sur-
faces are fewer. So global paint products are perfectly possible. But the low
value of paint relative to its bulk and weight renders it uneconomic for
long-distance shipment. So globally centralized manufacturing is not possible for most paints.

Managers should also avoid viewing strategies as global or not global.
They should focus on the extent to which different dimensions of strategy
are globalized. For example, M&M Mars, the confectionery manufacturer,
standardizes most of its products while maintaining different marketing
approaches and even, in some cases, different brand names.

MORE THAN ONE STRATEGY IS VIABLE

Although they are powerful, industry globalization drivers do not dictate
one formula for success. More than one type of international strategy can be
viable in a given industry.

Industry Variation Across Drivers

First, no industry scores high on every one of the many globalization drivers. A particular competitor may be in a strong position to exploit a driver that scores low on globalization. The dominance of national government customers offsets the globalization potential from other industry drivers, because government customers typically prefer to do business with their own nationals. In such an industry a competitor with a global strategy can use its other advantages, such as low cost from centralization of global production, to offset this drawback. At the same time, another multinational competitor with good government contacts can pursue a multilocal strategy and succeed without globalization advantages. And single-country local competitors can succeed on the basis of their very particular local assets. The hotel industry provides examples of both successful global and local competitors.27

Global Effects Are Incremental

A second factor affects why globalization drivers are not deterministic. The appropriate use of global strategy levers provides *additional* competitive advantage that is *incremental* to other sources of competitive advantage. These other sources may allow individual competitors to thrive with international strategies that are mismatched with industry globalization drivers. For example, superior technology provides a major source of competitive advantage in most industries, but it can be quite independent of globalization drivers. A competitor with sufficiently superior technology can use that to offset disadvantages in globalization.

Position and Resources of Business and Parent Company

The third reason why drivers are not deterministic has to do with resources (see the top left box in exhibit 1–2). A worldwide business may face industry drivers that strongly favor a global strategy. But global strategies are typically expensive to implement initially even though there should be great cost savings and revenue gains later. High initial investments may be needed to expand within or into major markets, to develop standardized products, to relocate value activities, to create global brands, to create new organization units or coordination processes, and to implement other aspects of a global strategy.

The strategic position of the business is also relevant. Even though a global strategy may improve the business's long-term strategic position, its immediate position may be so weak that resources should be devoted to short-term, country-by-country improvements. The automobile industry has very strong globalization drivers. But Chrysler Corporation, in avoiding bankruptcy, had to deglobalize by selling off most of its international automotive businesses. Financial survival was more important at that point. Last, there may be greater returns in investing in nonglobal sources of competitive advantage, such as superior technology, than in global ones, such as centralized manufacturing.

Limitations in Organization

Finally, organization factors such as structure, management processes, people, and culture affect how well a desired global strategy can be implemented. Differences in organization among companies in the same industry will, therefore, constrain the extent to which the companies can, or should, pursue the same global strategy.

CHALLENGES OF IMPLEMENTATION

Implementing strategy is always difficult. Implementing global strategy is particularly challenging because of the multiple countries and nationalities involved. Furthermore, in many cases a key part of the global strategy is not so much the content of the strategy (e.g., a standardized global product) but the decision to operate with a globally integrated management process (e.g., a global product development process). Implementation can be so disruptive and difficult that there may not be enough benefit in pursuing a highly global strategy. In particular, strategy globalization often requires changes that involve one or more countries having to give up long-established strategies, products, and the like. A European consumer packaged goods business had, under a multilocal strategy, developed different versions of the same basic product. One major country marketed a product made of *opaque* plastic parts and another major country marketed the same product made of *translucent* plastic parts. There seemed to be no real reason why consumers might prefer opaque over translucent or vice versa. But the managers of each country felt committed to their version and were loathe to risk the potential market place disruption involved in change. It was such implemention issues that posed roadblocks for this business's attempt to rationalize its worldwide product lines.

Four key organization and management factors determine a busi-

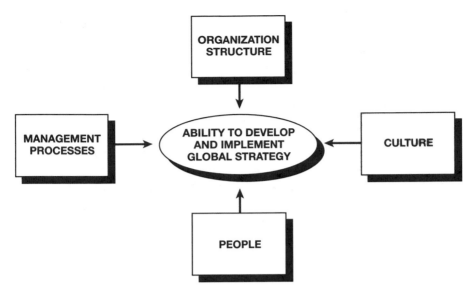

EXHIBIT 1–6　Management and Organization Factors Affecting Global Strategy

ness's ability to develop and implement a global strategy. Exhibit 1–6 summarizes these factors.

- *Organization structure* comprises the reporting relationships in a business—the "boxes and lines."
- *Management processes* comprise the activities such as planning and budgeting, as well as information systems, that make the business run.
- *People* comprise the human resources of the worldwide business and include both managers and all other employees.
- *Culture* comprises the values and rules that guide behavior in a corporation.

Chapter 8 will elaborate on the application of these organization and management factors.

GUIDE TO THE CHAPTERS

Chapter 2 describes in detail the operation of industry globalization drivers and finishes with an application of globalization drivers to Europe 1992. The next five chapters focus on each global strategy lever in turn: Chapter 3 on the use of global market participation, Chapter 4 on the use of global products and services, Chapter 5 on the use of global activity location, Chapter 6 on the use of global marketing, and Chapter 7 on the use of global competitive moves. Chapter 8 then addresses the organization and management issues in implementing global strategy. The chapter presents a framework of the organization and management factors that determine a business's ability to implement global strategy. Chapter 9 provides operational measures for all the industry globalization, global strategy, and global organization concepts discussed earlier. The chapter is particularly helpful for those undertaking a global strategy analysis of the type described in the last chapter. Chapter 10 pulls together the concepts of the book into a systematic, step-by-step approach to conducting a global strategy analysis.

DISCUSSION AND RESEARCH QUESTIONS

1. In addition to those listed in this chapter, what other trends are there in general globalization drivers?
2. What forces currently work against globalization?
3. Select a company (not one discussed in this chapter) and describe its total global strategy in terms of its core business strategy, its internationalization strategy, and its globalization strategy. How successful has this company been in each aspect of its total global strategy?
4. What are the most globally successful companies from your country (region)? Why?

NOTES

1. Hout et al. (1982) coined the term "multidomestic" to apply to industries rather than strategies. See Thomas Hout, Michael E. Porter, and Eileen Rudden, "How Global Companies Win Out," *Harvard Business Review,* September–October 1982, pp. 98–108. The term "multilocal" seems better when applied to strategies, in that "domestic" implies a company competing in its home market, while a great deal of local competition occurs between companies, none of which are in their home markets.
2. See Theodore Levitt, "The Globalization of Markets," *Harvard Business Review,* May–June 1983, pp. 92–102, and Kenichi Ohmae, *Triad Power: The Coming Shape of Global Competition* (New York: The Free Press, 1985).
3. From the U.S. Commerce Department, reported in "The Takeover of American Industry," *New York Times,* May 28, 1989, Section 3, pp. 1, 8, 9.
4. Alfred Rappaport questions the logic of using exchange rates as the justification for paying a premium for a foreign asset ("Foreign Companies Pay Too Much," *New York Times,* May 28, 1989, Section 3, p. 3).
5. See Philip Kotler, Liam Fahey, and S. Jatusripitak, *The New Competition* (Englewood Cliffs, N.J.: Prentice Hall, 1985).
6. For works on Japanese management see James C. Abegglen and George Stalk, Jr., *Kaisha: The Japanese Corporation* (New York: Basic Books, 1985); William G. Ouchi,

Theory Z: How American Business Can Meet the Japanese Challenge (Reading, Mass.: Addison-Wesley, 1981); and Richard Tanner Pascale and Anthony G. Athos, *The Art of Japanese Management: Applications for American Executives* (New York: Simon & Schuster, 1981).

7. This example is adapted from George S. Yip, Pierre M. Loewe, and Michael Y. Yoshino, "How to Take Your Company to the Global Market," *Columbia Journal of World Business,* Winter 1988, pp. 37–48. Copyright 1988. *Columbia Journal of World Business.* Reprinted with permission.

8. This accepted wisdom is laid out in one of the rejoinders provoked by Levitt's article—see Susan P. Douglas and Yoram Wind, "The Myth of Globalization," *Columbia Journal of World Business,* Vol. 22, No. 4, Winter 1987, pp. 19–29.

9. There are many sources of guidance on core business strategy. See, for example, Michael E. Porter, *Competitive Strategy: Techniques for Analyzing Industries and Competitors* (New York: The Free Press, 1980); Michael E. Porter, *Competitive Advantage* (New York: The Free Press, 1985); Kenichi Ohmae, *The Mind of the Strategist* (New York: McGraw-Hill, 1982); and Arnoldo C. Hax and Nicolas S. Majluf, *Strategic Management: An Integrative Perspective* (Englewood Cliffs, N.J.: Prentice-Hall, 1984); and Pankaj Ghemawat, *Commitment: The Dynamic of Strategy* (Boston: Harvard Business School Press, 1991).

10. See Derek F. Abell, *Defining the Business: The Starting Point of Strategic Planning* (Englewood Cliffs, N.J.: Prentice-Hall, 1980), for an extensive framework for business definition.

11. For a complete framework on how to select and enter foreign markets, see Franklin R. Root, *Entry Strategies for International Markets* (Lexington, Mass.: Lexington Books, D. C. Heath, 1987). For a general review of how to conduct international business, see, for example, Michael R. Czinkota, Pietra Rivoli, and Ilkka A. Ronkainen, *International Business* (Chicago: The Dryden Press, 1989).

12. The term "Europe 1992" is widely used to refer to the common market being created in the European Community. The end of 1992 is merely the target date for the enactment of a large series of liberalizing and harmonizing regulations. See, for example, Paolo Cecchini, *The European Challenge: 1992, The Benefits of a Single Market* (London: Wildwood House, 1988).

13. The concept of industry conditions affecting the potential for global strategy was first developed by Michael E. Porter in "Changing Patterns of International Competition," *California Management Review,* Vol. 28, No. 2, Winter 1986, pp. 9–40; and in his "Competition in Global Industries: A Conceptual Framework," *Competition in Global Industries,* ed. Michael E. Porter (Boston: Harvard Business School Press, 1986). The concept of industry globalization drivers was first presented in Yip, Loewe, and Yoshino, "How to Take Your Company to the Global Market," and more fully developed in Yip, "Global Strategy . . . In a World of Nations?" and George S. Yip, "An Integrated Approach to Global Competitive Strategy," in *Frontiers of Management Research and Practice,* ed. Roger Mansfield (London: Routledge, 1989).

14. *Fortune,* March 14, 1988, p. 53.

15. See Kotler, Fahey, and Jatusripitak, *The New Competition,* p. 174.

16. For a full description of the value-chain concept, see Porter, *Competitive Advantage.*

17. I thank Pierre M. Loewe of The MAC Group for this example.

18. Ohmae, *Triad Power.*

19. Levitt, "The Globalization of Markets."

20. Gary Hamel and C. K. Prahalad, "Do You Really Have a Global Strategy?" *Business Review,* July–August 1985, pp. 139–148; and Bruce Kogut, "Designing Global Strategies: Profiting from Operational Flexibility," *Sloan Management Review,* Fall 1985, pp. 27–38.

21. Peter G. P. Walters, "International Marketing Policy: A Discussion of the Standardization Construct and Its Relevance for Corporate Policy," *Journal of International Business Studies,* Summer 1986, pp. 55–69.

22. The possibilities and merits of uniform marketing have been discussed by Robert D. Buzzell, "Can You Standardize Multinational Marketing?" *Harvard Business Review,*

November–December, 1968, pp. 102–113; and by John A. Quelch and Edward J. Hoff, "Customizing Global Marketing," *Harvard Business Review*, May–June 1986, pp. 59–68.

23. Two very experienced consultants who worked for the Boston Consulting Group have estimated the potential cost savings in focused production. They found that if the number of products produced is halved, total factory labor costs should fall 30%, and total costs including materials should fall 17%, while breakeven should be reduced to 60% of capacity. See Abegglen and Stalk, *Kaisha: The Japanese Corporation*.

24. The Toyota Camry was first introduced into Japan in 1980. An export version was created in 1985. Another long-lived Japanese automobile model is the Honda Accord, first introduced into Japan in 1976. See Kiyonori Sakakibara and Yaichi Aoshima, "Company Growth and the Wholeness of Product Strategy," Working Paper No. 8904, Graduate School of Commerce, Hitotsubashi University, April 1989.

25. Reported in Marquise R. Cvar, "Case Studies in Global Competition: Patterns of Success and Failure," in Porter, "Competition in Global Industries."

26. See George S. Yip, "Do American Businesses Use Global Strategy?" Working Paper No. 91–101 (Cambridge, Mass.: Marketing Science Institute, January 1991).

27. This particular concept of management and organization factors affecting global strategy was first presented in Yip, Loewe, and Yoshino, "How to Take Your Company to the Global Market." Other authors such as Christopher Bartlett, Yves Doz, Sumantra Ghoshal, and C. K. Prahalad have done a great deal of work on the role of management and organization in global strategy. See Christopher A. Bartlett and Sumantra Ghoshal, *Managing Across Borders: The Transnational Solution* (Boston: Harvard Business School Press, 1989); and C. K. Prahalad and Yves L. Doz, *The Multinational Mission: Balancing Local Demands and Global Vision* (New York: The Free Press, 1987).

Chapter 2

Diagnosing Industry Globalization Potential

Industry globalization drivers are the underlying conditions in each industry that create the potential for using global strategy. Here we will examine each driver in more depth and, in addition, discuss how drivers affect two industry competitive forces—the threat of entry and rivalry among competitors. We will also review Europe 1992 as an example of changing globalization drivers.

To achieve the benefits of globalization, the managers of a worldwide business need to recognize when industry conditions provide the opportunity to use global strategy levers. These industry conditions can be grouped in four categories of globalization drivers: market, cost, government, and competitive. Each key industry globalization driver affects the potential use of global strategy levers (global market participation, global products and services, global location of activities, global marketing, and global competitive moves). The drivers are as follows:

Market Globalization Drivers

- Common customer needs
- Global customers
- Global channels

- Transferable marketing
- Lead countries

Cost Globalization Drivers

- Global scale economies
- Steep experience curve effect
- Sourcing efficiencies
- Favorable logistics
- Differences in country costs (including exchange rates)
- High product development costs
- Fast-changing technology

Government Globalization Drivers

- Favorable trade policies
- Compatible technical standards
- Common marketing regulations
- Government-owned competitors and customers
- Host government concerns

Competitive Globalization Drivers

- High exports and imports
- Competitors from different continents
- Interdependence of countries
- Competitors globalized

Industry globalization drivers relate to, but are different from, the industry competitive forces identified by Michael E. Porter: threat of entry, rivalry among existing firms, pressure from substitute products or services, bargaining power of suppliers, and bargaining power of buyers.[1] In most cases, but not always, increases in industry globalization will increase the strength of competitive forces. Particularly for the threat of new entrants and rivalry among existing firms, increased industry globalization heightens competition by widening its geographic scope. The specific effects on these two competitive forces vary in interesting ways depending on the specific industry globalization driver and will be addressed shortly for each of the drivers. Increased industry globalization also increases the pressure from substitutes by increasing the geographic scope of where these substitutes might come from. This effect is fairly straightforward and consistent and need not be discussed for individual industry globalization drivers. Last, the effects of industry globalization on the power of suppliers and the power of buyers can be positive in some cases and negative in others. In particular, the globalization of customers themselves (the "global customers" driver) increases their bargaining power relative to industry competitors, while the globalization of competitors (the "competitors global-ized" driver) reduces the bargaining power of customers. Analogous effects apply for the bargaining power of suppliers.

Globalization can also change the fundamental strategy required for managing competitive forces. In *Competitive Strategy,* published in 1980, Porter, in effect, recommends that companies seek to compete in markets with weak competitors and weak customers.[2] In *The Competitive Advantage of Nations,* published in 1990, Porter argues instead for participating in na-tional markets with the strongest rivals and most demanding customers, in order to build international competitiveness.[3] The difference between his two positions is explainable by the difference between a closed, domestic industry and an open, globalized industry. In a closed, domestic industry, a company accustomed to weak competitors and undemanding customers has little to fear—there is no source of new competitors that might grow strong in more demanding competitive arenas. In an open, globalized in-dustry, such newly strong competitors abound. *That is why it is important to understand how industry globalization drivers affect the threat of entry and rivalry among existing competitors.*

MARKET GLOBALIZATION DRIVERS

Market globalization drivers—common customer needs, global customers, global channels, transferable marketing, and lead countries—depend on the nature of customer behavior and the structure of channels of distribution. These drivers affect the use of all five global strategy levers. As illustrated in Exhibit 2–1, different industries have different levels of market globaliza-tion drivers. *These comparative rankings are approximate only and will also change with time.*

Common Customer Needs

Common customer needs represent the extent to which customers in different countries have the same needs in the product or service category (or the group of products and services) that defines an industry. Many fac-tors affect whether customer needs are similar in different countries. These factors include whether differences in economic development, climate, physical environment, and culture affect needs in the particular product or service category as well as whether the countries are at the same stage of the product life cycle.[4] Common customer needs particularly affect the op-portunity to use the global strategy levers of global market participation, global products and services, and global competitive moves. Common needs make it easier to participate in major markets because a few product

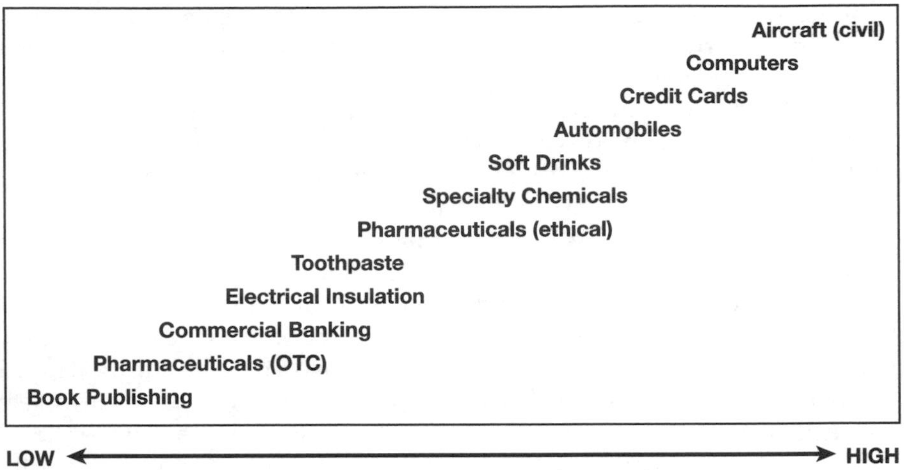

Aircraft (civil)

Computers

Credit Cards

Automobiles

Soft Drinks

Specialty Chemicals

Pharmaceuticals (ethical)

Toothpaste

Electrical Insulation

Commercial Banking

Pharmaceuticals (OTC)

Book Publishing

LOW ◄──────────────────────────────► HIGH

**EXHIBIT 2–1   Strength of Market Globalization Drivers
for Selected Industries**

varieties can serve many markets. Thus, fewer different product offerings need to be developed and supported. Japanese automotive companies have been particularly successful at exploiting common needs when they first entered world automotive markets. Toyota, Nissan, and Honda chose to focus on fundamental needs common to all countries—such as reliability and economy—rather than to focus on peripheral differences—such as styling. The underlying commonality of needs meant that their highly standardized global products were quite acceptable in most countries. Common needs also allow the sequenced invasion of markets with highly standardized products—again, a successful approach of many Japanese companies in different industries.

Common customer needs make entrants more dangerous by reducing the number of products or services that they need to develop for different countries. Success in one country with a global product can be used as a springboard for entering other countries. Thus, it is not surprising that Japanese entrants have been most successful in the last twenty years in markets with fairly common customer needs—electronic and automotive products. The Japanese are now turning to financial services. The common need of corporations around the world for sources of financing from debt or equity has encouraged the Japanese big four brokers—Yamaichi, Nomura, Daiwa, and Nikko—to try their luck in the U.S. and European financial markets. The Japanese are entering the New York Market by selling the "financial equivalent of Toyotas" (simple, high-quality products): Treasury bills, mortgage-backed securities, corporate bonds, and commercial paper. At the same time, they are establishing a presence in European financial markets.[5]

Global Food and Beverages

Even in food and beverages, where national taste seems dominant,[6] the speed of change of eating habits has been one of the most
dramatic events of the postwar decades, spurred primarily by travel,
tourism, and immigration. In only a few years, Japanese were converted to eating donuts, gradually with more cinnamon, until they
are now the same recipe as the American donut, but a littler smaller
to fit the Japanese hand.[7] The conservative British are increasingly
abandoning their warm "pint of bitter" beer for cold American and
European-style lager. Heineken has successfully created a globally
standardized beer that its adherents buy all over the world. Americans now drink more and more French mineral water. According to
executives in a leading multinational food and beverage concern, it
seems to be modern products without a tradition (or at least without
a tradition in most countries) that can most easily be globalized. Recent examples of such products include pizza and yoghurt.

Common needs across countries also make it more difficult for competitors to differentiate themselves from one another. Rivalry, therefore, becomes more severe. (It might be argued that globalization creates larger,
global segments that should have more room for competitors and, therefore, less rivalry. In practice, however, the lure of the large global market
seems to raise the ambitions of competitors.) Consumer tastes in magazines
are sufficiently common in Europe that publishers can now sell pan-
European offerings. Cultural differences do not seem great enough to prevent some magazines from crossing borders; consequently, publishing
firms are making an effort to sell those magazines to all of Europe with only
slight changes in content. The result is significant heightening of rivalry. In
the mid-1980s, *Bella* was successfully launched as a European women's
magazine, first in West Germany, then in Britain and Spain.

How common customer needs are across countries clearly varies
greatly by industry and depends on such factors as the importance of national culture and tastes, income elasticity, and physical conditions that
might affect the use of the product or service. For consumer businesses, the
book publishing and magazine industries fall at the low end of the spectrum in commonality of needs because of differences in both content and
language, although both these factors are changing rapidly. At the other
end of the spectrum, travel-related industries, like airlines and traveler's
checks, have needs that are inherently common across countries. Among
consumer packaged goods, most food products tend to lie at the low end
while household and personal care products are nearer the middle of the

---

Global Differences in Pharmaceutical Products

Pharmaceutical products provide an interesting contrast between prescription (ethical) drugs and over-the-counter (proprietary) drugs. The types of prescription drugs used for a given ailment tend to be more similar across countries than the types of over-the-counter drugs. In the latter case national habits in treatment tend to create differences in what consumers buy for themselves. For example, executives in one major drug company consider that Americans focus on head pains while Japanese focus on stomach pains. The pharmaceutical industry also illustrates the critical difference between the *incidence* of a particular type of need and the *specific products* used to meet those needs. While the incidence of each disease varies greatly geographically, the products used to treat each disease are mostly identical.

---

spectrum. For industrial businesses, commodities, such as many chemicals and other raw materials, tend toward very high commonality of needs. In contrast, more complex industrial products, such as computer equipment and process controls, range from moderate to highly common needs.

Customer needs may be more common than most executives think. *Managers, particularly those with single-country responsibilities, tend to focus on the differences between countries, because it is the differences that require effort in adaptation. But executives can find more commonality if they look for it.* This may also explain the varying strategies of companies. Some companies have looked for commonality and acted accordingly. Canon, for example, did this in developing a global photocopier that sacrificed the ability to copy certain sizes of Japanese paper.

Global Customers and Channels

Global customers buy on a centralized or coordinated basis for decentralized use, or at the least they select vendors centrally. As such, "global customers" can be distinguished from "international customers," "foreign customers," and "local customers," as shown in Exhibit 2–2. Global customers, compared with other types, have both more internationalized purchasing (in the sense of buying outside domestic markets) and more globalized purchasing (in the sense of global control by headquarters).

There are two types of global customers: national and multinational.

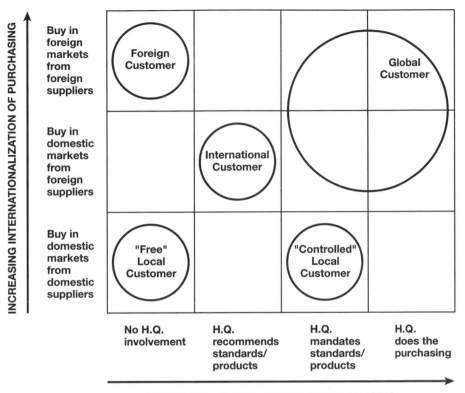

EXHIBIT 2–2   Types of Customers

A *national* global customer searches the world for suppliers but uses the purchased product or service in one country. National defense agencies are a good example. A *multinational* global customer also searches the world for suppliers and uses the purchased product or service in many countries. Examples are the World Health Organization for medical products and some automotive companies. The existence of global customers affects the opportunity or need for global market participation, global products and services, global activity location, and global marketing. Even if they do not purchase centrally, having global customers drives a business toward developing globally standardized products. Similarly, global customers can compare prices charged by the same supplier in different countries and tend to be unhappy with unexplainable discrepancies. Global customers usually occur in industrial categories, although in some consumer categories, such as cameras, watches, and luxury handbags, a significant portion of sales is accounted for by those buying while outside their home country.

The definition of a global customer or channel can be extended to "influencers" such as physicians who prescribe drugs, architects who specify building materials, and engineers and other technical experts who specify or recommend equipment and the like. Japanese trading companies, such as Mitsubishi and Mitsui, also act very much like global channels, although they typically make most of their "purchases" in one country—Japan.

To serve its global customers, the business needs to be present in all the customers' major markets. The U.S. advertising agency that used to have the Coca-Cola account (one of the largest in the world) had no local office to serve Coca-Cola when it expanded to Brazil. So McCann-Erickson, another American, but more global, agency, took the account in Brazil. Then McCann used the Brazilian relationship to win the entire Coca-Cola account worldwide.[8] One reason for AT&T's push to expand globally is the fact that many of its customers are global, and these customers will use rivals such as NEC, Siemens, or IBM for advanced voice and data networks if AT&T cannot meet their needs. Offering standardized products can also be a necessity for serving global customers. Increasingly, such global customers are requiring their suppliers to play the role of global coordination. General Electric has told many of its suppliers that it expects them to be responsible for ensuring that GE businesses get uniform products around the world. Citicorp has asked telecommunications suppliers to submit plans for a global network service. The company has also set up a centralized network unit to manage its telecommunications vendors. Some activities, such as development engineering, selling, and after-sales service, may need to be concentrated, or at least globally coordinated, in order to serve global customers effectively. Last, uniform marketing programs may be needed. Global pricing policies may be particularly important. But suppliers who implement global account management programs have to beware of global customers using the unified account management to extract lower global prices.

The latter provides an example of how the existence of global customers requires the content of the marketing mix to be uniform. It is also important to recognize potential global customers. These are multinational customers who currently do not buy or coordinate centrally but may start to do so. A global supplier can gain a first-mover or preemptive advantage by being the first to treat a potential global customer as an actual global customer.

Analogous to global customers, there may be channels of distribution that buy on a global or at least a regional basis. Global channels or intermediaries are also important in exploiting differences in prices by performing the arbitrage function of transshipment. Their presence makes it more nec-

---

Flying Globally

The international airline industry has a unique type of global customer. Most travelers, except the most patriotic, will consider all carriers that serve the route to be traveled and will select on the basis of quality, reliability, and other real and perceived attributes. At the same time, few travelers are free to start their travel in another country in order to find the best service (an exception would be Belgians who choose to fly KLM out of Amsterdam rather than Sabena out of Brussels). On the other hand, even if airlines do not compete on points of origin and final destination, they certainly compete on intermediate destination. So Swissair and Lufthansa compete partly on the basis of the relative superiority of Zurich and Frankfurt as airports through which to make connections in Europe.

---

essary for a business to rationalize its worldwide pricing. Global channels are rare, but regionwide ones are increasing in number, particularly in European grocery distribution and retailing. Aldi, the giant German supermarket chain, has recently set up a buying arm in Britain. Three other major European supermarket chains—Casino of France, Ahold of the Netherlands, and the Argyll Group of Britain—as noted earlier, agreed in 1989 to cooperate in purchasing and marketing. The existence of global (or regionwide) channels requires, like the existence of global customers, globally coordinated marketing and uniform marketing mix content.

Global customer and channel issues also apply to regional (e.g., Asian or European) customers. Indeed, regional customers are probably growing at a faster rate than are global customers, particularly in Europe.

The existence of global customers or channels cuts both ways for the threat of entry. On the one hand, it is much more difficult to displace an incumbent who is serving a customer in many countries. On the other hand, the essence of a global customer—centralized buying for multinational use—also makes a global account vulnerable to rapid total capture. A competitor may be able to capture a global account by selling to the head office only. Global or regional channels of distribution can also be exploited for rapid entry. Owing to the different regulatory, currency, and tax environments across Europe, many insurance companies have found the need to form alliances with foreign banks in order to enter new markets. By forming these alliances, insurers plan to take advantage of the banks' distribution networks (branches). Under a joint venture, Germany's Allianz sells life insurance policies through the branches of Spain's Banco Popular. In addition, Commercial Union, based in the United Kingdom, sells both life and nonlife insurance through Credito Italiano's branches in Italy.

The presence of global customers or channels increases rivalry among existing competitors. Global customers or channels become prizes to be fought over, and the fight is global in scope. As marketers aim to expand their brands to more countries, advertising agencies have been reorganizing in order to meet the demands of their global customers. In a preemptive move with its double-page advertisement in *The Wall Street Journal* and *The Financial Times* in 1984, Saatchi & Saatchi was the first agency to publicize its global capabilities. This move annoyed many rivals with more extensive global experience and customers. Some of these rivals then moved to enhance their own credentials. Both BBDO and Lintas created European boards of directors; Ogilvy & Mather removed three subregional posts and appointed a European creative director and a new European chairperson; DDB Needham relocated its international headquarters to Paris from New York.

The reinsurance industry provides a more classic type of global customer. In the search for reinsurance, insurance companies, many of them multinational, scour the globe for the lowest premiums and best contracts. The high information content and relatively standardized nature of the product make it easy for reinsurance buyers to behave as global customers.[9]

Transferable Marketing

The nature of the buying decision may be such that marketing elements, such as brand names and advertising, require little local adaptation; that is, brand names and advertising are readily transferable. Transferable marketing makes it easier to expand participation in markets—the business need not develop a new marketing approach. A worldwide business can also adapt its brand names and advertising campaigns to make them more transferable or, even better, design global ones to start with. Exxon chose its new name after an intensive worldwide search for a unique and easily pronounced name to replace Esso and a mixture of other brand names. The Exxon example also highlights the importance of trademark availability. Many companies are hampered in their efforts at consolidating around one global trademark or name because other companies own the rights to the names desired. By definition, transferability enables the use of uniform marketing strategies. Offsetting risks include the blandness of uniformly acceptable brand names or advertising and the vulnerability of relying on a single-brand franchise.

The accepted wisdom in international marketing has long been that marketing approaches need to be tailored for each country. For example, advertising should be developed locally and designed to appeal to the local audience. But companies are finding ways to succeed with uniform or only slightly modified marketing.[10] Such transferable marketing greatly lengthens the reach and punch of global competitors.[11]

Marketing elements that are transferable across countries can both raise and reduce entry barriers. On the one hand, incumbent competitors can leverage global marketing to build high barriers in almost every market. Coca-Cola has created not just national but global barriers to entry with its global brand franchise. This franchise has been built in part through global advertising and packaging. On the other hand, potential entrants can use transferable marketing as a "gateway to entry."[12] Entrants can apply the advertising, packaging designs, and so on that they have developed elsewhere. Transferable brand names and reputation need the additional factor of spillover media, foreign travel by potential customers, or other vehicles of communication before they can be used to reduce international entry barriers.

Transferable marketing adds a dimension to rivalry among existing competitors. Not only must rivals try to develop the best marketing programs in each country, but they must compete in their ability to transfer successful programs from country to country. Companies without a transfer mechanism can find themselves out marketed one country at a time by a rival that globally leverages a successful approach. In the toothpaste market, Colgate-Palmolive has achieved global share leadership partly through its successful application of a global approach to branding, packaging, and advertising. In contrast, rivals like Unilever and Beecham have lagged with different approaches in different countries.

Overall, it seems that global marketing is more acceptable than indicated by its fairly low level of use. Furthermore, general globalization forces, such as increasing travel, will increase the level of acceptance.

Lead Countries

Innovation in products or processes may tend to occur in just one or a few "lead countries." Such concentration of innovation may spring from the concentration of innovative competitors or of demanding customers or both. In that case it becomes critical for global competitors to participate in these lead countries in order to be exposed to the sources of innovation. Customers may view market position in a lead country as a surrogate for overall quality. Companies frequently promote a product in one country as, for example, "the leading brand in the U.S.A." Lead countries can be easily identified as those in which the most important product or process innovations occur.13

In many industries, there are lead countries in which major global competitors are based and where the bulk of innovations occur. For example, Japan is a lead country for consumer electronics, Germany for industrial control equipment, and the United States for computer software. In such industries it is critical for all competitors with global ambitions to participate in the lead countries. In many industries the key lead countries are the United States, Japan, and major European countries such as Germany or the United Kingdom. Other countries, of course, do take the lead in particular industries, such as Denmark for insulin and Italy for ceramic tiles.14 Most American and European companies have a very small presence in Japan and increasingly worry that they are missing out on innovations in that country. A few American companies have started to make the major commitments needed to set up R&D operations in Japan so as to be able to tap into the growing stream of Japanese innovations.

The existence of lead countries can increase the threat of entry. Potential entrants can readily identify the key innovations, even if they choose to enter other countries first. Furthermore, the lead countries become prized targets for entry. *As Japan increasingly becomes an innovator rather than an imitator in many industries, American and European companies need to recognize the criticality of Japan as a lead country.* There is certainly a gap to date in the seriousness with which American companies address Japan. This gap is symbolized by the far higher ratio of patents filed in the United States by Japanese companies relative to the number filed by American companies in Japan.

Rivalry is fiercer in lead countries as competitors recognize the strategic as well as financial importance of success there. In particular, companies need to recognize the value of investing to build a strong position in lead markets, particularly if those markets are the home of major global rivals.

COST GLOBALIZATION DRIVERS

Cost globalization drivers—global scale economies, steep experience effects, sourcing efficiencies, favorable logistics, differences in country costs, high product development costs, and fast-changing technology—depend on the economics of the business. These drivers particularly affect the use of the global activity location lever, as well as the global market participation and global product levers. Exhibit 2–3 ranks on cost globalization drivers the same industries ranked in Exhibit 2–1 on market globalization drivers. Notice some of the differences: Pharmaceuticals (ethical) rise to the top of the cost rankings while soft drinks fall to the bottom.

```
                                      Pharmaceuticals (ethical)
                                          Aircraft (civil)
                                         Automobiles
                                         Computers
                                    Electrical Insulation
                                  Specialty Chemicals
                                Book Publishing
                             Pharmaceuticals (OTC)
                         Toothpaste
                    Credit Cards
                Commercial Banking
           Soft Drinks
```

LOW ◀──▶ HIGH

EXHIBIT 2–3   Strength of Cost Globalization Drivers for Selected Industries

Global Economies of Scale and Scope

Global economies of scale apply when single-country markets are not large enough to allow competitors to achieve optimum scale. Scale at a given location of activity can then be increased through participation in multiple markets, combined with product standardization and/or concentration of selected value activities. But corresponding risks of increasing scale at one location include rigidity and vulnerability to disruption. There has been a shift in the economics of the electronics industry. As the cost of circuits has decreased, the cost advantage has gone to companies that can produce the lowest cost components. Size has become a major asset. Among others, Thomson, the French electronics maker, has realized the need to have a worldwide presence in an industry characterized by economies of scale. Accordingly, Thomson instituted a major global expansion that included the acquisition of General Electric's RCA consumer electronics business.[15]

In many cases it seems to be *global economies of scope* (the gains from spreading activities across multiple product lines or businesses) rather than economies of scale (the gains from increasing the volume of an activity) that push businesses to internationalize or to globalize. Economies of scale at the manufacturing level, in consumer household products, such as detergent and toothpaste, can typically be achieved by national plants in most but the smallest countries. Yet these industries are dominated by handful of multinational firms: Unilever, Procter & Gamble, and Colgate-Palmolive. It seems that the economies of scope involved in consumer research, product development, and the creation of marketing programs, provide a major source of the competitive advantage enjoyed by multinational companies in these industries.

Global scale economies reduce the threat of entry, particularly from potential entrants that are national companies. Where global scale economies apply, it will not be possible for an entrant to achieve competitive economic scale by entering a single national market. A nonmultinational will find it very difficult to get started in such an industry. In the disposable syringe industry, the minimum economic size in production has been estimated to be 60% of the combined markets in the United States and Japan.[16] As a result, national competitors play little role in this industry that is dominated by multinational companies like Becton Dickinson (U.S.) and Terumo (Japan). Conversely, where economies are not at a global scale, an entrant can start in a smaller country-market and gradually build the experience that will allow it to export to larger markets. That is why the U.S. market has become so vulnerable to imported personal computers and other products that can be effectively manufactured in low volumes.

Global scale economies also broaden the scope of competitive rivalry. With national scale economies, competitors have to worry about national market share in order to stay at the economically efficient scale. In the presence of global scale economies, competitors have to worry about their global share. Loss of share in any country will directly affect the cost position of any other country with which activities are shared.

Steep Experience Curve

Even if scale and scope economies are exhausted, expanded market participation, product standardization, and activity concentration can accelerate the accumulation of learning and experience effects (learning effects apply to direct manufacturing while experience effects apply to the entire production process). The steeper the learning and experience slopes, the greater is the potential benefit. *Managers should beware, though, of the usual danger in pursuing experience curve strategies—overaggressive pricing that destroys not just the competition but the market also.* A steep experience curve has similar effects as global scale economies on the threat of entry and rivalry among competitors.

Global Sourcing Efficiencies

The international market for supplies may allow centralized purchasing to achieve global sourcing efficiencies. Himont, at one time a joint venture between Hercules, Inc., of the United States and Montedison SpA of Italy, is the leader of the global polypropylene market. Central to Himont's strategy is global coordination among manufacturing facilities in the purchase of raw materials, particularly monomer, the key ingredient in polypropylene production. Rationalization of raw material orders significantly strengthens the venture's low-cost production advantage. Sourcing efficiencies have a similar effect as global scale economies on the threat of entry and rivalry among competitors.

Favorable Logistics

A favorable ratio of sales value to transportation cost enhances the ability to concentrate production. Other logistical factors include nonperishability, the absence of time urgency, and little need for location close to customer facilities. Low transportation costs allow concentration of production. Even the shape of the product can make a crucial difference. Cardboard tubes, such as those used as cores for textiles, are not economically shippable because the tubes are mostly air. In contrast, cardboard cones are transportable because they can be stacked, allowing many more units in the same space. In general, higher-priced/higher-quality products within any category face more favorable logistics. So French "vin de table" stays home while good Burgundies travel everywhere.

Favorable logistics increase the threat of entry. The low costs make it much easier for foreign entrants to enter markets by exporting. Favorable logistics also increase rivalry among existing competitors by expanding the geographic scope of competition. Rivals can readily shift products from country to country, such that competition is between global production capabilities.

Differences in Country Costs

Differences in country costs can provide a strong spur to globalization. Factor costs generally vary across countries, and more so for particular industries. The availability of particular skills also varies. Concentration of activities in low-cost or high-skill countries can increase productivity and reduce costs. But managers need to anticipate the danger of training future offshore competitors.[17]

Large variations in costs among the countries that produce or might produce a particular product increase the threat of entry from foreign sources. Japan and then the "four tigers" of South Korea, Taiwan, Hong Kong, and Singapore have very successfully leveraged low factor costs in entering many international industries. Other Southeast Asian countries such as Thailand are making similar entries in high–labor-cost industries such as construction wallboard. Eastern European countries may be the next to exploit low-cost, but high-skill, labor in threatening entry. Having a

---

Volkswagen's Relocation of Production

Under attack from lower-priced cars, Volkswagen has been under pressure to reduce its costs. One of the primary ways it has done this is by concentrating its production in various locations to take advantage of the differences in country costs. In Spain, hourly labor costs have been less than half those in Germany. To take advantage of this cost differential, the company moved production of Polos from Wolfsburg to Spain, freeing up the high-wage German labor to produce the higher-priced Golf cars. Another example of this concentration occurred when Volkswagen shut down its New Stanton, Pennsylvania, plant that manufactured Golfs and Jettas. The lower end of the U.S. market was served instead by its low-wage facility in Brazil that produced the Fox. The higher end of the product line (Jetta and Golf) was exported from Europe. This concentration and coordination of production has enabled the company to make substantial cost savings.

---

low cost of goods sold, relative to the selling price, is often an industry's best protection from cheap imports. Thus, marketing-intensive consumer products businesses, such as disposable razors, are still the preserve of American and European producers.

Differences in country costs increase rivalry among existing competitors by creating differential sources of competitive advantage. Rivalry heightened between Japanese and European consumer electronics manufacturers when the Japanese discovered that it was cheaper to produce Europe-bound products in the United States than at home. Ricoh assembles photocopiers containing 90% Japanese parts in California and reexports them to Europe. Furthermore, Sony produces audiotapes and videotapes at an Alabama plant, and audio recorders at a Florida plant, and ships them to Europe for sale. Similarly, the United Kingdom has become the preferred European manufacturing site for many Japanese companies. As a result the U.K. government has been embroiled in a dispute with other European Community governments on the extent of local content needed to qualify as "Made in Europe."

Exchange rates, and changes in them, provide a major source of the variation in costs between countries. But the effect of exchange rates works in one direction for the cost of local inputs, such as labor and some raw materials, and usually in the opposite direction for imported inputs and foreign services. So it is usually only labor-intensive industries, or those in which local materials and supplies are both important and plentiful, where exchange rates can have a major impact on relative country costs.

High Product Development Costs

High product development costs relative to the size of national markets act as a driver to globalization. Philips, the Dutch multinational, has estimated that technology developments in public telecommunications increased the cost of product development by enormous multiples. In the 1950s development costs for conventional electromechanical switching systems were about $10 million and they had an expected life cycle of about 25 years. By the beginning of 1970 when the analog system was introduced, development costs had jumped to $200 million, while the life cycle fell to twelve to fifteen years. In the 1980s, when the first digital systems were developed, costs had risen to $1 billion for a life expectancy of eight to twelve years. Philips calculates that digital development expenses of $1 billion require roughly 8% share of the world market just to recover costs. The largest single market in Europe—Germany—can in total deliver less than that share.[18]

Managers can reduce high product development costs by developing a few global or regional products rather than many national products. But the process for designing global products must not be so cumbersome as to slow the entire process. The automobile industry is characterized by long product development periods and high product development costs. One reason for the high costs is duplication of effort across countries. Ford Motor Company's "Centers of Excellence" program aims to reduce these duplicating efforts and to exploit the differing expertise of Ford specialists worldwide. As part of the concentrated effort, Ford of Europe is designing a common platform for all compacts, while Ford of North America is developing platforms for the replacement of the midsized Taurus and Sable. This concentration of design is estimated to save "hundreds of millions of dollars per model by eliminating duplicative efforts and saving on retooling factories."[19] One payoff comes in the new Mondeo model; introduced in 1993 as Ford's first only global car. High product development costs also have a similar effect as global scale economies on the threat of entry and rivalry among competitors.

Fast-Changing Technology

Fast-changing technology, in products or processes, usually accompanies high product development costs and in itself already increases industry globalization potential:

- The cost of embodying the technology changes typically drives companies to amortize that cost across as many markets as possible.
- Companies that pioneer a particular technology usually feel pressured to

globalize that innovation rapidly in order to exploit it before imitators do so. So both the cost and preemption reasons just cited spur companies to increase their global market participation.

- A company can better exploit and protect its new technologies by using globally integrated competitive moves that include a clear prioritization of when and where to use the technology against competitors.

GOVERNMENT GLOBALIZATION DRIVERS

Government globalization drivers—favorable trade policies, compatible technical standards, common marketing regulations, government-owned competitors and customers, and host government concerns—depend on the rules set by national governments and affect use of all global strategy levers. Exhibit 2–4 ranks on government globalization drivers the same industries as those ranked on market and cost globalization drivers in Exhibits 2–1 and 2–3. Again, notice some of the differences: Toothpaste rises to the top while electrical insulation falls near the bottom of the rankings.

Favorable Trade Policies

Host governments affect globalization potential in a number of major ways: import tariffs and quotas, nontariff barriers, export subsidies, local content requirements, currency and capital flow restrictions, ownership restrictions, and requirements on the technology transfer.[20] Governments' ex-

**EXHIBIT 2–4   Strength of Government Globalization Drivers
for Selected Industries**

```
                                                        Toothpaste
                                                    Soft Drinks
                                                Book Publishing
                                            Computers
                                        Automobiles
                                    Specialty Chemicals
                                Pharmaceuticals (ethical)
                            Aircraft (civil)
                        Commercial Banking
                    Electrical Insulation
                Credit Cards
        Pharmaceuticals (OTC)
```

LOW ◄───► HIGH

Where's the Beef? In Japan.

Favorable trade policies, by definition, increase the threat of foreign entry. Japan's agreement to eliminate the quota on American beef enabled many U.S. producers to enter the coveted Japanese market. U.S. trade representatives convinced Japan to replace the quota, which was equivalent to a tariff of almost 400%, with a tariff of 70% in 1989 and a tariff of 50% three years later. American beef may become as successful in Japan as American credit cards, which benefited from a similar removal of restrictions in the late 1970s.

---

ercise of these trade barriers makes it difficult for companies to use the global levers of global market participation, global products and services, global activity location, and global marketing and affects the need to use the lever of global competitive moves.

Government policies greatly restrict global market participation in the media industries. In many countries, foreign control of the media is restricted or prohibited. Some countries also impose other special restrictions. In Canada magazines must be printed in the country or else be charged a higher postal rate—in effect a local content requirement that restricts a company's choice on activity location.[21] France has strict rules on cultural content, limiting the quantity of foreign material that can be broadcast on radio and television. The newsprint industry also faces unfavorable trade barriers, probably because of its political salience as part of the natural resource sector. In the 1970s many national governments responded to the oil crisis and consequent business bankruptcies by intervening in the newsprint industry with subsidies, tax laws, cartels, and delays in scheduled tariff reductions and quota increases.[22]

National trade policies particularly constrain the extent to which companies can concentrate manufacturing activities. Aggressive U.S. government actions and threats on tariffs, quotas, and protectionist measures have helped convince Japanese automobile manufacturers and other manufacturers to give up their concentration of manufacturing in Japan. Reluctantly, Japanese companies have opened plants in the United States. Honda even made a public relations virtue out of necessity. It gave great publicity to the first shipment of an American-made Honda car to Japan.

The easing of government restrictions can set off a rush for expanded market participation. European Union (EU) regulations for banking and financial services are among those being harmonized in the 1992 process. The EU decision to permit free flow of capital among its member countries in 1992 has led to a jockeying for position among European financial institutions. Until recently, the Deutsche Bank had only fifteen offices outside Germany, but it has now established a major presence in the French market. In 1987, Deutsche Bank also moved into the Italian market by acquiring Bank of America's one hundred or so branches there. Other financial organizations from different countries, such as J. P. Morgan of the United States, Swiss Bank Corporation, and the S. G. Warburg Group in Britain, have increased their participation in major European markets through acquisitions.

Favorable trade policies increase rivalry among existing international competitors by making it easier for them to compete in each other's markets. The opening up of European financial markets, created by the Europe 1992 changes, has made rivals of national European banks. Until the changes, banks such as Germany's Deutsche Bank, Britain's Barclays Bank, and France's Banque Nationale de Paris competed only in fringe activities. Now they increasingly recognize each other as major rivals.

Compatible Technical Standards

Differences in technical standards among countries affect the extent to which products can be standardized. Government restrictions in terms of technical standards can make or break efforts at product standardization. Often, standards are set with protectionism in mind.

Motorola, a leading American electronics manufacturer, has found that many of its products were excluded from the Japanese market on the grounds that these products operated at a higher frequency than that permitted in Japan. Motorola has spent many years, with some notable successes, to get Japan to change its standards. Over-the-counter pharmaceuticals, being sold directly to the public, face strict standards that vary from country to country. Maximum allowed dosage is perhaps the greatest source of incompatibility. In contrast, while still strict, governments are more liberal with prescription pharmaceuticals, so that standards are typically more compatible. At the other end of the scale, the airline industry has to have highly compatible technical standards in order to function at all. For example, all international airports have similar runway lengths to accommodate the largest passenger jets, and the universal language used around the world in cockpits and control towers is English.

Telecommunications have been regarded by governments as contributing to national security. As a result, they have tended to rely on domestic suppliers. The world now faces a hodgepodge of standards in telecommunications. In Europe, Spain has a three-second busy tone while Denmark has a two-second one. France's telephone numbers have to be seven digits long while Italy's can be any length. German telephones operate on 60 volts, while other European countries use 8 volts. And so on.[23]

Compatible technical standards can make it easier for new entrants to achieve needed scale. With one product they can enter many markets at once. Lack of major differences in country technical standards greatly helped Japan's Canon enter the photocopier market in the early 1970s. Canon was able to design a single global product that needed minor modifications only for individual countries.

Compatible technical standards increase rivalry among existing competitors by making it easier for them to invade each other's markets. In telecommunications, the emergence of a new set of international standards, synchronous optical networking (SONET), is increasing global rivalry among existing competitors. Currently, the process of digitizing voice calls and data traffic into computer languages and speed transmitting them is an extremely inefficient process. Incompatible equipment must repeatedly code the digital streams and amplify them to reach their destinations. SONET will, however, permit a single fiber optic strand to carry 32,000 channels of voice and data messages simultaneously, quadrupling existing capacity.[24] Northern Telecom of Canada introduced its SONET-based system in 1989, while AT&T of the United States and Alcatel of France were developing their own SONET-based lines. Another example of the competitive power of compatible standards is the new electrical plug for the European Union. To avoid giving an advantage to any one country, the EU even considered standardizing on a new plug that is *in*compatible with any current EU or non-EU plug!

Common Ma/rketing Regulations

The marketing environment of individual countries affects the extent to which uniform global marketing approaches can be used. Certain types of media may not be allowed or may have restrictions on their use. The United States is far more liberal than Europe in the kinds of advertising claims that can be made on television. The British television authorities even veto the depiction of socially undesirable behavior, such as scenes of children pestering their parents to buy a product. And, of course, the use of sex is different. At one extreme, France is far more liberal than the United States about sex in advertising. There can also be limitations on various promotional devices, such as lotteries. In the United States, promotional competitions cannot require skill or special knowledge!

Common marketing regulations increase rivalry among existing international competitors by making it easier for them to invade each other's markets. British Airways has used a uniform global advertising campaign to help increase its market share in many countries around the world.

Government-Owned Competitors

The presence of government-owned competitors can increase the globalization potential of an industry. Such competitors frequently enjoy subsidies as well as protected home markets and are often a major source of foreign exchange earnings. That combination both allows and spurs them to pursue foreign markets aggressively. In response, other competitors need to have a global plan for fending off government-owned competitors.

The existence of government-owned competitors increases the threat of entry. Similarly, government-owned competitors increase rivalry because of their differing motivations from private competitors. According to a disgruntled American competitor, Spanish and Italian government-owned manufacturers of aluminum products typically act to depress prices in the European market.

Government-Owned Customers

In contrast to government-owned competitors, the presence of government-owned customers provides a barrier to globalization. Such customers usually favor national suppliers. The recent privatization of some European telecommunications companies has spurred greater global competition in the equipment-supplying industry.

Host Government Concerns

Last, in addition to the specific government drivers just discussed, firms pursuing a global strategy need to be aware of the concerns of host governments. According to Yves Doz:[25]

- Global businesses will quickly respond to shifts in the relative factor cost competitiveness of various manufacturing locations by relocating to different countries.
- Global integration gives multinational companies more opportunity to bias the financial results of subsidiaries to decrease total tax liability.
- Value-chain specialization within global businesses will keep key competencies outside their countries.
- The weakening of national decision centers under global strategy makes it more difficult for governments to deal with multinational companies.

In addition, governments and companies usually have a desire for local reliance in major or strategic industries, for example, the textile industry in a number of Asian countries. So governments will seldom allow such major industries to depend for key inputs on supply from foreign countries, particularly distant ones.

COMPETITIVE GLOBALIZATION DRIVERS

Competitive globalization drivers—high exports and imports, competitors from different continents, interdependence of countries and globalized competitors—raise the globalization potential of their industry and spur the need for a response on the global strategy levers. Exhibit 2–5 ranks on competitive globalization drivers the same industries ranked on market, cost, and government drivers in Exhibits 2–1, 2–3, and 2–4. Civil aircraft and computers probably rank highest in competitive drivers while book publishing ranks lowest.

High Exports and Imports

The most basic competitive driver is the level of exports and imports of both final and intermediate products and services. The more trade there is between countries the more do competitors in different countries interact with each other. A global strategy is, therefore, more necessary. Furthermore, high levels of trade change the nature of competitive forces as the earlier discussion on the threat of entry indicated.

EXHIBIT 2–5   Strength of Competitive Globalization Drivers for Selected Industries

```
                                                    Aircraft (civil)
                                                Computers
                                            Automobiles
                                        Specialty Chemicals
                                    Pharmaceuticals (ethical)
                                Electrical Insulation
                            Toothpaste
                        Soft Drinks
                    Commercial Banking
                Pharmaceuticals (OTC)
            Credit Cards
    Book Publishing
```

LOW ◄──► HIGH

Unilever's Failed Bid for Richardson-Vicks

The need to preempt a global competitor can be the spur to increased market participation. In 1986 Unilever, the Anglo-Dutch consumer products company, sought to increase its participation in the American market by launching a hostile takeover bid for Richardson-Vicks, a U.S.-based multinational manufacturer of toiletry and health care products. Unilever's global archrival, Procter & Gamble, saw the threat to its home turf and outbid Unilever to capture Richardson-Vicks. With Richardson-Vicks' European system P&G was able to greatly strengthen its participation in Unilever's base markets in Europe. So Unilever's attempt to expand participation in a rival's home market backfired to allow the rival to expand participation in Unilever's home markets.

Competitors from Different Continents and Countries

Another driver of industry globalization potential is the extent to which major competitors come from different continents or countries. Because their differing backgrounds spur different objectives and approaches, global competition among rivals from different continents tends to be more severe.

Interdependent Countries

A competitor may create competitive interdependence among countries by pursuing a global strategy. This effect arises from the sharing of activities. For example, a business may use a plant in Mexico to serve both the U.S. and Japanese markets. So market share gains in Japan will affect volume in the Mexican plant, which, in turn, will affect costs and ultimately the business's market share in the United States. Thus, with interdependent countries, a competitor's market share in one country contributes to its overall cost position and, therefore, its share position in another country. Such interdependence helps a company to subsidize attacks on competitors in different countries. But it also requires the company to manage its competitive position jointly in each country rather than leave that task just to local management. Other competitors then need to respond via increased global market participation, global marketing, or globally integrated competitive strategy to avoid a downward spiral of sequentially weakened positions in individual countries.

Interdependence among countries makes entry more difficult. An in-

---

GE's Global Moves in Major Appliances

In the appliance industry, globalized competitors have greatly increased industry rivalry. The formation of strategic alliances between Whirlpool and Maytag in efforts to give them a global advantage has provoked General Electric to alter its strategy and globalize its efforts as well. In the 1960s, GE had closed down its production operations in Italy to get out of the European appliance market altogether. By concentrating on the U.S. market, GE increased its market share to a comfortable 30% level. But the recent globalization of its competitors has exerted pressure on GE. In an effort to match its competitors' globalizing moves, GE decided to enhance its world market position before 1992, when the European Community would remove its remaining barriers to internal trade. In 1989, GE formed a joint venture with Britain's General Electric Company (GEC) whereby GE purchased 50% of GEC's European appliance business for $575 million.

---

cumbent competitor can be expected to retaliate more fiercely in order to protect its interdependent position. Protecting the share of a subsidiary becomes doubly important when that also means preserving the cost position of subsidiaries in other countries. Interdependence among countries also increases rivalry among existing international competitors. It requires competitors to worry about their market share in multiple countries simultaneously. In particular, they should be much more willing to give up profits in one country in order to protect their position in other, dependent countries.

Globalized Competitors

Competitors are globalized to the extent that they use the global strategy levers of global market participation, global products and services, global location of activities, global marketing, and global competitive moves. When a business's competitors use global strategy to exploit industry globalization potential, the business needs to match or preempt these competitors. These moves include expansion into or within major markets and being the first to introduce a standardized product or the first to use a uniform marketing program. Competitors pursuing a global strategy place pressure on the industry as a whole to globalize. For example, competitors that push globally standardized products or use globally uniform marketing will influence customers to find global products and marketing more acceptable.

Globalized existing competitors reduce the threat of entry from new entrants—there are more likely to be powerful multinational incumbents defending each market. Incumbents with integrated global strategies can draw on their worldwide assets and resources to suppress potential national entrants. Major U.S. consumer goods companies have typically viewed Europe as a single, broad market and, consequently, deployed their assets across national boundaries. This globalized posture has made it more difficult for their European competitors to enter and compete in markets other than their home country. In contrast, until spurred by Europe 1992, European companies have tended to focus their efforts in a single, national market. A recent study of 45 major European food companies found that half had a presence in only one or two countries.[26]

Globalized existing competitors also increase industry rivalry by increasing the geographic scope of competition. Competition between globally integrated competitors becomes battles between global systems, not just single-country one-on-one combat. In one household products category, competitors began to pay more attention to each other once one company clearly became global and started to make major inroads into the other competitors' markets.

THE CASE OF EUROPE 1992

Europe 1992 provides an intriguing and highly important example of how industry globalization drivers can be analyzed for an entire region, the European Union, across all its industries.[27] Europe 1992 increases the strength of all globalization (or Europeanization) drivers within the EU and also affects overall globalization drivers for any industry of which Europe is part of the world market.

Changes in EU Government Globalization Drivers

The legislation creating Europe 1992 can be viewed as direct changes of each of the government globalization drivers in Europe:

- *Trade policies* will be made fully favorable among all member countries by eliminating all tariff and nontariff barriers and all subsidies. "Mutual recognition," whereby (with few exceptions) products accepted for sale in any member country will have to be accepted by all member countries, represents a very powerful weapon against nontariff barriers. So Germany can no longer rely on its "beer-purity" laws to keep out British and other European beers.
- *Subsidies* will be outlawed. When Mercedes wanted to set up a plant in Baden-Wurtemberg, the wealthiest state in Germany, the European Commission prevented the state government from offering a subsidy.
- *Technical standards* are being made compatible through harmonization of each industry's standards, although each industry is proceeding at its own pace. The European Union distinguishes between those areas where European har-

monization is needed and those where mutual recognition of national standards is sufficient. The European Commission is restricting itself to laying down essential health and safety requirements that are obligatory in all member states.[28]

- *Marketing regulations* may, however, take somewhat longer to become compatible because of the strong cultural attitudes toward the role of advertising and other forms of promotion.
- *Government-owned competitors* can remain, but they will lose much of their subsidy-based advantages when competing within the community.
- *Government-owned customers* will lose their ability to favor national suppliers, openly so at any rate. Given that public procurement now accounts for about 15% of the community's gross domestic product, this is a particularly powerful change.[29]

Changes in Competitive Globalization Drivers

Europe 1992 increases the strength of each of the competitive globalization drivers. *Exports* and *imports* within the EU will increase, as will the number of *competitors from different countries* in each single country. The large size of the integrated European market will also attract more *competitors from different continents*. Both American and Japanese companies are gearing up to participate more in Europe. The competitive *interdependence of countries* will also increase as companies build manufacturing and distribution networks that are continental in scope rather than national. As a result, competitive battles will be Europewide in scope. Last, *Europeanized competitors* will increase in number and scope, as companies increasingly adopt pan-European strategies.

Changes in Market Globalization Drivers

Market drivers for globalization or Europeanization will increase. *Customer needs* and tastes will become more common across countries through exposure to other products. This is not to say that needs and tastes will reduce in number and variety. Rather, in most markets there will arise both a large "Euromass" segment and smaller national segments at the fringe, instead of the current largely separate national segments. In support of the idea of convergence toward global segments, the Brewers Association of Canada conducted a study that suggests the convergence, over the period 1960 to 1985, of many countries around the world (United States, Canada, Belgium, Netherlands, France, Italy, United Kingdom, West Germany, Japan and Australia) to the same mix in consumption of wine, beer, and liquor.[30]

Europewide customers and *channels* will increase in importance. Companies will increasingly search all the EU for suppliers. Distribution channels are already merging and forming alliances in order to provide pan-European coverage. *Transferable marketing* will increasingly become the norm, as buyers get more exposed to multilanguage packaging, to German sales representatives in France and vice versa, and to pan-European advertising created by pan-European marketing teams. Furthermore, *lead countries* will play a greater role with the freer movement of products and services.

Changes in Cost Globalization Drivers

Last, strengthening of cost globalization drivers is a major objective of Europe 1992. The potential for European *scale economies* greatly increases because the elimination of barriers to trade will allow the concentration of production and the harmonization of standards enhances the potential for standardized products. Similarly, the increasing acceptability of pan-European products makes *experience curve* strategies more viable. One of the strongest cost drivers will be *favorable logistics* as the elimination of frontier checks speeds the flow of trucks from their current average of 15 mph or so.[31] Combined with the elimination of tariff and nontariff barriers, these favorable logistics will make *sourcing efficiencies* from centralized purchasing more achievable. In the short term, *differences in country costs* will become more significant in the absence of trade and logistical barriers, as companies find it easier to shift from high-cost to low-cost countries. (In the longer term, such movements will push costs closer together.) Companies will feel encouraged to invest in high-cost pan-European *product development* efforts because there will be larger markets for the results.

This chapter has described the external, industry-based globalization drivers that affect whether businesses should use globally integrated strategies. The next five chapters will address the use of each of the five major types of global strategy levers available to a business: global market participation, global products and services, global location of activities, global marketing, and global competitive moves.

GUIDELINES FOR DIAGNOSING INDUSTRY GLOBALIZATION POTENTIAL

Getting a good understanding of industry globalization potential is the starting point for developing an effective total global strategy. In diagnosing this potential, managers should find the following guidelines useful:

- Do not assume that industries are either global or not global. Instead, nearly every industry has globalization potential in some aspects and not others.

- Different industry globalization drivers can operate in different directions, some favoring globalization and others making it difficult and inadvisable.
- Businesses can respond selectively to industry globalization drivers, by globalizing only those elements of strategy affected by favorable drivers.
- The level of globalization potential changes over time.
- Industry globalization drivers can work at a regional or continental scale as well as at a global scale.
- Industry competitors can themselves affect some globalization drivers. The competitors that stimulate these changes typically reap the major benefits.

DISCUSSION AND RESEARCH QUESTIONS

1. Select an industry and analyze its globalization drivers as they were five years ago, today, and what they are likely to be in five years' time.
2. Which aspects of this industry are most in favor of the use of global strategy? Which aspects are least in favor of its use?
3. Research and evaluate the different trade agreements and trading bloc agreements—the European Union, the North American Free Trade Agreement, Mercosur, GATT, and so on—in terms of how they affect global strategy.
4. What other drivers of globalization are not included in this chapter but should be?

NOTES

1. Michael E. Porter, *Competitive Strategy: Techniques for Analyzing Industries and Competitors* (New York: The Free Press, 1980).
2. Ibid.
3. Michael E. Porter, *The Competitive Advantage of Nations* (New York: The Free Press, 1990).
4. See also Pradeep A. Rau and John F. Preble, "Standardization of Marketing Strategy by Multinationals," *International Marketing Review*, Autumn 1987, pp. 18–28, 24.
5. William Glasgall, "Japan on Wall Street," *Business Week*, September 7, 1987, pp. 82–90.
6. The strength of national preference is illustrated by the French dictionary of food that devoted numerous paragraphs to each of the many types of French cheese but had this entry only for cheddar: "a cheese much eaten by the English." Charles de Gaulle once complained that it was impossible to govern a country that had a thousand different cheeses. America, of course, has instead 31 flavors of ice cream (according to Baskin-Robbins, at any rate).
7. According to David A. Stout, head of economics, Unilever PLC, "Competition in Foods on the World Stage," *Financial Times* Centenary Conference, London, February 8, 1988.
8. David J. Collis, "Saatchi and Saatchi Company PLC," Case No. 1–387–170 (Boston: Harvard Business School, revised 4/88).
9. Takayuki Amano, Sheila Colgan, and Mika Palosuo, "Reinsurance Industry," unpublished study (Washington, D.C.: Georgetown Business School, 1989).
10. See John A. Quelch and Edward J. Hoff, "Customizing Global Marketing," *Harvard Business Review*, May–June 1986, pp. 59–68; and Dean M. Peebles, "Don't Write Off Global Advertising: A Commentary," *International Marketing Review*, Vol. 6, No. 1, 1989, pp. 73–78.

11. Gatignon and Abeele suggest that one test for the transferability of marketing is the extent to which sales response elasticities to marketing expenditures are the same across countries. Thus, if the response of sales to advertising expenditure is similar in two countries, that is a starting point for assuming that the content of the advertising may be transferable. See Hubert Gatignon and Piet Vanden Abeele, "Can You Standardize Marketing Programs Internationally? Cross-country Determinants of Marketing Mix Effectiveness," Marketing Science Institute Mini-Conference on Global Marketing, Cambridge, Mass., May 1990.

12. See George S. Yip, "Gateways to Entry," *Harvard Business Review,* September–October 1982, pp. 85–92.

13. See Thomas Hout, Michael E. Porter, and Eileen Rudden, "How Global Companies Win Out," *Harvard Business Review,* September–October 1982, pp. 98–108; and Porter, *The Competitive Advantage of Nations.*

14. See Porter, ibid., who searched ten countries, including smaller ones such as Denmark and Switzerland, for industries in which these ten countries led.

15. See also Janice McCormick and Nan Stone, "From National Champion to Global Competitor: An Interview with Thomson's Alain Gomez," *Harvard Business Review,* May–June 1990, pp. 127–135.

16. Marquise R. Cvar, "Case Studies in Global Competition: Patterns of Success and Failure," in *Competition in Global Industries,* ed. Michael E. Porter (Boston: Harvard Business School Press, 1986), pp. 483–516.

17. See Constantinos C. Markides and Norman Berg, "Manufacturing Offshore Is Bad Business," *Harvard Business Review,* September–October 1988, pp. 113–120.

18. Estimates provided by Gerrit Jeelof, vice chairman, Board of Management, Philips N.V. See Gerrit Jeelof, "Global Strategies of Philips," *European Management Journal,* Vol. 7, No. 1, 1989, pp. 84–91.

19. "Can Ford Stay On Top?" *Business Week,* September 28, 1987, pp. 78–86.

20. See also Yves Doz, *Government Control and Multinational Management* (New York: Praeger, 1979); and Yves Doz, "Government Policies and Global Industries," in *Competition in Global Industries,* pp. 225–266. In addition Spence cites three public sector activities that can protect domestic competitors: blocking access to the domestic market, providing subsidies, and creating spillovers in research and development. See A. Michael Spence, "Industrial Organization and Competitive Advantage in Multinational Industries," *American Economic Review,* Vol. 74, No. 2, May 1984, pp. 356–360.

21. Jane Ashton, William Kummel, Elizabeth Powell, and Mary Colman St. John, "The Magazine Publishing Industry: A Global Strategy Analysis," unpublished report (Washington, D.C.: Georgetown Business School, 1989).

22. Susan B. Berg, Richard B. Bruno, Michael J. Derr, R. Scott Handel, and Stephen B. Straske, "The Newsprint Industry: An Analysis of Globalization Potential," unpublished report (Washington, D.C.: Georgetown University, 1989).

23. From Stephen Bowen, senior vice president, Northern Telecom Limited (Canada).

24. *Business Week,* August 14, 1989, pp. 84–85.

25. These four concerns are raised by Yves L. Doz, "Government Policies and Global Industries," in *Competition in Global Industries.* See also Doz, *Government Control and Multinational Strategic Management,* and Dennis J. Encarnation and Louis T. Wells, Jr., "Competitive Strategies in Global Industries: A View from Host Governments," in *Competition in Global Industries.*

26. Study conducted by The MAC Group for *The Cost of Non-Europe,* Basic Findings, Vol. 12, Part B, Commission of the European Community, Brussels, 1988.

27. For a detailed explanation of Europe 1992, see, among others, Paolo Cecchini, *The European Challenge: 1992, The Benefits of a Single Market* (London: Wildwood House, 1988); and John A. Quelch, Robert D. Buzzell, and Eric R. Salama, *The Marketing Challenge of Europe 1992* (Reading, Mass.: Addison-Wesley, 1990). For a quantification of how much EC 92 might improve business profitability, see George S. Yip, "A Performance Com-

parison of Continental and National Businesses in Europe," *International Marketing Review*, Vol. 8, No. 2, 1991, pp. 31–39.

28. See Chris C. Burggraeve, "Meeting Product Standards in the Single Market," *The Journal of European Business*, May–June 1990, pp. 22–26.

29. Speech by Peter Sutherland, former commissioner of the European Community, to the Planning Forum Conference on "The Challenge of Europe 1992," Boston, October 16, 1989.

30. See James Espey, " 'The Big Four': An Examination of the International Drinks Industry," *European Journal of Marketing*, Vol. 23, No. 9, 1989, pp. 47–64.

31. Estimate by McKinsey & Company.

Chapter 3

Building Global Market Participation

This chapter presents a new, global strategy–oriented way of viewing market participation. Instead of selecting country-markets on the basis of stand-alone attractiveness, managers need to consider how participation in a particular country will contribute to globalization benefits and the global competitive position of the business.

Participating in markets outside the home country acts as a lever for both internationalization (the geographic expansion of activities) and globalization (the global integration of strategy). But in the internationalization mode, managers select countries based on stand-alone attractiveness. In contrast, when used as a global strategy level, market participation involves selecting countries on the basis of their potential contribution to globalization benefits and to the global competitive position of the business. The same considerations also apply to determining the level at which to participate—primarily the target market share; and to determining the nature of participation—building a plant, setting up a joint venture, and so on. Managers may, of course, often make market selection decisions from a mixture of motives, and many multinational companies have grown that way.[1] The key is to recognize that there is a difference in the two motivations and in their potential consequences.

Heineken's First International Markets

The internationalization history of Heineken, the Dutch brewer, provides a classic example of choices made on the basis of stand-alone attractiveness. Heineken's first international markets were Egypt, Ceylon, Singapore, Indonesia, the West Indies, and the Congo. What did these six countries have in common? Heineken chose the first five countries because they were either Dutch colonies or on shipping routes to them. These factors made those markets very attractive to Heineken, even though each country had little effect on Heineken's global position. The last country on the list, the Congo, came about because a Belgian brewer that also had business in the Congo had been sold to a Belgian bank, which then asked Heineken to take care of the company.[2] Most other multinational companies can tell a similar story of one-by-one decisions based on country-by-country stand-alone attractiveness and happenstance. As the world's most global beer company (in terms of international revenues), Heineken now recognizes the global strategic importance of key markets like North America. The company has a major target of building up its business in the United States and Canada, which in 1990 accounted for less than 10% of sales.

TYPES OF GLOBAL MARKET PARTICIPATION

The traditional view of being international tends to focus on the percentage of a business' revenues outside the home country and the number of countries in which the business participates. Corporate annual reports of both American and European companies almost invariably report these two statistics. But these two measures are of little use when we take a global strategy view of market participation. Knowing that a concern has 50% of its revenues outside the home market is meaningless without knowing the percentage of the worldwide market that is outside the home country. Similarly, being present in ten countries that include the United States, Japan, and Germany is far more important, in most industries, than is being present in thirty countries that exclude these three but include many small, less advanced countries.

To have a global level of market participation requires significant global market share, a reasonable balance between the business's geographic spread and the market's spread, and presence in globally strategic country-markets. Allianz Versicherungs AG, Europe's largest insurance group headquartered in Germany, has a global strategy of gaining leading market positions in the

---

Japanese Companies' Expansion Paths

In contrast to Heineken's experience, the internationalization of Japanese companies provides many examples of a global strategy approach to market selection. According to Philip Kotler, Liam Fahey, and S. Jatusripitak, there have been three typical paths of expansion, each exhibiting a clear global plan.3 The most common has been to move from Japan to developing countries to developed countries. This occurred in steel, automobiles, petrochemicals, consumer electronics, home appliances, watches, and cameras. In this path the Japanese companies built up experience and capacity in the smaller and easier developing countries. Typically, the United States has then been the first developed country to be penetrated, because of its large size; its relative closeness to Japan; and the lower level of tariff, cultural, and language barriers than in Europe. The second expansion path—going straight to developed countries, particularly the United States—occurred in high-technology industries such as computers and semiconductors. In this expansion mode the Japanese also sometimes used countries similar to the United States as trial markets. Fujitsu used Australia this way in computers. A third expansion path was to start directly with developed countries. This happened with products for which the Japanese home market was still not developed or too small—videotape recorders, color televisions, and sewing machines.

United States, Europe, and Asia. Allianz built up a strong position in Europe primarily through acquisitions and pursued a similar strategy in the United States with its 1990 purchase of Fireman's Fund, one of the largest insurance companies in the country.

Global Market Share

Achieving high market share in single-country markets has long been a key objective for most managers. The benefits include being able to exploit economies of scale, possessing greater bargaining power with suppliers and distribution channels, and enjoying more ready acceptance by customers. Some researchers have recently questioned these benefits.4 But these benefits of high share seem even greater in highly global industries. That is because the advantages of high market share can be leveraged across many countries, not just one. The advantages can be used again and again. A business that takes a global approach to manufacturing—by concentrating production in one or a few countries—in an industry where economies of scale are large can exploit the resultant low-cost advantage in country after country. The strategy has worked for Japanese companies in industry after industry. Low-share competitors may be able to resist in individual countries by developing specialized strategies, but that approach is unlikely to be available in the majority of countries.

Global Balance

High global market share is important but not sufficient for global market participation. A global business also needs to have its geographic distribution of revenues in reasonable balance with that of the worldwide market. That is, the business should usually not have most of its revenues concentrated in just a few countries, and its market share in each country should not be too different from its global market share. Global balance is important as a counterpoint to large market share, because the business usually needs to have significant presence in many countries in order to benefit fully from a global strategy. On a country-by-country basis, in some industries it may be better to have a large, significant share in some countries and a small share in others than to have a moderate share level everywhere.[5] But this effect may well be offset by the damaging effect of uneven market share on the ability to operate a global strategy.

An imbalanced level of market participation weakens the use of each of the other four global strategy levers. A business with revenues concentrated in a few businesses will find it difficult to develop global products that have wide appeal. Inevitably, the desires of the few dominant countries will take precedence. While this may be fine in the short term, such a situation makes it more difficult to expand geographically in the future. For the same reasons, and with the same consequences, such a business will find it difficult to develop global marketing programs. A concentrated business may also find it difficult to develop a globalized network of value-adding activities. Ideas for where to locate activities may be biased toward the needs of the dominant countries. In addition, there is usually a strong reluctance to move away from the status quo. Perhaps, most important, *a business with imbalanced market participation will find it difficult to make effective integrated competitive moves.* Because of its weakness in many markets, such a business will have fewer opportunities and leverage points for making preemptive and counterparry moves against competitors. Being aware of global balance can change the perception of competitive threats. A competitor with a large share but limited presence can be less of a threat than a competitor with a smaller share but broader market presence.

Most American companies probably have a significant imbalance with too great a proportion of revenues in the United States. Furthermore, in most industries the U.S. market is growing more slowly than the rest of the world, so that the imbalance will probably get worse.

Presence in Globally Strategic Markets

Last, a large global market share and global balance need to be combined with presence in key or globally strategic country-markets. Perhaps the most important difference between market participation for the sake of internationalization and that for the sake of globalization is the role of *globally strategic countries.* Such countries are important beyond their stand-alone attractiveness. There are several ways in which a country can be globally strategic as a market:

- Large source of revenues or profits
- Home market of global customers
- Home market of global competitors
- Significant market of global competitors
- Major source of industry innovation

Large Source of Revenues or Profits

The size of a market is, of course, a major factor in country stand-alone attractiveness. Size is also important for global strategic reasons. The larger the market, the more it can contribute to a competitor's global scale economies. Success in a large market can, therefore, drive down worldwide costs for a competitor that shares costs across countries. Success in a large market can also provide funds to subsidize the business in other markets. Active subsidization across countries is a key feature of a global strategy. For these reasons it is critical to succeed in large markets and to deny success in such markets to global rivals. American and European companies suffer a common disadvantage in that Japan, the third major market after Western Europe and the United States, is so much more difficult for foreign competitors than are these other two markets.

In most industries, Japanese competitors enjoy at home a well-protected major source of revenues and profits.[6] Conversely, the size of the U.S. market is rapidly turning from an advantage to a liability for American companies. When they had little global competition, American businesses could use their home scale advantage to muscle their way into overseas markets. But new, tough, and newly tough foreign competitors are irresistibly drawn to the U.S. market—still the largest single country-market in the world.

Markets that are large relative to their region can also be strategically important, particularly where it is impractical to ship between continents.

For that reason, Brazil is commonly regarded in many industries as strategically important. That is despite the difficulties of doing business there. Brazil has had some of the highest trade barriers in the world, so that in most industries multinational companies have had to set up local production rather than being able to import. Under its new, democratic government Brazil is now gradually reducing these trade barriers.

Home Market of Global Customers

Global competitors need a strong presence in the home market of global (and other major) customers. Relationships can be maintained best at the customer's home. The customer's foreign subsidiaries will also look askance at a supplier that does not have a major share of its home country business. Major customers are also the key source of ideas for innovation. So it is important to have a research and development presence in these customers' home markets. Having demanding customers can also be a key to global success.[7]

Home Market of Global Competitors

For many global competitors their home market represents a major source of revenues or profits, although the home market need not be the country in which the parent company has its head office.[8] A business needs a strong presence in these enemy home markets in order both to limit funds flow to its competitors and to act as a hostage for good behavior. One executive characterizes this motivation as an "in your face" strategy. Equally important, the business can learn firsthand how the competitor operates and more closely monitor developments. Being in the home market of major competitors greatly reduces the chance of being surprised. Kodak has now greatly strengthened its position in Japan, but at a far higher cost than if it had committed to Japan much earlier.

The air-conditioning industry provides an example of the dangers of ignoring the Japanese market. Major U.S. producers, who have long dominated the world market, made much less of an effort in Japan, now the world's largest (in revenues). Japanese manufacturers have successfully applied a technology invented in the United States in the 1960s, the ductless split (which provides a smaller and quieter central air-conditioning system than conventional methods), and now seek international markets. A stronger presence in Japan might have alerted American producers to the growing attraction of this technology rather than having to make up lost time now.

Competing in Japan

In contrast to many other American (and European) companies, IBM's early and high successful commitment to Japan has probably helped to reduce the global threat it faces from Fujitsu and other Japanese computer manufacturers. Stunting the domestic growth of foreign competitors (as IBM did) is, of course, cheaper than fighting them after they have grown to global scale. Motorola has succeeded in this much tougher, latter task. In the early 1980s, Motorola found itself under attack in its home market by Japanese competitors in both its semiconductor and communication businesses. At the same time, Motorola faced seemingly insuperable barriers protecting its rivals' home markets. But undeterred, Motorola mounted a sustained effort to both defend its U.S. markets and invade markets in Japan. This effort included soliciting the threat of U.S. congressional action. Motorola's reward has been the gradual yielding of barriers in Japan and an increasing number of contracts won. In 1990 the Japanese Ministry of Post and Telecommunications even selected a Motorola design for a digital cellular telephone component as a national standard. Perhaps, more important, Motorola has been able to preserve its market leadership at home.[9] Citibank provides another example of an American firm that has undertaken the hard task of building a position in Japan. As part of this effort, Citibank has been willing to cut opportunistic deals with local partners such as the postal-savings system to build an automated teller network system and to lease space in Mitsubishi Bank offices. Furthermore, Citibank is making progress in part by offering services that are new to Japan but successful in the United States, such as telephone transfers and its CitiGold account for large depositors.

Significant Market of Global Competitors

Participating in significant markets of global competitors brings similar benefits to those from participating in competitors' home markets.

Major Source of Industry Innovation

As discussed in Chapter 2, most industries have a few markets that act as "lead countries" in the sense of being the primary source of innovations. Very often, lead countries are also the home markets of global customers and global competitors. But identifying lead countries further helps the process of making the correct decisions on market participation.

GLOBALLY UNIMPORTANT COUNTRIES

Just as less important markets need not be entered as part of a global strategy, the same markets, if already entered or entered for reasons of stand-alone attractiveness, can be left out of the global integration effort. So these countries need not be included when applying the other four global strategy levers of global products and services, global location of activities, global marketing, and global competitive moves or can be left to last in the globalization effort. In addition to the factors affecting global strategic importance, other factors should be considered in deciding whether a country should be integrated into the global strategy. These other factors include market size; competitive position; extent of ownership and control of the subsidiary; quality of the subsidiary's management; and the benefits, costs, and risks of change.[10]

BENEFITS OF GLOBAL MARKET PARTICIPATION

A global approach to market participation helps a company to achieve each of the categories of global benefits: cost reduction, improved quality, enhanced customer preference, and competitive leverage.

Cost Reduction

Expanding market participation helps reduce costs by increasing volume for economies of scale. That benefit applies whether the expansion takes place for internationalization or for globalization reasons. But a global strategy approach to selecting the markets into which to expand, and in which to participate, can make choices that have a more direct effect on the ability to achieve global scale economies.

Improved Quality

Presence in lead countries, and exposure to their demanding customers and innovative competitors, can help a business improve the quality of its products. But a company reaps such benefits only if it is willing to learn from these countries. In general, Japanese companies have been much better at applying such lessons than have American and European companies.

Enhanced Customer Preference

As in the case of McCann-Erickson serving the Coca-Cola account, global market participation can enhance customer preference through global availability, global serviceability, and global recognition. The greater the percentage of purchases accounted for by global customers (whether organizations or consumers), the more benefits arise from global market participation.

Competitive Leverage

A global strategy approach to market participation can increase competitive leverage in the various ways already described. In summary, these gains include the advantages of allowing earlier entry into key markets, providing more sites for attack and counterattack, and creating hostages for good behavior. If choices need to be made among countries for participation, an important consideration is the choice among countries where global competitors are present and where they are not.

A global presence also helps guard against complacency and gives the ability to retaliate against competitors in their home markets, as mentioned in Chapter 1. For example, the strength of the Kellogg Company in global markets for ready-to-eat cereals has been a major reason why large foreign competitors such as Nestlé have a limited presence in the U.S. cereal market.[11] Indeed, Kellogg's archrival, General Mills, has had to resort to establishing a partnership (Cereal Partners Worldwide) in Europe with Nestlé, which will manufacture and market General Mills' products.[12]

DRAWBACKS OF GLOBAL MARKET PARTICIPATION

A global approach to market participation also has the clear drawback of an earlier or greater commitment to a market than warranted on its own merits. In addition, the more the business is managed on a globally integrated basis across many geographic markets, the more coordination costs will be incurred. The cost of coordinating across countries depends in part on the differences and barriers between the countries. Other drawbacks of global market participation arise from the crossing of national frontiers and the loss of customer focus. Using PIMS (Profit Impact of Market Strategy) data, this author found that continental-scale businesses in Europe performed financially worse than national-scale businesses in the period 1972 to 1987, that is, before the 1992 creation of the single European market would reduce barriers. This study also found that in the United States, where barri-

---

Going National by Going Global

Fosters Brewing provides a special case of using global market participation to strengthen a business's position in its home market. Fosters beer used to be a small regional brand in the state of Victoria in Australia. Fosters wanted to expand nationally but recognized that Australians were very loyal to their regional beers. So Fosters decided not to go head-to-head with its Australian competitors by directly challenging them in their home markets. Instead, Fosters hit on a global strategy of exploiting the *wanderlust* of young Australians. Fosters decided to seed its beer in those foreign locations where young Australian tourists congregated, such as Earls Court in London. Thus, many young Australians acquired a taste for Fosters while overseas. When they returned home and wanted to celebrate their foreign memories, they would choose Fosters. This global market participation strategy greatly helped Fosters to become the leading brand in all of Australia.[13]

---

ers and differences between regions are much less than in Europe, continental-scale businesses performed better than regional-scale businesses.[14]

Coordination Costs

Expansion in geographic scope across national boundaries is particularly likely to increase coordination costs. The simple need to set up separate legal entities much of the time provides one major source of additional complexity. Furthermore, the legal entity usually requires some management structure to be responsible for it. Thus, a multicountry business will typically require more layers of management than will a national business covering the same geographic territory size. Other sources of increased coordination cost include international differences in technical standards, language, culture, and operating practices.[15]

Crossing National Frontiers

A business that operates across national frontiers incurs trade barrier costs, transportation costs, and inventory costs. Tariff and nontariff trade barriers hurt performance by reducing sales and increasing costs. Transportation is slower and more costly because of border checks. Also, the combination of trade barriers and transportation difficulties may require a multicountry business to maintain more inventory relative to sales than would a single-country business.

Losing Customer Focus

Multicountry businesses are also less likely to be able to customize for buyer needs than single-country businesses. A multicountry business may have to offer many more product versions or else provide less customer satisfaction than single-country competitors. Offering more products incurs more cost, while providing less customer satisfaction hurts sales.

THE SPECIAL CASE OF JOINT VENTURES

International joint ventures represent a special case in market participation.[16] They provide a rapid way of expanding the geographic scope of a business. For example, in the late 1980s British Airways formed a marketing joint venture with United Airlines in order to increase its participation in major markets. Overseas carriers are unable to establish hub-and-spoke systems within the U.S. market because U.S. law prevents them from flying routes between American cities. The joint venture, however, ameliorated the situation for British Airways. By sharing ground facilities and customer services with United at U.S. airports, British Airways was able to route passengers from United's domestic flights onto its international flights. But dependence on joint venture partners can also be precarious. As United Airlines sought direct global expansion, British Airways found its partner becoming a direct rival. By late-1991, British Airways was negotiating to ally itself with a new U.S. partner, Northwest Airlines. By 1993, British Airways had yet another American partner, U.S. Air.

Managers need to beware, however, of thinking that setting up a joint venture in a country means that the market is covered and can be counted as part of a business's global presence. Whether joint ventures represent genuine market participation depends on how the venture is set up and on how the partners behave. Strategic success in global joint ventures may depend more on such behavior than on organization.[17] Let's look at one situation. An American multinational company, "AMSUPP," had very strong market positions in an industrial supplies business in all major countries except Japan. There it had set up a joint venture with the leading Japanese company, "NIPPONSUPP," in the industry. The venture gave AMSUPP a 45% ownership in return for technology transfer as well as capital investment. In discussing global coverage and global market share, the AMSUPP managers included Japan in their calculations. With Japan, AMSUPP's global market participation looked very complete. Japan's inclusion was particularly important because, using the criteria discussed earlier in this chapter, the AMSUPP managers identified Japan as the most globally strategic country, more so even than the United States. Unfortunately, the way in which the venture was set up and the way in which the AMSUPP managers operated really negated the possibility of genuine participation by AMSUPP.

First, AMSUPP owned a share only of the manufacturing subsidiary of NIPPONSUPP, and not a share of the parent company that was responsible for marketing and sales. AMSUPP, therefore, had no legal right of access to NIPPONSUPP's markets and customers. Second, while NIPPONSUPP had sent marketing representatives to the United States to learn about the American market from AMSUPP, AMSUPP had not done the same in Japan. Many American companies have found that in joint ventures with Japanese companies, the latter have gained far more access to their American partners' knowledge than have the former to their Japanese partners' knowledge. In effect, AMSUPP did not participate in the Japanese market in any strategic sense—it had merely a financial investment, and not a very profitable one either. When the AMSUPP managers understood their problem and tried to change it, they found that they were in the proverbial position of riding a tiger—it could not get off for risk of being eaten. In this case, if AMSUPP ended the joint venture it would lose all its business in Japan. Worse, it had created the tiger itself by setting up NIPPONSUPP with the best technology. That, combined with NIPPONSUPP's manufacturing skills, resulted in NIPPONSUPP's products being of higher quality than those manufactured by AMSUPP. AMSUPP now had to maintain the relationship in order to prevent NIPPONSUPP from becoming a fearsome global competitor. So joint ventures and alliances help much more in strengthening the core strategy and the internationalization strategy than the globalization strategy.

DIFFERING STRATEGIC ROLES FOR EACH COUNTRY

A global strategy approach to market participation also means that different countries should have different roles within the total business. The collection of country-businesses should be viewed as a strategic portfolio rather than as a passive one. The Boston Consulting Group (BCG) popularized the use of cross-subsidization of businesses within a corporate portfolio. The same approach can be applied to countries in global strategy. Typically, the home country needs to subsidize markets that are newer to the business. That contrasts with what has been a common mindset in companies dominated by the home business. Such companies often treat international markets opportunistically as ways to balance capacity utilization.

Business Growth/Competitive Strength Matrix

A comprehensive way of allocating country roles is to use an adaptation of the BCG matrix.[18] In Exhibit 3–1, the horizontal axis uses competitive strength (which includes market share) instead of BCG's relative market share (and is reversed in direction from the BCG matrix), and the vertical axis uses growth potential of the business instead of BCG's industry growth rate. In this business growth/competitive strength matrix "cash cow" countries provide funds for investment in "wildcat" countries that may become future "star" countries. For a typical U.S.-based business, the cash cow countries might include the United States and the United Kingdom; the star countries might include Italy; and the wildcat countries might include Japan, Spain, and Hungary.

Global Strategic Importance/ Competitive Strength Matrix

Another important way of allocating roles to countries is to take a competitive approach based on the global strategic importance of each country. The country strategic importance/competitive strength matrix in Exhibit 3–2 keeps the same horizontal dimension as Exhibit 3–1 but uses as

EXHIBIT 3–1   Business Growth/Competitive Strength Matrix

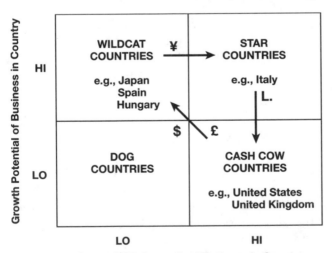

Note:
- Adapted from the Boston Consulting Group's growth share matrix.
- Arrows indicate desired directions of cash flow.
- Countries are for illustration only.

HI	DANGER/ FIX e.g., Japan	MAINTAIN/ ENHANCE/ PREEMPT e.g., United States Germany
LO	AVOID/ RAID e.g., Australia	DEFEND e.g., Brazil
	LO	**HI**

Global Strategic Importance of Country

Competitive Strength of Business in Country

Note: Countries are for illustration only.

EXHIBIT 3–2   Country Strategic Importance/Competitive Strength Matrix

the vertical axis the global strategic importance of each country. Countries in each cell of the matrix have a different competitive prescription. *Maintaining* and *enhancing* the business's position in countries that are of high global strategic importance and where the business is strong (upper right cell) must be viewed as a very high priority. It may also be important to *preempt* possible competitive threats. For a typical U.S.-based business, countries in this cell might include the United States and Germany. The top left cell, where countries have high global strategic importance but the business has a weak competitive position, presents a *danger* area that managers need to *fix*. For many, perhaps most, American (and European) businesses today, Japan looms large in this cell. As the arrow indicates, the business should seek to move itself in Japan to the upper right cell. The lower right cell represents countries with low global strategic importance but where the business has high competitive strength. The business should *defend* its position in these countries, but not at exorbitant cost. For a typical American business, many Latin American countries might today be in this cell. Last, the lower left cell indicates countries with low global strategic importance where the business has low competitive strength. These countries should probably be treated opportunistically. Managers should *avoid* them or *raid* them for short-term profits. For many American businesses, countries like Australia might fall in this cell. A key challenge for governments in such countries is to increase the global strategic importance of their markets.

Implementation Issues

In using both matrices shown, attention should be paid to likely changes over time as country-markets evolve. Users may also want to use refinements such as placing businesses in positions that straddle two cells or designating likely or planned directions of movement. Another very important consideration is the organizational and political aspects of designating portfolio roles to countries. The corporate portfolio approach came to some grief in the 1980s because of both conceptual flaws and the demotivating effects it had on managers responsible for businesses dubbed as dogs or cash cows.[19] The issue of motivation is part of the larger topic of global organization and management that will be covered in Chapter 8.

INDUSTRIES THAT NEED MULTIMARKET PARTICIPATION

Industry globalization drivers affect the importance in each industry of participating in multiple markets and of defining the market globally. Are there particular industries where companies have chosen multiple- rather than single-market participation? Various studies have identified the industries dominated by multinational rather than national companies. But the fact that industries have multinational companies does not mean that the industries are inherently global. They could just as easily be inherently multilocal.

Many of the industries most dominated by multinational companies are very multilocal. For example, most consumer packaged goods industries—detergents, toiletries, many food categories—are dominated by multinationals—Unilever, Procter & Gamble, Nestlé, and so on. But in these industries the primary strategy has been to transfer the multinational's expertise—in product development, quality manufacturing, and marketing—but then to manage each country on a more or less stand-alone basis. But, as cited elsewhere in this book, even in these industries companies are beginning to take a more global approach.

GUIDELINES FOR BUILDING GLOBAL MARKET PARTICIPATION

Participating in the right countries and at the right level provides the foundation on which a successful total global strategy needs to be built. The following guidelines summarize the global, rather than multilocal, approach to building market participation:

- Managers need to select countries for entry and investment on the basis of global strategic importance as well as of stand-alone attractiveness.
- The most strategic countries can often be the most expensive ones in which to build up significant market presence.
- Managers should particularly worry about the home countries of major global competitors or *potential* global competitors.
- Managers need to evaluate multiple, sometimes conflicting, criteria in identifying globally strategic markets. So selecting the markets in which to participate is somewhat more complicated than is using a simple rule of thumb like "be in the 'Triad' markets of the United States, Europe, and Japan."
- Different countries can play different strategic roles as part of the total global strategy.
- Alliances and joint ventures can provide a quicker and easier way to build global market participation, but also weaken the potential for a fully integrated global strategy.

DISCUSSION AND RESEARCH QUESTIONS

1. What are the most important countries in which a global business should participate today, and why? What will this list of countries look like in ten years' time?
2. How should a company select countries for market participation?
3. Compare and contrast the "multilocal" and "global" approaches to market participation.
4. What priorities should be assigned by a multinational computer company to North America, Latin America, Western Europe, Eastern Europe, the Middle East, Japan, East Asia, and other regions? How would your answer differ for other types of companies? How would your answer differ based on the home country of the company in question?

NOTES

1. The literature on foreign direct investment (FDI) provides extensive treatment of companies' motivations for internationalization. See, for example, Peter J. Buckley and Mark Casson, *The Future of the Multinational Enterprise* (New York: Holmes and Meier, 1976); Alan M. Rugman, *International Diversification and the Multinational Enterprise* (Lexington, Mass: Lexington Books, D.C. Heath, 1979); Peter J. Buckley, *The Theory of the Multinational Enterprise, Acta Universitatis Upsaliensis, Studia Oeconomiae Negotiorum,* Vol. 26 (Uppsala, Sweden), 1987; and John H. Dunning, "The Eclectic Paradigm of International Production: A Restatement and Some Possible Extensions," *Journal of International Business Studies,* Spring 1988.
2. This history was provided by G. Van Schaik, vice chairman and executive board director, Heineken N.V., at the Annual Conference of the Strategic Management Society in Amsterdam on October 19, 1988. Mr. Van Schaik went on to say that if Heineken were going international for the first time today, it would choose some very different markets.

3. This section is based on Philip Kotler, Liam Fahey, and S. Jatusripitak, *The New Competition* (Englewood Cliffs, N.J.: Prentice Hall, 1985), p. 174.

4. There is significant controversy in the academic literature about the direction of causation between market share and profitability, and some even question whether there is a positive association. The key literature on this topic includes Robert D. Buzzell, Bradley T. Gale, and R. G. M. Sultan, "Market Share—A Key to Profitability," *Harvard Business Review*, January–February 1975, pp. 97–106; Richard P. Rumelt and Robin Wensley, "In Search of the Market Share Effect," *Proceedings*, Academy of Management Annual Meeting, 1981, pp. 2–6; Robert Jacobson and David A. Aaker, "Is Market Share All That It's Cracked Up to Be?" *Journal of Marketing*, Vol. 49, No. 4, Fall 1985, pp. 11–22; John E. Prescott, A. K. Kohli, and N. Venkatraman, "The Market Share–Profitability Relationship: An Empirical Assessment of Major Assertions and Contradictions," *Strategic Management Journal*, Vol. 7, 1986, pp. 377–394; Robert D. Buzzell and Bradley T. Gale, *The PIMS Principles: Linking Strategy to Performance* (New York: The Free Press, 1987); and Robert Jacobson, "Distinguishing Among Competing Theories of the Market Share Effect," *Journal of Marketing*, Vol. 52, No. 4, October 1988, pp. 68–80.

5. See for example, Porter's ideas about the disadvantages of being "stuck in the middle": Michael E. Porter, *Competitive Strategy: Techniques for Analyzing Industries and Competitors* (New York: The Free Press, 1980).

6. Yoffie and Milner argue that, contrary to classical trade theory, preserving access to large markets can justify government intervention in trade, when competitors practice protectionism in industries characterized by large economies of scale, steep learning curves, or sizable R&D requirements. See David B. Yoffie and Helen V. Milner, "An Alternative to Free Trade or Protectionism: Why Corporations Seek Strategic Trade Policy," *California Management Review*, Summer 1989, pp. 111–131.

7. See Michael E. Porter, *The Competitive Advantage of Nations* (New York: The Free Press, 1990).

8. Ibid.

9. See David B. Yoffie and John Coleman, "Motorola and Japan, Case No. 9–388–056 (Boston: Harvard Business School, 1988).

10. See also Pradeep A. Rau and John F. Preble, "Standardization of Marketing Strategy by Multinationals," *International Marketing Review*, Autumn 1987, pp. 18–28.

11. Kasra Ferdows et al., *The Internationalization of U.S. Manufacturing: Causes and Consequences* (Washington, D.C.: National Academy Press, 1990), p. 13.

12. This partnership was announced in 1991.

13. See also Geoff Lewis, "Carlton & United Breweries," in *Cases in Australian Management*, eds. Geoff Lewis and Peter Fitzroy (Sydney: Prentice Hall, 1991).

14. See George S. Yip, "A Performance Comparison of Continental and National Businesses in Europe," *International Marketing Review*, Vol. 8, No. 2, 1991, pp. 31–39.

15. Hofstede's classic study has highlighted the major differences in culture within one multinational corporation. See Geert Hofstede, *Culture's Consequences: International Differences in Work Related Values* (Beverly Hills, Calif.: Sage Publications, 1984).

16. Joint ventures are a very large topic in their own right. See, among others, Larry G. Franko, *Joint Venture Survival in Multinational Corporations* (New York: Praeger, 1971); Kathryn R. Harrigan, *Strategies for Joint Ventures* (Lexington, Mass.: Lexington Books, 1985); Kathryn R. Harrigan, *Managing for Joint Venture Success* (Lexington, Mass.: Lexington Books, 1986); and Joseph L. Badaracco, *The Knowledge Link* (Boston: Harvard Business School Press, 1991). See also Michael E. Porter and Mark Fuller, "Coalitions and Global Strategy," and Pankaj Ghemawat, Michael E. Porter, and Richard E. Rawlinson, "Patterns of International Coalition Activity," in *Competition in Global Industries*, ed. Michael E. Porter (Boston: Harvard Business School Press, 1986).

17. See Gary Hamel, Yves L. Doz, and C. K. Prahalad, "Collaborate with Your Competitors and Win," *Harvard Business Review*, January–February 1989, pp. 133–139.

18. See also Jean-Claude Larreché, "The International Product-Market Portfolio," in *Read-*

ings in Marketing Strategy, eds. Jean-Claude Larreché and Edward E. Strong (Palo Alto, Calif.: The Scientific Press, 1980).

19. See Philippe Haspeslagh, "Portfolio Planning: Uses and Limits," *Harvard Business Review*, January–February 1982, pp. 58–73; and Richard G. Hamermesh, *Making Strategy Work: How Senior Managers Produce Results* (New York: John Wiley, 1986).

Chapter 4

Designing Global Products and Services

Using global products and services constitutes the second global strategy lever. Globally standardized products or "global products" are, perhaps, the one feature most commonly identified with global strategy. But *the idea of a fully standardized global product that is identical all over the world is a near myth that has caused great confusion.* Such products are very rare and hard to attain, like an "edible Walkman"—the dream of multinational food companies.[1] Standardization occurs, of course, along a continuum. The benefits of global products (or services) can be achieved by standardizing the core product or large parts of it, while customizing peripheral or other parts of the product. For example, most of Sony's consumer electronic products are primarily standardized except for the parts that meet national electrical standards.

The passenger automobile industry provides an excellent example of the wide range of global standardization, both between companies and between model lines within a company. At one end, both Mercedes and Honda, for example, sell products that are highly standardized globally. At the other end, General Motors has had little in common between its North American and European product offerings, although that is now changing. Furthermore, all the automotive manufacturers are striving to increase their

---

Volkswagen's Overcustomization

Volkswagen's experience as the first foreign manufacturer to locate in the United States provides a poignant story of the risks of not standardizing enough, that is, customizing *too much* for local tastes. Volkswagen had set a target of increasing its U.S. market share from 2% to 5% by targeting the 60% of buyers who normally considered domestic models only. So Volkswagen adapted its products to American tastes by softening the suspension and the seats, placing carpeting instead of map pockets on the insides of the doors, and color coordinating the interiors to liven up the standard gray Volkswagen interiors. The result was disastrous. Subsequent market research showed that instead of attracting domestic-loyalists, the changes merely drove away import-loyalists! Volkswagen has taken this lesson very much to heart and today insists on retaining the special German and Volkswagen characteristics whenever localization to suit different market conditions is undertaken.

---

level of standardization. Ford does this in part by assigning responsibility to different parts of the company in developing major portions of a new car for world markets. Mazda, in Japan, of which Ford owns 25%, has the main responsibility for small cars, Ford of Europe for medium-sized cars, and Ford in North America for larger cars.

In passenger automobiles product standardization comes primarily in the "platform" (the chassis and related parts) and to a lesser extent the engine. Developing the platform can account for 30% of the total development cost of a new vehicle. So automobile companies hardly ever design different platforms for different countries, but they may use different bodies on standardized platforms. For example, the Toyota Camry in the United States appears to be a somewhat different car from the Toyota Carina in the United Kingdom, but both use the same platform and engine family.

Steelcase, a major U.S. manufacturer of office furniture, offers its mostly standardized Ellipse "desking system" in the United States, Germany, and France in spite of very different customer preferences in each country. For the U.S. market, Steelcase makes the colors more subtle, makes the wires and cables reachable from the user side of the desk, and changes top sizes to reflect U.S. norms. Herman Miller, another U.S. furniture manufacturer, sells its Newhouse desk system on five continents. The only modification that Herman Miller makes in this line is to use lower heights for Japan.

Faster new product development methods coupled with flexible manufacturing have also allowed manufacturers to develop and produce many more models than before, making it easier to customize for local markets while enjoying global scale economies. So, for example, Toyota, which used to field fewer passenger car models than its American rivals, by 1990 offered more models than did Ford (59 versus 44). But Toyota developed and makes these 59 models from just 22 basic designs. So the company still benefits from a focus on a relatively small number of core products. Improvement in design and development methods, particularly in the use of overlapping rather than consecutive stages of development, have allowed Toyota and other Japanese manufacturers to shorten drastically the time from drawing board to market.[2] Flexible manufacturing, including the use of just-in-time inventory management, has allowed Toyota to produce efficiently the large number of models put out by the development process. In summary, Toyota now seems to be able to benefit from both the global benefits of product and production focus and the local benefits of product proliferation.

Recording companies sell records, discs, and tapes that are essentially globally standardized. But they have also learned to make small local adaptations. For a "pop" record that is marketed in several countries, a company may sometimes get the recording artist(s) to add a single line in the local language. This single line then allows local audiences to relate better to a song that is otherwise foreign. "Shout lines" for disco dancing are particularly suitable for such local translation.

In services, McDonald's allows little variation on its core formula of restaurant design, service approach, and key menu items, but it allows peripheral customization like the serving of alcohol in France and of pork in England. In opening its Moscow restaurants, McDonald's made great efforts to maintain its standard formula, right down to the smiles of the servers.

Some Japanese companies have been particularly successful at getting countries to accept their standardized version of a product. This was a case of necessity because, when they first entered international markets, Japanese companies simply could not afford to offer different models to each country, or even a broad product line within the same country. Where they succeeded was in identifying those core product features that customers truly wanted and then providing that basic product at a price low enough and at a quality high enough that customers would give up the frills. American manufacturers' position of being able to afford many versions of a product turned out to be an Achilles' heel. This was particularly the case in automobiles, where domestic manufacturers were wedded to the multioption approach—and most of the options were superficial to the basic function of an automobile. Furthermore, American automobile manufacturers made no attempt until very recently to market the same product around the world. They had trained the U.S. consumer to want a product that was very different from what the rest of the world could afford.

Businesses can standardize the worldwide *mix* of products as well as the *content* of a product. A globally standardized product mix means that the business sells the same range or list of models around the world. In contrast, global content standardization involves the extent to which individual product items or models are the same around the world. For example, candy companies such as M&M Mars try to sell pretty much the same range of products around the world, even though the products themselves vary in content to allow for differences in tastes. It can be helpful to map mix standardization against content standardization for the business and its competitors. Exhibit 4–1 illustrates a situation in an American chemical additives business. The business had long pursued a product line strategy of customizing to meet differing customers' needs. The result was a very broad product line, most of which was offered in every country. Furthermore, there was little standardization within each product line, so that the business maintained an inventory of many thousands of individual items. In contrast, its leading competitor, a European firm that was just as profitable, sold a much narrower product line that was also much more standardized across countries.

Presenting the information in the manner of Exhibit 4–1 raises two questions: First, did the competitor's approach suggest that customer needs were as different as this business's executives assumed? Second, did this business's product line strategy incur unnecessary costs?

BENEFITS OF GLOBAL PRODUCTS AND SERVICES

I have identified four categories of benefits from globalization: cost reduction, improved quality, enhanced customer preference, and competitive leverage. Each of these benefits applies to global product or service standardization.

Cost Reduction

Reducing costs is probably the most common motivation in standardizing products. These cost savings include development, purchasing, production, and inventory costs. Thus, as described in Chapter 2, high product development costs acts as a globalization driver of product standardization. The higher the development cost relative to expected revenues, the more need there is to develop a few global or regional products rather than many national products. It is important to distinguish between technical and mar-

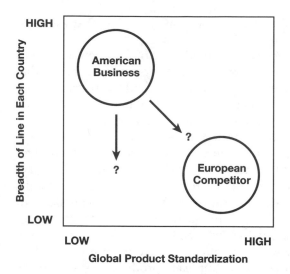

EXHIBIT 4–1   Options in Global Product Line Strategy

ket development costs. Technical, rather than market, development costs act as a driver for product standardization. For example, in the pharmaceutical industry, ethical (prescription) drugs require many years and great expense in technical development, perhaps $200 million for a major new drug. As a consequence, pharmaceutical companies try to develop as few national variants as possible—drugs such as Smith Kline's Tagamet and Hoffman-La Roche's Valium are essentially the same worldwide. In contrast, proprietary (nonprescription or over-the-counter) drugs cost relatively little in technical development but a great deal in market development. Since national regulations for nonprescription drugs vary a great deal from country to country (more so than for prescription drugs), and developing variants is relatively cheap, companies are happy to market many national versions of over-the-counter drugs. The expensive market development costs are mostly incurred locally and, therefore, cannot be much reduced by globalization.

Product standardization also multiplies the gains from concentrating production to exploit economies of scale. As will be discussed in the next chapter, activity concentration can reduce costs even without product standardization, but with it the potential savings become far greater.

Improved Quality

Less obvious than cost reduction, but potentially as important, product standardization can also improve the quality of the products themselves. Reducing the worldwide number of products, through standardiza-

---

Standardizing to Reduce the Number of Products

Savings on purchasing, production, and inventory accrue when standardization reduces the number of products and increases the volume per product. Black & Decker has been particularly successful in reducing its number of products. Before Nolan Archibald became CEO of Black & Decker in 1985, the company was a collection of highly independent subsidiaries, where British, French, and German country managers developed and sold their own products in their own countries. For example, the company made over one hundred different motors worldwide. Not surprisingly, Black & Decker had tremendous overhead that was not offset by any efficiencies or economies of scale. When Archibald came on board, he instituted the development of standardized products that could be sold around the globe. By 1989, Black & Decker made only twenty different motors and was planning to reduce that number to five. Philips, the Dutch multinational company, has also drastically reduced its product lines, such as in television receivers, over the last few years.

---

tion, allows financial and management resources to be focused on the smaller number of products. Braun, the German manufacturer of shavers, coffee makers, and other consumer durable goods, and now a subsidiary of Gillette, maintains a very high reputation partly by restricting the number of products it offers. This parsimony applies across countries as well as across the product line. Braun does little tailoring for national tastes, but single-mindedly maintains its distinctive, global design style.

Enhanced Customer Preference

Although product standardization can reduce customer preference by failing to tailor for national needs, in many situations standardization can actually increase preference. For consumer products and services that are bought while abroad as well as in the consumer's home country, the availability of the same product or service can often be a plus that reinforces preference. Frequently consumed products such as soft drinks, fast food, cigarettes, and candy lend themselves most to this effect. Not surprisingly, Coca-Cola, McDonald's, Philip Morris, and Nestlé derive much of their revenues from globally standardized products. In contrast, products that are seldom purchased while abroad, like detergent or floor wax, do not gain preference from global standardization. Similarly, all travel-related consumer services, from credit cards and traveler's checks to airlines and automobile rental, need to be as standardized as possible. Some companies, such as American Express, do an excellent job, while others are surprisingly lax. Automobile rental companies such as Hertz and Avis have failed to standardize the way in which they classify their types of vehicles and do not even provide a guide to comparing American and European classifications. Because few American travelers are familiar with individual European models, they sometimes wind up renting cars in Europe that are too small for their families and baggage. Europeans have the opposite problem. They can find themselves trying to drive an "intermediate" in North America that is larger than any passenger car on European roads.

Global standardization also enhances consumer preference when being global is an essential part of the category's or brand's appeal. Thus, part of Benetton's appeal to teenagers is the implication that wearing its (globally standardized) clothes somehow contributes to world unity; part of Louis Vuitton's appeal is that wealthy and discerning buyers around the world have the same taste in luggage and accessories. Furthermore, when users of Benetton or Vuitton products travel, the items bring global recognition of the travelers' affinity, taste, or wealth.

Industrial or commercial products and services sold to multinational customers can also gain increased preference from standardization. The more the customers themselves have a global strategy, the more need they have to purchase globally standardized products and services. Some executives worry that standardizing products will make it easier for competitors to steal business with imitative products. But this risk can be greatly reduced by continuing to differentiate *among* multinational customers while standardizing *within* a given multinational customer.

Competitive Leverage

Globally standardized products can increase competitive leverage by providing low-cost products that act as the basis for invading markets. When they first entered international markets, most Japanese companies lacked the resources to develop and support different products for different countries. Turning this weakness into a strength, they focused on a small number of globally standardized products that initially via low cost, then via superior quality, allowed them to conquer market after market. In contrast, Western companies that are market share followers tend to defend against larger competitors by offering locally customized products. The Japanese experience suggests that smaller competitors may have greater need for standardized products. One research study found that the market share and profit performance of seventy-one European and Japanese firms serving the U.S. market was *negatively* related to the extent to which products were adapted for the U.S. market; that is, the firms with standardized products performed better.[3]

DRAWBACKS OF GLOBAL PRODUCTS AND SERVICES

The most important drawback of global product standardization is that some aspects of national needs may have to be sacrificed. As a result, customer preference in some countries may be less than for a product customized for the local market. Stories abound of companies that have made mistakes by not customizing for local needs, such as American appliances that are too large for Japanese kitchens or Japanese calculator pads too small for American fingers. The key is to find a balance between the benefits and drawbacks of standardization. Furthermore, the benefits can be increased and the drawbacks reduced by designing global products from scratch. These global products (or services) should seek to satisfy the most important common needs of the most important markets.

WHEN TO USE GLOBAL PRODUCTS AND SERVICES

As with the other global strategy levers, industry globalization drivers affect the use of global products and services.

Market Globalization Drivers for Global Products

Among market globalization drivers, the extent of *common customer needs* and of the importance of *global customers* provides the main stimuli to using globally standardized products and services.

Canon's Global Photocopier

Canon's product strategy when it first entered the photocopier business in the early 1970s provides one of the most powerful examples of sacrificing the ability to meet local needs. Canon chose to design from scratch a global product. In doing so Canon realized that it could not keep the feature of being able to copy all sizes of Japanese paper if the product cost was to meet its target. Canon willingly gave up the ability to meet all the needs in its *domestic* market in order to maximize its prospects in the *global* market.[4] Few American companies would find it easy to make such a decision.

Common Customer Needs

The extent to which customers in different countries have the same needs and tastes in a given product or service category provides the primary determinant of how much to standardize. In the pharmaceutical industry fundamental customer needs are highly common as disease and ailments strike all of humanity and in mostly similar ways. Many afflictions are universal: from the common cold to heart disease. There are some geographic differences, with tropical diseases being the largest group of location-specific afflictions. Similarly, national diets and lifestyle affect the relative incidence of different diseases, such as the well-known high incidence of heart disease in Western countries arising from high-fat diets and the high incidence of hypertension in Asian countries arising from high-salt diets. But, like other differences in national habits, these dietary differences and their related health consequences are declining. Ice cream is becoming increasingly popular in Japan while Oriental food is joining the menu of American fast food. Overall, needs are highly common. But even if the *incidence* of a particular disease varies, its treatment is usually the same. So multinational drug companies are able to market nearly identical products around the world, and successes in one country can rapidly become global successes.

At the same time, national practices differ somewhat in how ailments are treated. Some countries are more eager users of surgery, some rely more on medicines prescribed by doctors, and others depend on over-the-counter remedies suggested by pharmacists. In particular, the preferred form of the medicine varies greatly. For example, in Britain many people prefer to take aspirin in powder form dissolved in water instead of the tablet or capsule form popular in the United States. People in some countries like to take medicine via suppositories. Preference for folk remedies over manufactured medicines also varies. Recently, the return-to-nature trend has created the new category of "phaetopharmaceuticals," which are made from natural, nonchemical ingredients. These new medicines have captured a very large share of the market in Germany. Even diagnosis can be affected by national culture—Americans tend to focus on head pains while Japanese tend to focus on stomach pains. National differences in treatment tend to be much greater for over-the-counter drugs, which consumers select for themselves, than for prescription drugs, which are chosen by doctors.

Computer products also have high levels of global standardization. While local business practices and government regulation may affect the content, format, and frequency of, for example, accounting reports, the need for hardware is not fundamentally affected by these variations. So in the computer industry companies usually find it easier to standardize globally hardware than software. But various cultural factors affect both hardware and software—computing is particularly affected by language differences. For example, Japanese *kanji* characters require two bytes to store, in contrast to one byte for Western alphabetical characters. One computer company accommodated these differences by designing a global product from the start, with broad capabilities. Also, in Japan, dedicated word processors (capable of handling Japanese characters) are far more common than in Western Europe and the United States, where dedicated word processing machines have dwindled as a product segment. The need to translate software and documentation for the various European and Asian markets also poses a barrier to the easy dissemination of application software. In health care software systems, the key distinction between countries in the commonality of software needs turns on whether medicine is socialized.

In textbook publishing, the potential for global products is limited by the desire of teachers to use books that reflect the national perspective on history, sociology, psychology, and other subjects. Other than primary sources and some scholarly books, college textbooks in the social sciences and humanities remain largely domestic in origin. Textbooks at the precollege level are even more restricted to national markets. One significant exception to the lack of global textbooks is English as a second language (ESL) instruction, where standardized texts abound. Even so, the world market has long been divided between instruction in American English and British English, with textbook sales following the relative influence of the two countries. For example, American English is taught in Japan, but British English is taught in Malaysia. In some countries, such as Brazil, there is competition between the two forms of English.

Global Customers

Global customers often demand global products and services. So the incidence of global customers has a major effect on the need and potential for product standardization. In the computer industry, customers who globally coordinate their purchases are becoming an increasingly important driver. As customers become more sophisticated computer system buyers, and as they become globalized themselves, they are also becoming more willing to look beyond a single vendor. Their purchasing criteria have changed from focusing on the security provided by a single vendor to maximizing system performance at minimal cost. Further, as companies adopt "open systems" architectures, they frequently do so with the realization that their corporate information systems need to be coordinated on a global scale. But as yet, only perhaps 10% to 15% of buyers act as global customers. A large number of buyers (perhaps 20% to 25%) look regionally.[5] But because of their investment in proprietary systems, many buyers are reluctant to consider new suppliers. Multinational firms may choose to replicate their headquarter's computer system in their foreign affiliates instead of adopting a newer global hardware standard if the costs of transferring software, writing new programs, and training staff on new systems are too great.

In the process control industry, many multinational customers now demand globally standardized products. For example, Royal Dutch Shell, a major customer, might order sixteen identical units for its different plants around the world because it wants each plant to be a mirror image of the others.

Most consumer packaged goods industries have few global customers, but the chocolate industry provides an interesting exception. The chocolate industry has global customers in one special sense. Many consumers buy chocolate as a gift for others (or for themselves) while traveling abroad. The ease of customizing chocolate to incorporate local specialties (chocolate with macadamia nuts in Hawaii or with kiwi fruit in New Zealand) also encourages purchases by travelers. Such purchases abroad expose consumers to different types of chocolate around the world, helping to establish global standards in perceived quality and perhaps taste also. So companies can benefit by maintaining similar brand image, packaging, and quality standards for their chocolates around the world. The impact of global customers is even greater for more frequently purchased consumer packaged goods items such as soft drinks and cigarettes.

Cost Globalization Drivers for Global Products

Among cost globalization drivers *global scale economies, high product development costs,* and *fast-changing technology* have the most effect on the need for global products and services.

Global Scale Economies

Global-level scale economies in the production process encourage businesses to centralize production. Typically, the technological imperatives that yield global scale production economies also yield important production economies in product rationalization. Thus the gains from centralized production can usually be multiplied when combined with a focused, global product line. Both Black & Decker in small appliances and Becton Dickinson in disposable syringes have greatly benefited from using global product ranges with limited items.

High Product Development Costs/
Fast-Changing Technology

High product development costs provide a major motivation for using globally standardized products and services. This motivation is particularly important in industries with rapidly changing technology, such as electronics, or risky development efforts, such as pharmaceuticals. As technology becomes more important in more and more industries, companies in even the food industry are finding that it no longer pays to develop national products. In the coffee industry, for example, the cost of developing new forms of soluble coffee is so great now that companies work on developing new forms (e.g., freeze dried) for global markets only, even though they may adapt blends (e.g., types of coffee beans used) for individual markets.

Government Globalization Drivers
for Global Products

Among government globalization drivers *favorable trade policies* and *compatible technical standards* have the greatest effect on the potential for global products and services.

Favorable Trade Policies

Trade barriers, particularly nontariff ones, such as quotas and local content rules can greatly restrict a company's ability to produce and market a globally standardized product line. In products where the source of raw materials is critical, or the production process is difficult to reproduce in some countries, trade restrictions can prevent the use of global products.

Compatible Technical Standards

Differences in technical standards and related rules directly affect the extent to which products can be globally standardized. Fortunately, differing national standards are converging in many industries toward common global standards. The increasing convergence of standards in telecommunications is making it easier to design global products in that industry. For example, instead of designing products for just the North American market, as it used to do, Northern Telecom, the Canadian telecommunications company, now designs global products for all of its markets, making only minor software modifications for individual countries.

Global Standardization in Financial Services

Despite regulatory barriers, many companies in financial service industries manage a surprisingly high degree of global standardization. Although differences in financial products exist, many are becoming increasingly standardized.6 Barclays, the leading British bank, aims to ensure through its global customer information system that its multinational corporate customers can have access to a uniform range of products at a uniform level of service in a familiar Barclays environment. Because credit cards have become standardized, Citicorp is introducing its bank cards into Europe with little modification. American Express is, perhaps, the master of offering a standardized global product in financial services. French banks have introduced standard leasing arrangements with particular success in Spain and Portugal. Letters of credit have been standardized to the extent that they are almost exclusively written in English to facilitate international transactions and to ensure consistency of contract language. Some products, however, are difficult to standardize because of long-standing differences in national practices. In the United States, the thirty-year mortgage is now standard, while in Europe the ten-year mortgage is more common. Despite these differences, many financial product modifications are not too costly, so that national differences can often be accommodated. The potential for further global standardization seems high as regulatory changes continue to standardize further banking practices and foster greater international competition.

Competitive Globalization Drivers for Global Products

Last, having *globalized competitors* who themselves use globally standardized products or services can provide a powerful spur to developing global products of one's own. It is Japanese companies that have tended to lead in this strategy, forcing their rivals to play catch-up in designing global products, for example, American and European manufacturers in both automobiles and consumer electronics.

DEVELOPING GLOBAL PRODUCTS AND SERVICES

There are two primary ways to develop global products and services. The first, and preferred, method is to develop products and services with the global market in mind, as Canon did for its first photocopier. This approach

USG's Successful European Product Standardization

The experience of USG Interiors, a subsidiary of USG Corporation (formerly U.S. Gypsum), with acoustic ceiling tiles in Europe provides a useful example of why and how one company pushed for product standardization.7 While limited to Europe, the same principles apply in a global program. In 1986, USG had acquired a German-based manufacturer of building products, DONN, which was the dominant supplier of ceiling suspension products in the commercial construction market in Europe. The four DONN companies, in Germany, France, the United Kingdom, and Scandinavia, operated very independently, and the localized approach seemed to be one of DONN's greatest strengths. The acquisition by USG brought a new name, USG Interiors Europe, and a whole new product line—the APCO line of acoustic ceiling tile, manufactured by USG in the United States, that seemed a natural fit with the DONN suspension product. USG Interiors Europe decided to introduce APCO as a standardized pan-European product that had minor modifications from the North American product and did not take DONN's old multilocal approach of allowing each country to develop its own products and programs.

Europe 1992 provided the impetus for this change in approach. The European interior building industry had been very fragmented for many years, as the different national, and even local, requirements made it very difficult to ship and install materials across boundaries. As a consequence, many small manufacturing and installation companies existed, and most of them operated within a limited geographic range only. But with Europe 1992, regulations, style, norms, and quality standards would be harmonized within the different countries in Europe. USG Interiors predicted that business opportunities would increase, and the industry would consolidate into fewer but larger manufacturing companies producing very similar products for all EC markets at lower costs.

The second reason for standardization was that all manufacturing of the new line would be done in the United States. Given that Europe would use different sizes from the United States and would require short production runs, it was imperative for the U.S. factory that Europe standardize on one product line and not require many different, national lines. Even so, it was the first time that the U.S. operations would have to deal with packaging restrictions, stock quantities in non-U.S. sizes, as well as different colors and formulas for what appeared on the surface to be the same product. The U.S. workers would also have to deal with the aesthetic requirements of a European-based community that was decidedly different from North America. European standards for color and tolerances on sizes and texture were more stringent than those in the U.S. market.

USG's approach to anticipating the 1992 changes involved taking the most strict national standards and making them their overall European standards. USG also used a team approach to specify the product requirements and marketing needs and to develop an integrated approach to launching into the different markets. Most important, this integrated approach was sensitive not to upset the local marketing practices already established and that had proven so effective historically in each of its four European companies. The new product line was introduced from late 1987 through 1989. USG judged the new pan-European approach to be highly successful—by late 1989, revenues and profits had tripled from those in 1983.

has the obvious advantage of taking into consideration the needs of major markets right at the start, rather than having to retrofit a product developed for one national market. *Managers should start by identifying globally strategic markets and then understanding the needs of those markets. Perhaps most important, managers should search for commonalities rather than for differences.* Such an approach should allow managers to design the largest possible standardized core, while allowing for necessary customization at the same time.[8]

The second, less desirable but more common, approach is to adapt existing products or services. In adapting from an existing mix of national products, managers need to start by understanding the causes of the national variants. Have these variants arisen from a deliberate response to real differences in needs and tastes? Or are they accidents of independent development? Very often the answer is much more accident than deliberation. Many businesses wind up with product lines that are much less standardized than they could be, simply by not having a global perspective, so that countries make decisions independently of each other.

A European manufacturer of semidurable consumer products found itself with half the countries in the world selling products in one set of colors and the other half in another set. These were not major color differences, but differences, for example, in the shade of blue. This situation arose because most of the world was supplied out of two manufacturing plants, one in the United Kingdom and one in Germany, and the two general managers in these two countries made decisions independently. When first asked to explain the difference, the executives in this business tried to justify their decisions on the basis of differences in consumer preference. But when pushed, the executives admitted that the differences did not arise from perceived consumer differences but from the independent decision-making process. In contrast, the business's major competitor had great success with a highly standardized product line, confirming that customer preferences were not that different.

GUIDELINES FOR DESIGNING GLOBAL PRODUCTS AND SERVICES

Successfully designing global products and services requires managers to make tough trade-offs between global and local demands. Several guidelines apply, including the following:

- Globally standardized products and services can bring the benefits of not just cost savings, but also those of improved quality and customer preference.
- The best global products are usually those that are designed as such from the start rather than being adapted from national products later.
- Designers of global products and services should try to maximize the size of the common global core while also providing for local tailoring around the core.
- In investigating needs around the world, managers should look for similarities as well as for differences.

DISCUSSION AND RESEARCH QUESTIONS

1. What is the difference between a local product and a global product?
2. Identify a global product or service. Describe what is standardized about it, and what is localized.
3. Which of the following products and services are more globally standardized and why?

   Apple Macintosh
   Sony Walkman
   American Express Gold Card
   Disney theme parks
   Mercedes automobiles
   Nestlé coffee

4. How should a company go about developing a global product?
5. Select one product or service and discuss which aspects of it are global and which local, and why.

NOTES

1. This term was coined by David Stout, head of economics, Unilever PLC.
2. See George Stalk, Jr., and Thomas M. Hout, *Competing Against Time* (New York: The Free Press, 1990).
3. Masaaki Kotabe and Glenn S. Omura, "Sourcing Strategies of European and Japanese Multinationals: A Comparison." *Journal of International Business Studies,* Vol. 20, No. 1, Spring 1989, pp. 113–130.
4. See also Michael E. Porter, "Changing Patterns of International Competition," *California Management Review,* Vol. 28, No. 2, Winter 1986, pp. 33 and 34.
5. These estimates of global customers and global channels were made by senior executives in a major computer manufacturer.
6. This paragraph is based on Julie Carson, Sanjay Dube, Shyhjaw Chien, Eric Crabtree, and Mitsuhisa Ashida, "Worldwide Commercial Banking in the Late 1980s," unpublished report (Washington, D.C.: Georgetown Business School, 1989).
7. This example is based on a presentation by Dietmar Neupert, managing director, USG Interiors, Inc. (Germany), at the Planning Forum Conference on Europe 1992, in Boston, on October 16, 1989.
8. See also Ilkka A. Ronkainen, "Product-Development Processes in the Multinational Firm," *International Marketing Review,* Winter 1983, pp. 57–65. For a comprehensive description of how to develop multinational product policy, see, for example, William H. Davidson, *Global Strategic Management* (New York: John Wiley, 1982).

Chapter 5

Locating Global Activities

The global location of activities represents the third global strategy lever. Where to locate a business's activities and how to coordinate them constitute critical choices in global strategy. Michael Porter calls these choices configuration (location) and coordination and suggests a four-cell matrix of types of international strategy: high foreign investment with extensive coordination, country-centered strategy, export-based strategy, and pure global strategy.[1] While these types provide helpful summaries, my approach views location and coordination choices as providing a continuum rather than discrete choices. Furthermore, the location and coordination of activities constitute only one of the five global strategy dimensions and one of the four organization dimensions.

Every functional or value-adding activity, from research to manufacturing to customer service, is a candidate for globalization.[2] Traditionally, multinational companies have faced two choices in activity location. On the one hand, they can duplicate an activity in multiple foreign locations. The classic multinational strategy has been to reproduce activities in many countries, particularly the production function by setting up factories and other manufacturing assets. On the other hand, multinational companies can keep activities concentrated in the home country.

The classic export-based strategy has been to locate as much of the value chain as possible back home, while locating overseas only down-stream activities, such as selling, distribution, and service, that have to be performed close to the end customer. But a global strategy for activity location involves a third approach, locating each individual activity in the one (or a few) countries most appropriate for that activity. *So a business pursuing a global activity strategy might locate research in the United Kingdom, development in Germany, raw material processing in Mexico, subassembly in the United States, final assembly in Ireland, and so on.* Some writers suggest that a primary determinant of a global, as opposed to a country-centered, strategy is having a large amount of value added in upstream activities located in one country.[3] But this constitutes an export rather than a global strategy.

Exhibit 5–1 shows an extreme case of a fully global value chain in which every activity occurs in one, different country only. In reality most companies would, and should, provide for some duplication of most activities. Such duplication provides security against supply disruptions and provides some flexibility in the system.

Another way of viewing the global approach to activity location is the following: Global activity location means deploying one integrated, but globally dispersed, value chain or network that serves the entire worldwide business rather than separate country value chains or one home-based value chain.[4] But managers should bear in mind that some countries may have to be kept out of the global value chain, typically because their markets have too high protective trade barriers to allow imports. Of the large

EXHIBIT 5–1   The Extreme Global Value Chain

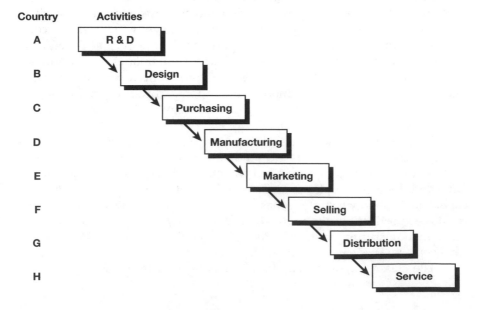

noncommunist countries, it is usually Brazil and India that have had the highest all-around trade barriers to manufactured goods, and not Japan as many believe. (It is too early to characterize the trade policies of the many newly ex-communist countries.)

Perhaps the most important consideration in a global strategy approach to activity location is to take a "zero-based" view and to ask what would be the optimal pattern and location of each activity if the company could start from scratch. Hardly any company is likely to be able to conclude that its current pattern of location is optimal. Because globalization conditions have changed, and continue to do so, and because of a lack of global thinking in the past, many, perhaps most, companies find themselves saddled with activity networks unsuited to the globalization potential of the industries in which they operate. Companies in Europe provide the most extreme example. With the arrival of a single European market, many companies there find themselves with factories fifty kilometers apart on either side of a frontier that will no longer exist. Clearly, changing the location of activities, particularly of major fixed assets such as factories, is expensive and, in many cases, not justified. But global managers need to operate with an understanding of where their activities ought to be located even if they cannot easily move them there. Such knowledge is essential in planning investments to upgrade or expand existing facilities and to create new ones.

ROLE OF NATIONAL FACTORS

Many factors affect the choice of location for activities. Global managers need to distinguish between traditional country considerations and global strategic importance, among other factors.

Traditional Country Considerations

Traditional international economic theory has stressed the importance of "comparative advantage" in addressing where multinational companies should locate their activities.[5] In particular, they should locate in countries where the costs of raw materials, labor, and other production inputs ("factor costs") are lowest for a given level of productivity. But production cost is only one consideration. Furthermore, production costs themselves are subject to broader influences such as tax benefits and other forms of aid that may be provided by national and other country authorities. Japanese automobile manufacturers seem particularly astute in garnering the maximum governmental benefits from their production location decisions. In placing their American production plants, not only did they extract many concessions from states eager for their patronage, but Honda, Nissan, and Toyota have each located in a different state (Ohio, Tennessee, and Kentucky, respectively), perhaps to maximize their political lobbying effectiveness by each having two senators to represent their concerns. Interestingly, BMW and Mercedes are locating their new factories in yet two other states—South Carolina and Alabama.

Other considerations include broader issues of productivity and quality, convenience for shipping to other countries, reliability of the workforce, the cost of capital, the economic infrastructure, and the extent of political risk. Some Third World countries with low costs and high productivity may seem ideal but may need to be avoided because of their high level of political risk. While the risk of outright expropriation has declined, the risk of government interference and political and economic disruptions continue. Many Western companies manufacturing in China have suffered from a sudden clampdown on foreign exchange that they needed to purchase raw materials, equipment, and supplies. Another type of issue concerns the so-called "country-of-origin" effect, in which customers give preference to goods produced in certain countries or that they believe to come from those countries.6

The country-of-origin effect in the U.S. automobile market partly explains why the Toyota Corolla, a nearly identical car to General Motors' Geo Prizm, and produced on the same assembly line in the United States, commands a 10% or so price premium in the market. (The next chapter, on global marketing, will also address this effect.) All these considerations in the location of activities, including from where to source production inputs, should be familiar to multinational companies in developing their internationalization strategy. So in keeping with the focus of this book on globalization rather than internationalization, I assume a basic understanding of these issues and address them only in terms of how they affect globalization strategy.7

Globally Strategic Countries for Activity Location

Just as countries can be globally strategic from the viewpoint of market participation, they can be globally strategic in terms of activity location, for some of the same, but also some different, reasons. Two activities, R&D and production, particularly need to be located in globally strategic countries.

For R&D Location

For R&D, globally strategic countries have the following characteristics:

- Major source of industry innovation
- Presence of highly skilled and/or how cost R&D workers
- Highly demanding customers

As in the case of market participation, the R&D activity benefits from location in countries that are major sources of industry innovation. R&D workers in those countries can gain direct access to the many sources of the innovations being created—via face-to-face contacts with university researchers, participation in conferences, quicker access to publications, competition in the job market, and so on. Monitoring from a distance cannot achieve the full benefits possible through physical location. For example, many scientific journals in Japan are published only in Japanese and circulate little outside the country. While the countries making the major innovations in an industry also tend to have the most skilled R&D workers, other countries can also be important sources of highly skilled or low-cost staff. Several Asian countries have demonstrated this capability.

With the opening up of Eastern Europe, similar opportunities may emerge. The former Soviet Union, for example, has very well-trained scientists who may have much to contribute to commercial R&D efforts. Last, locating R&D in countries with highly demanding customers helps the R&D staff there to better understand the nature of their needs. Furthermore, the same tactic might bring benefits even for the home market. American automobile manufacturers, facing severe attacks from Japanese and European competitors, have made some efforts at designing cars with a European or Japanese feel (e.g., General Motors' Chevrolet Celebrity "Eurosport" model and the Ford Taurus). If they seriously want to do this, they might consider moving their design staff to Europe or Japan or using their European divisions to design some of the models for their American market.

For Manufacturing Location

For manufacturing, globally strategic countries are those that offer an attractive investment climate as well as factors and conditions on which to build comparative and strategic advantage. Companies choosing to make investments in manufacturing facilities, as opposed to sourcing from outside suppliers, need to consider a long list of factors affecting the investment climate. This list includes the level of political stability, government policies toward foreign investment, trade policies, tax policies, legal factors, the macroeconomic environment, and policies on international payments. These considerations are the usual ones that have to be dealt with when a company internationalizes through foreign direct investment.[8] The additional factors that produce comparative and strategic advantage and, therefore, render a country globally strategic for manufacturing include the following:

- Favorable factor conditions
- Close location to major markets
- Favorable country-of-origin effect
- Manufacturing presence of global competitors

Favorable factor conditions—such as low-cost raw materials or labor, or highly skilled or productive labor—form the traditional basis for comparative advantage of one country relative to others.9 Similarly, location close to major markets can be viewed as a type of factor advantage that lowers transportation cost or speeds up response time, thus providing both comparative and strategic advantage.10 Countries that lead in innovation, that produce high-quality products, or that have highly demanding customers often enjoy a positive country-of-origin effect, though typically only within specific product categories. Last, the manufacturing presence of other global competitors can create a positive spiral of rivalry and imitation that continually upgrades the level of manufacturing capability for all competitors in the country.11 So a global strategy for activity location can also be viewed as a means to get access to resources on which to build both comparative and strategic advantage.

ROLE OF EXCHANGE RATES

Currency exchange rates have a direct effect on relative country costs and, therefore, on the competitive positions of companies. In the construction equipment business, Caterpillar Tractor depended heavily on U.S.-based production, while its Japanese rival, Komatsu, manufactured mainly in Japan. In 1979 Caterpillar was the low-cost producer, but by 1985 most of its product lines were priced over 40% above Komatsu's. One reason was that the U.S. dollar had increased by 50% over the yen and most key European currencies. This price difference greatly helped Komatsu to penetrate many of Caterpillar's traditional markets.12 During the same period foreign film manufacturers made significant inroads into several markets. Eastman Kodak estimates that the strong dollar cost it $3.5 billion between 1980 and 1985 in terms of lost market share, inability to penetrate new markets, and lower profit margin. Similarly, companies that shift to low-cost countries for offshore production are taking a bet, in part, that these low costs will not be eroded by currency changes. Perhaps most important, *companies need to recognize the strategic as well as financial risk posed by currency changes.*

Traditional definitions of currency exposure concentrate mainly on foreign currency flows that relate to the company's own operations. This internal focus ignores the fact that an unfavorable currency movement may not just be unfavorable; it could be favorable to the competition. But exchange rate changes can also favor a company in the short term and hurt it in the long term. In the late-1980s, depreciation of the U.S. dollar relative to the Japanese yen improved the competitive position of American companies relative to their Japanese rivals. But the higher value of the yen also allowed Japanese companies to make many bargain acquisitions that would enhance their long-run competitive capabilities. So exchange rate changes can act as catalysts in the restructuring of companies and industries.[13]

But forecasting long-term exchange rates is generally acknowledged to be very difficult. About the only consensus is that the currencies of countries with high or fast-growing productivity tend to appreciate relative to currencies in countries with low or slow-growing productivity rates. Even so, differences in productivity did not account for the down-up-down, doubling, and halving path of the U.S. dollar against the Japanese yen, Deutsche mark, and other major currencies in the 1970s and 1980s. Nor were many experts able to predict this path. One view is that companies should locate production in countries with low productivity, with the expectation that the currency will stay weak. Furthermore, these companies can increase their advantage by increasing their productivity in the country faster than the country's overall rate of productivity growth.

Another view takes into account "parity purchasing power" exchange rates that adjust for differences between countries in the prices of similar goods and services. So a country with a high relative nominal (official) exchange rate but high relative prices also has a lower parity purchasing power exchange rate. Some studies provide evidence that nominal exchange rates tend to move toward their parity purchasing power exchange rate over time.[14] Then the latter rate can be used to forecast the movement of the official exchange rate. Perhaps the best that can be said is that companies looking for exchange rates that will stay weak should locate operations in countries with weak economies. Even then, it is only the nominal exchange rate that might weaken, and real exchange rates might still go up with wage and other factor price increases. Offsetting that exchange rate benefit is, of course, all the other disadvantages in terms of infrastructure and productivity inherent in weak economies. On the other hand, if a company wishes to locate in strong, or at least, developed economies, it should probably not make its choice between such countries on the basis of expected currency movements. Any likely differences in nominal exchange rates are likely to be offset by movements toward the parity purchasing power exchange rate. To maintain its comparative advantage over foreign competitors, a producer also needs to increase its productivity, *relative* to that of the country in which the production activity is located, *faster* than its competitor does in its country. Otherwise, the firm will find its productivity gains more than offset by increases in the currency exchange rate where it is located. So it is dangerous to invest in locating activities in a country with one strong sector, unless the activity is in that sector. For example, because of the effect of oil exports on strengthening Norway's exchange rate, other industries there have had great difficulty in being competitive internationally.[15]

So given the difficulty of forecasting exchange rates, global managers can choose among alternative ways of handling the uncertainty. According to Bruce Kogut, they can speculate, hedge, or be flexible.[16] *Speculation* involves committing to one or a small number of countries as production sites. This approach, of course, runs the risk of betting the wrong way. *Hedging* means spreading out production and other activities so that losses from exchange rate rises in one country can be offset by gains from exchange rate declines in other countries. But diversifying the manufacturing base around the world may be insufficient. Managers also need to consider what competitors are doing. So a global strategy needs to consider strategic foreign exchange exposure as well as operating exposure, and strategic flexibility as well as operating flexibility. A strategy of *being flexible* means investing in excess capacity in several locations and then shifting production with exchange rate shifts. This last option provides the best chance of reducing strategic risk as well as reducing operating risk. In particular, a really cautious strategic approach to being flexible would be to manufacture in some of the same locations as major global competitors. That way, the competitor would stand less chance of gaining an advantage from movements in exchange rates.

STRATEGIC ADVANTAGE VERSUS COMPARATIVE ADVANTAGE

The previous discussion of exchange rates highlights the difference between strategic advantage and comparative advantage. In global competition, companies need to exploit both. *Strategic* advantage springs from the core business strategy, as discussed in Chapter 1. This advantage can be spread and applied around the world without depending on country-based sources of *comparative* advantage such as low labor costs or superior technological infrastructure. Apple Computer's strategic advantage came primarily from its pioneering position in the personal computer business, its unique user-friendly designs, and the strong name recognition and loyalty that it quickly built. But as both domestic and international competitors encroached on Apple's turf, the company had to add comparative advantage also by shifting some of its production activities offshore to reduce costs. So today Apple's competitive advantage depends on a combination of strategic and comparative advantage.

Federal Express developed a core business strategy for the document and package delivery market that gave it significant strategic advantage in its home country, the United States. The company is now seeking to expand its business globally. Whether or not Federal Express succeeds will depend greatly on whether its core strategy can provide the same extent of strategic advantage abroad. But as a service business based in many countries, Federal Express's international prospects will depend little on comparative advantage. Indeed, its core strategy has not translated well to Europe, and Federal Express has had to abandon its intra-Europe services, although its U.S.-Europe business thrives. In contrast, Japanese automobile manufacturers, including Toyota, in the 1980s successfully added quality-based and design-based strategic advantages to the cost-based comparative advantage with which they entered international markets in the 1960s. *The best global strategies combine strategic and comparative advantage to yield global competitive advantage.*

Exhibit 5–2 illustrates some possible combinations of strategic and comparative advantage. Companies with only strategic advantage have a *core-formula strategy* (upper left cell), as Caterpillar, the construction equipment manufacturer, had in the 1970s and Federal Express has to date. Similarly, Disney's theme parks depend on the highly successful core formula that the company is now using to expand internationally. But Disney has not been able to bring American sunshine and low prices (comparative advantage) to northern France, with disastrous consequences for EuroDisney to this point. Companies with only comparative advantage tend to have to compete on the basis of low cost as many Japanese companies did in the 1960s, and many Korean companies did in the 1980s, in a *cost-based export strategy* (lower right cell). Some Korean concerns, like Samsung's microwave oven business, have now been able to move beyond low-cost–based comparative advantage to add quality-based strategic advan-

EXHIBIT 5–2   Strategic and Comparative Bases of Advantage

		No	Yes
Strategic Advantage	Yes	**CORE-FORMULA STRATEGY** Caterpillar in 1970s Federal Express in 1990s Disney theme parks	**GLOBALLY LEVERAGED STRATEGY** Sony Toyota in 1980s
	No	**UNTENABLE STRATEGY** British Leyland in 1970s Chrysler in 1980s	**COST-BASED EXPORT STRATEGY** Toyota in 1960s Samsung in 1980s Hyundai in 1990
		No	Yes

Comparative Advantage

Changing Locations in the Ceramics Industry

The ceramics industry provides an example of how the ideal country for activity location changed over time with changing sources of strategic advantage.[17] In the 1960s and 1970s, the central driving factor for strategic advantage was the conversion of a craft skill into high-volume industrial production. This conversion required highly skilled workers found most easily in Germany. So a German firm, Villeroy & Boch, pioneered and led the shift. In the 1980s, the basis of strategic advantage shifted to design, continuous process operation, and the new single-firing technology. These advantages were both developed by Italian firms and were most readily available in Italy where there were many designers, a low cost of capital, and less skilled but lower cost labor than in Germany.[18] In the 1990s having strong logistic systems and presence in key markets has been added to the sources of comparative advantage. Firms can gain advantage by locating in Milan and Paris for design, in Italy and Portugal for low-cost labor, and in Germany and United States for exposure to the customers in these very large and demanding markets.

---

tage. Others, such as Leading Edge in microcomputers, succeeded for a while on the basis of comparative advantage but lost their position when they could not develop high enough quality to achieve strategic advantage. Still other Korean concerns, such as Hyundai's passenger automobile business, are at the cusp of transition. Companies with both sources of advantage have a *globally leveraged strategy* (upper right cell), as Sony has had for a long time and that Toyota achieved in the 1980s. Companies with neither source of advantage have an *untenable strategy* (lower left cell) and will fail to hold their position, as happened to British Leyland and Harley-Davidson in the 1970s and Chrysler in the 1980s.

The sources of strategic and comparative advantage also change over time. They change for external reasons, such as differing productivity growth rates among nations and the advent of new technologies, and for competitor-driven reasons, such as one competitor committing to exploit an emerging technology, as Hattori-Seiko did to the quartz technology for watches in the 1970s. Similarly, Japanese competitors' commitment in the 1980s to multipurpose, rather than specialized single-purpose, industrial robots has dramatically enhanced their strategic advantage relative to American competitors. In the 1990s, investment in flexible manufacturing will probably provide one of the most important sources of strategic advantage.

BENEFITS OF GLOBAL LOCATION OF ACTIVITIES

A global strategy for activity location can achieve each of the major globalization benefits of cost reduction, improved quality, enhanced customer preference, and increased competitive leverage.

Cost Reduction

Multinational companies, whether using multilocal or global strategies, need to minimize the tariffs, taxes, and transportation costs they pay. In addition, compared with a multilocal approach, a global approach to activity location can reduce costs in further ways. It can *reduce duplication of activities* by eliminating and consolidating identical activities from many country locations into one or two globally centralized locations. In 1973, Unilever had 13 factories for soap production in Europe. As part of its globalization and Europeanization drive, Unilever had reduced these to three factories and one finishing plant by 1989. Similarly, N.V. Philips closed eighty factories in the 1970s to consolidate and to reduce duplication. In the 1980s Philips changed the role of the remaining factories from local production operations to "international production centers" that provide large-volume production for world markets.[19] Last, although a global approach to activity location means fewer locations than under a multilocal strategy, it may involve more locations and duplication than under a pure export approach.

A global approach to activity location can help exploit *economies of scale* by pooling production or other value-adding activities. For each activity, there can be an overall effect for the industry as a whole. The global benefits of manufacturing concentration are generally greater in the commercial aircraft business than in the apparel business—because the minimum efficient production scale requires a much higher share of the global market in aircraft than it does in apparel. But the specific effect for individual firms depends on the actual production technology used by the firm and by its market position. So firms that use a lower scale technology face fewer potential benefits from global concentration unless they change their technology approach also. Similarly, firms with a large share of large national markets will, other things being equal, gain less from global concentration than will firms with small market shares, because these larger firms may already be able to achieve the minimum efficient scale. Smaller firms usually face a tough choice. They can try to overcome their size disadvantage by concentrating more than their larger competitors, but they run the risk of being swamped if these competitors adopt the same strategy. Or the smaller firms can stay with multiple, low-scale national activities that depend on differentiation, quality, service, and other non–cost-based sources

---

Global Manufacturing of Disposable Syringes

Becton Dickinson's global manufacturing strategy in disposable syringes combines all three elements of global cost reduction: reducing duplication, exploiting economies of scale, and exploiting flexibility. The significant economies of scale and experience effects in the disposable syringe business encouraged Becton Dickinson to build a global manufacturing network that concentrated production primarily in the United States, Ireland, Mexico, and Brazil. Each production facility served multiple markets. For instance, in the early 1980s, 50% of the U.S., 90% of the Irish, and 70% of the Mexican and Brazilian production was shipped to other markets. This concentration and coordination of production was made possible by the company's use of highly standardized global products and standardized production processes. In addition to reducing duplication and increasing economies of scale, this global product and manufacturing strategy gave Becton Dickinson the flexibility to take advantage of exchange rate fluctuations. For example, when the Mexican peso plummeted in value, Becton shifted much of the production in Mexico to serve overseas markets. Sourcing out of Mexico then gave Becton Dickinson a cost advantage vis-à-vis its competitors who were locked into producing in higher cost countries.[20]

---

of strategic advantage. In industries where price is the primary customer concern, such strategies restrict the user to a small portion of the market. Furthermore, even in industries where product features and quality are also important, a cost advantage can be converted into not just lower prices but greater investment in improving product features and quality.

In the commodity chip market, economies of scale and learning/experience effects result in lower cost for high-volume plants. These drivers have resulted in huge factories in Japan belonging to companies such as NEC, Fujitsu, and Hitachi. The output of these factories is much more than one market can absorb, both allowing and requiring the Japanese companies to make large volume sales in the United States. In the United States, on the other hand, companies such as Texas Instruments and Micron Technology (of Boise, Idaho) have smaller plants and higher costs, putting them at a cost disadvantage. The consolidation of production by the Japanese chip makers and the global strategy that they have followed are two of the factors responsible for their greater competitiveness in the global commodity chip market. This greater competitiveness is illustrated by the growth of their world market share in all memory products from 25% in 1980 to 64% in 1986 (before declining to 59% in the face of new Korean competition).[21]

The global concentration of activities can exploit *economies of scope* (which apply to the gains from spreading activities across multiple product lines or businesses) as well as economies of scale. The same kind of issues apply, with the complicating need to coordinate across different product lines and businesses. These complications include the possibility that one link in the value-added chain should be global for one business but local for another business and will be further addressed later in this chapter.

Exploiting flexibility can be another way in which a global approach to activity location can reduce costs and applies primarily to production and sourcing activities. Partial concentration allows flexibility in regard to changes in exchange rates and in bargaining with suppliers, labor unions, and host governments. The requirement for achieving this benefit lies not so much in the existence of multiple locations, which a multilocal strategy would have, and even more so, but in the capability to switch activities between locations. According to Bruce Kogut, such a capability has to exist in the configuration of physical assets, in the product policy and in the management structure, policies, and processes of a company. First, flexibility in production requires investment in excess capacity that can produce to meet the needs of multiple countries. But such investment may be too costly in some industries and companies. Second, production flexibility is greatly enhanced by the use of global products—products with a high degree of cross-country standardization. (The specific strategy of "flexible manufacturing" will be discussed shortly.) Third, the management system must allow production to be switched between countries without penalizing the individual managers and units giving up that production. Often, these management issues pose the greatest barrier to global flexibility. Putting these three requirements together—excess capacity, global products, and a global management system—can create a global network that allows a business to profit from the uncertainty of the world market.[22]

Improved Quality

A global approach to activity location can improve product and program quality by focusing on a smaller number of products and programs than under a multilocal strategy. This quality-enhancing focus can occur in a number of elements in the value-added chain, particularly for R&D and production activities. Concentration of the R&D function allows a company to devote greater resources to the projects undertaken. At the same time, a concentrated R&D function can also be the center of a global network that taps into selected skills and knowledge in particular countries. In the late-1980s Texas Instruments set up a software design subsidiary in Bangalore, India, to access the low-cost, but highly skilled technical workers available there. This subsidiary communicates with Texas Instruments' R&D center in the United States via satellite each day, thus operating very much as part of a global network. This location strategy, and resulting benefit of high-quality design work at low cost, is made possible by the strength of the industry globalization driver, differences in country costs.

Concentration of production allows investment in better facilities and equipment than can be afforded under a multilocal strategy. These superior assets can then produce higher quality as well as lower cost products. *Studies increasingly show that low cost and high quality are not alternative, but complementary, strategies.*23 In highly globalized industries, combining low cost and high quality is particularly important because buyers have more choice in where they buy and have access to the best products or services offered in the world. In addition, competitors will be able to pursue low-cost strategies through global centralization and standardization. Concentration of production should also allow more consistent quality control.

Last, taking the zero-based approach inherent in a global approach to activity location may open up unlikely and fascinating possibilities. Many U.S. banks now fly batches of checks and other financial instruments to be processed in the Far East in order to benefit from the higher quality standards there as well as the lower costs and higher productivity. One American banker, who uses Asian financial processing, commented that "For Asian checkers, it's a matter of pride. They feel a deep sense of personal embarrassment if they make a mistake that results in a loss to the bank. This results in very high standards of accuracy."24

Enhanced Customer Preference

Globalized activity location has only an indirect effect on customer preference, via possible improvements in product design and quality. Other global strategy levers—global market participation, global products, and global marketing—have more direct effects.

Increased Competitive Leverage

A global strategy for activity location can increase competitive leverage by bringing the resources of the worldwide network to bear on the competitive situation in individual countries. Under a multilocal strategy in which products are supplied by local manufacturing facilities, each subsidiary's competitive position—as based on its cost and quality position—depends on that subsidiary's own market share and revenues. So a subsidiary that loses market share under competitive attack also loses the operating scale needed to maintain the very cost and quality advantages needed to defend its market position. This was the losing position in which

Philips, with its highly independent subsidiaries relying on local production, found itself in country after country, facing the Japanese electronics onslaught of the 1970s and early 1980s. In contrast, under a global strategy, each subsidiary's cost and quality position depends much more on the global market position of the worldwide business. So loss of local market share has little effect on cost and quality. In other words, *a global strategy for activity location can greatly reduce the dependence of each subsidiary's competitive position on local conditions.*

Such independence from local conditions also applies under an export strategy for activity location. But, as discussed in relation to exchange rates, a global approach with a network of locations provides more flexibility relative to exchange rate and other changes. So, again, a global approach can provide more leverage against competitors.

DRAWBACKS OF GLOBAL LOCATION OF ACTIVITIES

A global strategy for activity location also has drawbacks. Exhibit 1–5 in Chapter 1 summarized the major potential problems in such a strategy. These possible drawbacks include *lessened responsiveness to customers, increased currency risk, increased risk of creating competitors,* and *difficulties in managing the value-added chain.*

Lessened Responsiveness to Customers

In comparison with a multilocal strategy in which most activities are located in the same countries as customer-markets, a global strategy of partial concentration of activities distances many of these activities from customers. The same applies even more so, of course, to an export-based strategy of total concentration. Obvious drawbacks include increased inventory costs, transportation expenses, and tariffs. These additional costs need to be less than the cost savings discussed earlier.

Increased Currency Risk

Performing value-adding activities in countries where the company obtains little revenues means incurring costs in currencies different from that of revenues. As discussed earlier, this currency risk needs to be managed in a number of possible ways. Such management can verge on speculation, and companies need to beware of playing the foreign exchange markets for the sake of trading gains alone.

Increased Risk of Creating Competitors

One approach to building a global manufacturing network is to use "offshore manufacturing" in which the home country-market is supplied from production facilities located elsewhere. This strategy is, of course, a special case of the more general one of global activity location. But offshore manufacturing has received the most attention and criticism, particularly in regard to the danger of "hollowing out" the corporation as more and more parts of the value-added chain are moved offshore.[25] Offshore manufacturing is particularly risky when the suppliers are collaborators rather than fully owned subsidiaries. Numerous offshore suppliers have learned the business of their customers sufficiently well to develop into full-fledged competitors.[26] Even the use of fully owned subsidiaries runs the risk of creating new competitors if local managers spin off on their own.

Difficulties in Managing Value Chain

A global network of activities, in which interdependent elements of the value-added chain are spread across different countries, is inherently difficult to manage. In contrast, the centralized network of an export-based strategy or the mostly independent value-added chains of a multilocal strategy pose much less of a management task. If managed badly, a global network can be both less efficient and more costly.

LOCATING INDIVIDUAL ACTIVITIES

Thinking in terms of a global value-added chain makes it clear that a global strategy can be applied to different links of the chain. Some elements of the chain can be geographically concentrated while others are duplicated and dispersed. So how should each element of the value-added chain be located in a global strategy? The next sections discuss how to configure the elements whose locations are most affected by globalization drivers.

Global Financing

This book concerns global strategy at the business rather than the corporate level. So issues like financing, a corporate function, are not within the scope of this work. But one issue worth highlighting is how the financing task should differ between companies pursuing multilocal strategies and those pursuing global strategies. In particular, the finance function for global strategy needs to match *global* competitors' costs of capital, not just those of competitors in each national market.[27] Such matching requires in the first place that the company have a good understanding of global competitors' true cost of capital. That task is not so easy, as witness the current debate on whether or not Japanese firms have, on average, a lower cost of capital than Western companies.28

Global Research and Development

In parallel with the notion of global products, the essence of a global strategy for R&D is that it be conducted to serve the entire global market rather than individual countries. Most multinational companies have historically run their R&D operation to stress serving either the home market or individual foreign markets, rather than the global market as a whole.29 Most American companies have tended to do little of their R&D outside the United States. Studies estimate that only 10% of R&D expenditures for U.S.-based multinational companies were conducted outside the United States in 1976 and perhaps 12% in 1980.30 Furthermore, this foreign activity has been limited to a relatively small number of countries—the United Kingdom, Australia, Canada, Japan, France, Germany, Mexico, and Brazil in order of frequency in one study.31 Japanese companies have been even more limited in locating R&D activity overseas, partly because of the low level, until very recently, of Japanese overseas manufacturing investment and partly because Japanese companies do such a good job of scanning for foreign technical information.32 *But overseas Japanese R&D seems to be on the rise.* In a classic example of locating in a lead country to tap into its R&D resources, Japanese computer and electronics companies are opening laboratories to do basic research in the United States, partly it seems in order to lure the most creative American computer scientists to work for them. Japanese companies are also increasingly buying into already developed technology through acquisition of foreign companies.33

The location and management of the R&D activity can have a major effect on how well it serves such a global function. Many executives consider that the output of R&D activity serves end markets best when the activity is also located in those markets.34 But a global strategy for R&D needs to balance this need with several others:

- Global R&D needs to tap into sources of knowledge and information wherever they might be located on the globe.
- Global R&D needs to transmit that knowledge back to the central R&D management wherever that might be.
- The central management function needs to ensure that this knowledge is used as appropriate.
- There has to be a process for allocating priorities globally on the basis of strategic need rather than of proximity. Otherwise, the R&D staff are likely to

---

Conducting R&D in Japan

One American company, W. R. Grace, a large, diversified manufacturer of chemical and other products, has made the move to conduct R&D in Japan. Believing that the United States, Europe, and Japan are the leaders in technological innovation in the chemicals industry, the company recently opened a research center in Japan. Grace already had R&D facilities in the United States and Europe but felt the need to complete the triad by establishing a presence in Japan. Grace executives believe that this development will enable them to stay on top of, and potentially have access to, Japanese developments. Grace has made contacts with researchers in Japan's universities and governments and has hired Japanese scientists.

---

favor the projects of the managers they see regularly rather than those of distant foreigners.

- Global R&D has to be able to develop global products with the capability for customization for major national markets.

All these tasks have to be performed while balancing the need to achieve critical mass and economies of scale, which varies by industry. Analysis of the industry's globalization drivers helps determine how best to locate and manage the R&D activity to meet these needs.

Effects of Market Globalization Drivers on Global R&D

A number of market globalization drivers affect where R&D should be located and how it should be managed. *Common customer needs* make it less necessary to locate R&D in multiple countries, so favoring concentration to achieve scale benefits. The presence of *global customers* encourages companies to place some of their R&D activities close to their most important global customers. The existence of important *lead countries* strongly encourages companies to locate at least some of their R&D activities in those countries. As a minimum, companies should locate in lead countries a scanning function to gather information on developments. A recurring theme found in the research conducted for this book is the need for American companies to locate some R&D activity in Japan. Many of these companies face strong Japanese global competitors and are also very weak in the Japanese market. R&D presence in Japan would help them to better understand the sources of their Japanese competitors' technical capabilities, as well as to improve their ability to serve the Japanese market, and perhaps global markets also.

Effects of Cost Globalization Drivers on Global R&D

Cost is easily the most important globalization driver that affects the location of R&D activities. R&D activity seems, in most industries, to need a large amount of expensive equipment and many scientists to work in close collaboration to achieve significant results. So companies have traditionally favored concentrating the activity. In addition, the high cost of R&D makes the international duplication of facilities very difficult. Increasingly, however, the need to locate R&D in globally strategic countries and the spreading availability of R&D skills are encouraging companies to spread their R&D efforts and to find creative ways to maintain a globally integrated network of R&D workers, as mentioned earlier in the case of Texas Instruments' operation in India.

Effects of Government Globalization Drivers on Global R&D

While government trade policies—through tariffs, quotas, and local content rules—may force multinational companies to manufacture locally, government regulation can have a less direct effect on R&D. Companies may sometimes find it necessary to locate in particular countries in order to understand better the technical specifications and regulations. For example, the drug approval process is so complex that having a local R&D presence can help companies deal with the process more successfully. Governments are also eager for technology transfer into their countries. So a local R&D facility that operates as part of a global network can be used to enhance relations and bargaining power with host governments.

Effects of Competitive Globalization Drivers on Global R&D

As with other global strategy levers, companies need to be concerned if their competitors pursue a globally more astute strategy for R&D. In particular, companies that conduct their R&D primarily at home may well need to reciprocate when foreign competitors set up R&D on their territory. Last, companies may find acquisitions of competitors especially helpful in strengthening their global R&D, both as a way of obtaining technical expertise and as a way of enhancing the scale of R&D operations.

Global Purchasing

Using a global strategy for purchasing is the mirror image of catering to global customers. A globally centralized and integrated approach to purchasing can ensure that the business has access to the best possible materials and components as well as the best possible prices. Whether to incur the costs and additional management requirements of global purchasing depends on the specific potential benefits. For example, Singer Furniture found its own offshore sourcing to be inefficient and unable to exploit the potential for sourcing economies. So it contracted with another company, IMX, to be its exclusive agent for overseas purchasing. IMX uses its own global network to find low-cost sourcing opportunities that lower purchasing and shipping costs of Singer goods. In addition, Singer benefits from the increased purchasing clout and economies of scale from sharing this activity with another company. The automotive industry has probably gone the furthest in the use of global sourcing. For example, the European Ford Escort, which was originally designed to be a world car and wound up as a pan-European model, sources components from fifteen different countries: the United Kingdom and Germany, where it is final assembled, as well as Norway, Sweden, Denmark, Belgium, the Netherlands, France, Austria, Switzerland, Italy, Spain, the United States, Canada, and Japan.[35]

Global Manufacturing

Manufacturing covers a large number of activities, including the development of product and process technology, the building of production capacity and plant facilities, maintaining the manufacturing information system, managing materials and inbound and outbound logistics, maintaining quality and reliability standards, planning production, and managing the actual production operations. Typically, most of these activities need to be performed in close proximity to each other, so that location decisions tend to cover these activities as a package. Nevertheless, to the extent that a particular activity can be separated from the others, the location strategy for it can be different.

There are many arguments for and against foreign manufacturing, some of which were covered in the discussion of offshore manufacturing. Reasons for foreign manufacturing include enhancing customer relations outside the home country; getting closer to markets; gaining access to local, immobile factors of production and technological resources; reducing transportation costs, avoiding tariff and nontariff barriers; satisfying some demands of and gaining benefits from local governments; hedging against country-specific risks; and preempting competition.[36] I assume that the reader already understands these issues or can learn about them elsewhere[37] and concentrate instead on the issue of how to configure a global manufacturing network in the sense defined earlier.

Cost globalization drivers constitute the key reason for using global manufacturing, with government drivers also important, and market and competitive drivers less so.

Effects of Cost Drivers on Global Manufacturing

Probably the most important cost driver for global manufacturing is the nature of *scale economies.* As discussed earlier, globally centralized manufacturing is favored to the extent that the minimum efficient scale is greater than the volume the firm can sell in individual national markets. Steep *learning and experience effects* also favor global manufacturing in order to move down the curve faster. So it is no coincidence that competitors in the semiconductor industry, well known for its steep experience effects, primarily use globally centralized manufacturing.

Having *favorable logistics* is also a critical requirement for global manufacturing to work. Shipping costs must not be so great as to offset the cost savings from centralization. But creativity can sometimes be applied to reduce transportation barriers. An American manufacturer of medical sterilization equipment manufactured in its local markets because the product, with its large sterilization chamber, was too bulky to be shipped economically. But this manufacturing strategy left the company operating below full capacity in each of its minimum efficient scale plants. Eventually, the company hit on the solution of centralizing in the United States the manufacture of the sterilizing controls, which constituted the more valuable part of the product, shipping these high-value controls, using local suppliers to provide the low-value sterilizing chambers, and then conducting final assembly in the local countries. Similarly, Gettinger, a subsidiary of Electrolux, the Swedish appliance manufacturer, has set up in several countries local manufacturing of the bulky appliance shells. Some products, however, such as explosive chemicals, face other, more difficult, logistical barriers.

Differences in country costs also favor the use of global manufacturing by making it worthwhile to locate in specific countries. Particularly when looking to exploit low labor costs companies need to consider what percentage of total costs (both purchases and value added) are accounted for by labor costs and the differences in labor productivity between countries. Differences in tax rates also provide another source of differences in country costs. Using a global manufacturing network, rather than duplicated multilocal facilities or a single exporting facility, offers two ways to reduce taxes. First, the selective location of manufacturing facilities, inherent in global strategy, allows the company to pick countries with low (either official or negotiated) tax rates. Second, the transhipment of raw materials, and intermediate and final products, within a global manufacturing network provides opportunities to set transfer prices and subsidiary remittances so as to minimize total tax liability.

Some researchers argue that in most manufacturing industries, labor costs have been outweighed by market access, quality control, timely delivery, and responsiveness to customers as determinants of global competitiveness. Therefore, global site selections might hinge on the cooperation, flexibility, and trainability of the labor force rather than on its cost.[38]

Effects of Government Drivers on Global Manufacturing

Whether an industry has *favorable trade policies* greatly affects the potential for global manufacturing. In essence, greater protectionism reduces the ability to operate with a global manufacturing network.[39] Ironically, while mature industries with their more stable product and process designs suit themselves to global manufacturing, protectionism is often more prevalent in such industries also, both because local production has had time to spread and because jobs lost to imports cannot be readily recreated. Many trade barriers are now falling, which is one of the major drivers spurring companies to investigate global manufacturing. The global network can also be used to circumvent or reduce the impact of trade barriers such as through the judicious use of local content. By assembling and conducting some manufacturing operations in Britain, Japanese automobile manufacturers have been able to get their vehicles certified as of European origin even though a very high percentage of the content is originally imported from Japan. In the late 1980s the Goodyear Tire Company wanted to strengthen its production base in the global tire industry by setting up a manufacturing subsidiary in Korea. But Goodyear faced stiff government regulations against its move. Only by agreeing to become an exporting plant was Goodyear able to win government approval for the ownership that the company wanted.

Compatible technical standards also make it easier to use global manufacturing, by reducing the need for running different product lines. So the task of a centralized manufacturing plant is simplified.

Effects of Market Drivers on Global Manufacturing

Product designs that are changing rapidly to meet changing market needs tend to require a close linkage among marketers, designers, and manufacturing. So the stable product designs that dominate in the mature stage of the product life cycle should make it easier to use global manufacturing, provided that *common customer needs* across countries also apply. Furthermore, the cost savings from global manufacturing are most needed in the mature industries where customers use precise, hard criteria based on product price performance relationships in their purchasing decisions.[40] It is probably no coincidence that maturity in the U.S. and European automobile and consumer electronics markets has coincided with dominance by Japanese manufacturers using globally centralized manufacturing.

An additional market driver affecting global manufacturing is the country-of-origin effect discussed earlier. A dilemma that companies face in locating production facilities is that many low-cost countries do not have a high reputation for quality. One solution may be to use quality control managers from countries that have high reputations for quality, such as Germany or Japan, and to ensure that potential customers know about this fact. There is the apocryphal story that in the 1950s a town in Japan changed its name to Usa in order to be able to label products manufactured there as "Made in USA." In another example of how the preferred countries of origin have changed over time, nineteenth-century German tool makers used to imitate the Sheffield (England) trademark.

Effects of Competitive Drivers on Global Manufacturing

Last, as with the use of the other global strategy levers, global manufacturing may be mandated by competitive actions. If the industry has characteristics favoring global manufacturing, competitors that move first will gain scale, experience, or other advantages that can keep them ahead of slower movers. So in such industries firms need to match or preempt their *competitors' use of global manufacturing.*

Additional Factors

Each factory can also have a different role in a global network. That role then affects the degree of integration needed as well as the sophistication and content of the support activities that should be located at the factory.[41] These roles include getting access to low-cost production factors, using local technological resources, and gaining proximity to local markets. Furthermore, for each of those roles, a factory can play more passive or active roles within the global network. Integration of the different factories within a global network is becoming increasingly important. In a recent multicountry study of international manufacturing, managers at several U.S. multinational corporations reported that their primary challenge in coming years is integrating their existing global operations to perform as a single system rather than as islands of manufacturing and technological capabilities.[42]

In addition, some specific characteristics of a company's manufacturing process may make it easier to shift from a situation of duplicated independent plants to one of an interdependent global network. One characteristic is that the plants should have manufacturing processes that are more or less similar. A second characteristic is that the pattern of material flows between plants and warehouses be relatively simple. A third characteristic is that manufacturing configurations be relatively simple.[43]

Role of Flexible Manufacturing

As mentioned in the last chapter, the advent of computer-based "flexible manufacturing" (using computer-aided manufacturing—the CAM in CAD/CAM) is redefining the notion of globally standardized products.[44] While still a new practice, flexible manufacturing is an important option that needs to be factored into global manufacturing strategy.[45] In particular, the use of flexible manufacturing interacts with both the use of globally standardized products and the use of geographically concentrated manufacturing.

In terms of market globalization drivers, the presence of *common customer needs* favors product standardization and the subsequent manufacturing concentration to produce those products. But flexible manufacturing allows more scope for producing customized variants of a core global product. So even in industries where customer needs are not that common, a business with a flexible manufacturing capability can design a standardized global core that it then customizes, in a centralized manufacturing facility, for different national or regional markets. Markets at an earlier stage of the product life cycle typically face greater variety in product design, which would usually prevent the use of globally standardized products. But, again, a flexible manufacturing capability may allow earlier use of standardized core global products and concentrated manufacturing. In terms of cost globalization drivers, high *economies of scale* favor concentrated manufacturing but have conflicting effects on the need to use flexible manufacturing. On the one hand, companies will not be able to support many minimum efficient scale plants, so having the flexibility to produce many different products in each plant will be an advantage. On the other hand, by their nature, flexible manufacturing techniques tend to reduce the gains from large-scale production.

Some experts now believe that flexible manufacturing can be used to increase product variety without increasing costs.[46] But some increase in cost seems typically necessary. For example, the National Bicycle Industrial Company, a subsidiary of Matsushita, the Japanese electronics concern, has a factory that makes customized models, under the Panasonic brand, to individual order. With 20 employees and a computer capable of design work, its small factory can produce over 11 million variations on nearly 20 models in about 200 color patterns and almost any size. Customers are fitted for their order before any production begins. The finished bicycles sell for $500 to $3,000 compared with $250 to $500 for standard bicycles. But it might be argued that these customized bicycles are based on a standardized core set of parts and designs. Furthermore, the large price differential over the mass production models limits the share of the market that can be obtained by these customized products.

Managing Interdependence Between Businesses

Although not a central theme of this book, interdependence between different businesses within a company has implications for activity location. Many companies share activities across different businesses, and such sharing often takes place in several countries. For example, in many paper-based companies, different businesses share upstream pulp-processing facilities. Or different businesses in a company may share a distribution system or sales force as in many consumer packaged goods companies. In these cases, problems arise when one business requires a more globalized strategy in a shared activity than does another business. Two businesses in the same company may share two activities in their value-added chains, such as purchasing and manufacturing. But one business should have a primarily global strategy while the other business should not. So the first business should ideally have globally centralized manufacturing of standardized global products, while the second business needs locally adapted products and could use local manufacturing also. But the economics are such that both businesses' production costs are lower when they share centralized manufacturing facilities. So a possible compromise solution would be to allocate one part of the factory to work on customizing products for the second business. In addition, any extra costs that the second business incurs because of having to accommodate the first business's need for centralized production, such as for transportation of finished goods, should be ameliorated by giving some break in the transfer price to local subsidiaries.

Global Distribution

Most of the issues in the location of distribution activities relate to classic marketing and internationalization concerns. Logistical factors become doubly important in an international context. But globalization drivers can also change how these factors apply. In particular, changes in government globalization drivers can redefine the optimal configuration of a global distribution system. The advent of the single European market provides the most dramatic application of this effect. In Europe the coming removal of border controls is allowing distribution managers to redraw the maps that show time from their distribution centers to various delivery points. Maps that have been contorted by the time taken for trucks to pass frontier controls will show smooth concentric circles instead. As a result, distribution centers can be consolidated and centralized, as with manufacturing sites.

Thinking creatively about the global value-added chain can produce highly effective global distribution. Benetton provides one of the best examples of a global distribution strategy. From a single computerized warehouse in Treviso, Italy, Benetton ships its products all over the world directly to the independent, but contractually tied, retail stores that sell its clothing. This distribution centralization is made possible, in part, by Benetton's use of just-in-time ordering. Benetton makes no garment until it is ordered by one of its stores. So an innovative approach in its order-taking and manufacturing value-added activities allows Benetton to gain global strategic advantage via the distribution element of the value chain.

Global Service

The last activity in the value chain, customer service, usually, by its nature, has to be performed locally. Even so, some aspects such as information and communication systems can be centralized or relocated. An American software company now provides telephone support to its U.S. customers from Ireland. Furthermore, providing a uniform standard of service provides assurance to global customers—whether organizations or individuals. At the same time, differences in both culture and custom particularly affect what customers may expect in different countries. On weekends in Japan medical equipment company sales representatives wash the cars of the doctors that they call on! These representatives will even collect their customers' children from school.

GUIDELINES FOR LOCATING GLOBAL ACTIVITIES

An effective global network can locate activities to achieve the benefits of cost reduction, increased competitive leverage, and so on. At the same time this network must be able to serve the key needs of local markets around the world. The following guidelines summarize the key issues on this topic:

- In locating global activities, managers should free up their thinking by starting with the "zero-based" assumption that their business has no activities located anywhere in the world, then ask what the ideal pattern of location would be. Only then should managers bring back into consideration the reality of where the business's activities are actually located now, and what it would cost (in the broadest sense) to relocate activities.

- Different activities have differing needs for global centralization, local dispersion, or some combination in between.
- The ideal pattern of location changes with circumstances and the evolution of the business.
- The best pattern of location usually allows for some duplication in order to provide flexibility and safeguards against disruption.
- Some activities, particularly research and development, need to have presence in globally strategic countries.
- Coordination of geographically dispersed activities can substitute in some cases for global centralization.
- Managers should consider both strategic advantage and comparative (country-based) advantage in locating activities to maximize competitive advantage.

DISCUSSION AND RESEARCH QUESTIONS

1. What is the difference between a multilocal and a global approach to locating value-adding activities?
2. What is the difference between strategic and comparative bases of advantage?
3. Select one company or business and trace how it has developed its strategic and comparative bases of advantage over time.
4. What parts of its value chain should an American manufacturer of automobiles consider relocating, and where, in the light of the 1993 North American Free Trade Agreement? Would your answer be different for a major insurance company?
5. Select one company or business and describe how the location of its value-adding activities has shifted over time.

NOTES

1. Michael E. Porter, "Competition in Global Industries: A Conceptual Framework," in *Competition in Global Industries*, ed. Michael E. Porter (Boston: Harvard Business School Press, 1986), and Michael E. Porter, "Changing Patterns of International Competition," *California Management Review*, Vol. 28, No. 2, Winter 1986, pp. 9–40.
2. For an in-depth discussion of the role of value-adding activities in competitive strategy, see Michael E. Porter, *Competitive Advantage* (New York: The Free Press, 1985).
3. See Balaji S. Chakravarthy and Howard V. Perlmutter, "Strategic Planning for a Global Business," *Columbia Journal of World Business*, Summer 1985, pp. 3–10.
4. Both Prahalad and Doz (1987) and Bartlett and Ghoshal (1989) advocate the use of a global network in which subsidiaries and the center specialize in different activities. See C. K. Prahalad, and Yves L. Doz, *The Multinational Mission: Balancing Local Demands and Global Vision* (New York: The Free Press 1987), and Christopher A. Bartlett and Sumantra Ghoshal, *Managing Across Borders: The Transnational Solution* (Boston: Harvard Business School Press, 1989).
5. See, for example, Rudiger Dornbush, Stanley Fisher, and Paul A. Samuelson, "Compar-

ative Advantage, Trade, and Payments in a Ricardian Model with a Continuum of Goods," *American Economic Review*, Vol. 67, December 1977, pp. 823–839.

6. There is an extensive literature on the country-of-origin effect. See, for example, Johny K. Johansson, "Determinants and Effects of 'Made in' Labels," *International Marketing Review*, Vol. 6, No. 1, Spring 1989, pp. 47–58.

7. For a guide to these fundamental issues in internationalization, see, for example, Michael R. Czinkota, Pietra Rivoli, and Ilkka A. Ronkainen, *International Business* (Chicago: The Dryden Press, 1989), and Paul W. Beamish, J. Peter Killing, Donald J. Lecraw, and Harold Crookell, *International Management: Text and Cases* (Homewood, Ill.: Richard D. Irwin, 1991).

8. There are many sources of advice on evaluating foreign direct investment. See, for example, Franklin R. Root, *Entry Strategies for International Markets* (Lexington, Mass.: D. C. Heath, 1987), Chapter 5, on which this list is based. Root also characterizes four kinds of risk in foreign direct investment: general instability risk, ownership (expropriation) risk, operations risk, and transfer risk. See also Stephen J. Kobrin, *Managing Political Risk Assessment* (Berkeley: University of California Press, 1982).

9. But Michael E. Porter, *The Competitive Advantage of Nations* (New York: The Free Press, 1991) has challenged this traditional notion, by espousing a concept of the competitive advantage of nations that includes factor conditions, demand conditions, related and supporting industries and firm strategy, structure, and rivalry.

10. Some strategists now argue that time is a critical source of competitive advantage. See George Stalk, Jr., and Thomas M. Hout, *Competing Against Time* (New York: The Free Press, 1990).

11. See Porter's (*The Competitive Advantage of Nations*) discussion of the role of firm strategy, structure, and rivalry in spurring performance improvement.

12. This analysis is based on Abraham M. George and C. William Schroth, "Managing Foreign Exchange for Competitive Advantage," *Sloan Management Review*, Winter 1991, pp. 105–116.

13. See also W. Carl Kester and Timothy A. Luehrman, "Are We Feeling More Competitive Yet? The Exchange Rate Gambit." *Sloan Management Review*, Winter 1989, pp. 19–28.

14. See Donald R. Lessard, "Finance and Global Competition: Exploiting Financial Scope and Coping with Volatile Exchange Rates," in *Competition in Global Industries*, ed. Michael E. Porter (Boston: Harvard Business School Press, 1986).

15. See Marcus C. Bogue III and Elwood S. Buffa, *Corporate Strategic Analysis* (New York: The Free Press, 1986), pp. 69–74, 93.

16. Bruce Kogut, "Designing Global Strategies: Profiting from Operational Flexibility," *Sloan Management Review*, Fall 1985, pp. 27–38.

17. This example is developed from a presentation, "Competitive Market Strategy for the Global Business," by Dr. Burkhard Wittek, Boston Consulting Group, Munich, at the Strategic Management Society's 8th Annual Conference in Amsterdam, October 1988.

18. See also Porter, *The Competitive Advantage of Nations*, pp. 210–224.

19. Gerrit Jeelof, "Global Strategies of Philips," *European Management Journal*, Vol. 7, No. 1, 1989, pp. 84–91.

20. This example is adapted from Marquise R. Cvar, "Case Studies in Global Competition: Patterns of Success and Failure," in *Competition in Global Industries*, ed. Michael E. Porter (Boston: Harvard Business School Press, 1986), pp. 483–516.

21. From Dataquest, reported in Clyde V. Prestowitz, Jr., *Trading Places* (New York: Basic Books, 1988), pp. 144–145, and also from a private communication with a (U.S.) Semiconductor Association spokesman, March 8, 1991.

22. See Kogut, "Designing Global Strategies."

23. The need to choose between low-cost and differentiation strategies, suggested by Michael E. Porter, *Competitive Strategy: Techniques for Analyzing Industries and Competitors* (New York: Free Press, 1980), has been challenged in a number of studies. See, for example, Roderick E. White, "Generic Business Strategies, Organizational Context

and Performance: An Empirical Investigation," *Strategic Management Journal*, Vol. 7, 1986, pp. 217–231; G. Dess and P. Davis, "Porter's (1980) Generic Strategies as Determinants of Strategic Group Membership and Organizational Performance," *Academy of Management Journal*, Vol. 27, 1984, pp. 467–488; and Carolyn Y. Woo and Karel Cool, "Porter's (1980) Generic Strategies: A Test of Performance and Functional Strategy Attributes," Working Paper, Purdue University, 1983.

24. From a 1989 study conducted by Hamilton Consultants, Cambridge, Massachusetts.

25. See, for example, Constantinos C. Markides and Norman Berg, "Manufacturing Offshore Is Bad Business," *Harvard Business Review*, September-October 1988, pp. 113–120.

26. Markides and Berg, ibid., cite Hitachi, which made microprocessors for Motorola, introducing its own 32-bit microprocessor; Toshiba, which acted as a supplier of copying machines to 3M, now promoting its own brand name; and Daewoo, while still a subcontractor to U.S. companies, now selling its own personal computer.

27. See Lessard, "Finance and Global Competition."

28. See George N. Hatsopoulos, "High Cost of Capital: Handicap of American Industry," report sponsored by the American Business Conference and Thermo-Electron Corporation, April 1983, and Carliss Y. Baldwin, "The Capital Factor: Competing for Capital in a Global Environment," in *Competition in Global Industries*.

29. Jack N. Behrman and William A. Fischer, "Transnational Corporations: Market Orientations and R&D Abroad," *Columbia Journal of World Business*, Fall 1980, pp. 55–60.

30. "R&D by Foreign Affiliates of U.S. Companies, 1966–75" (New York: The Conference Board), reported in Robert M. Pierson, "R&D by Multi-Nationals for Overseas Markets," *Research Management*, July 1978, pp. 19–22, and Robert C. Hirschey and Richard E. Caves, "Research and Transfer of Technology by Multinational Enterprises," *Oxford Bulletin of Economics and Statistics*, Vol. 43, No. 2, May 1981, pp. 115–130.

31. Behrman and Fischer, "Transnational Corporations."

32. Robert Ronstadt and Robert J. Kramer, "Getting the Most Out of Innovation Abroad," *Harvard Business Review*, March-April 1982, pp. 94–99.

33. *Business Week* cites Hitachi Koki Co. and Nissei Sangyo Co.'s acquisition of Dataproducts Corp. (computer printers), Chugai Pharmaceutical's acquisition of Gen-Probe (biotechnology), Fujisawa Pharmaceutical's acquisition of Lyphomed (drugs), NKK's acquisition of Silicon Graphics (3-D workstations), and Niko's acquisition of Electro-Scan (electromicroscope): "A Shopping Spree in the U.S.," Special Issue on "Innovation: The Global Race," June 15, 1990, pp. 86–87.

34. Ronstadt and Kramer, "Getting the Most Out of Innovation Abroad."

35. See Peter Dicken, *Global Shift: Industrial Change in a Turbulent World* (London: Harper & Row, 1986), p. 304.

36. See M. Therese Flaherty "Coordinating International Manufacturing and Technology," in *Competition in Global Industries;* and Kasra Ferdows, "Mapping International Factory Networks," in *Managing International Manufacturing*, ed. Kasra Ferdows (Amsterdam: Elsevier Science North Holland, 1989).

37. See, for example, William H. Davidson, *Global Strategic Management* (New York: John Wiley, 1982), Chapter 5, and Wickham Skinner, *Manufacturing: The Formidable Weapon* (New York: John Wiley, 1985).

38. See Kasra Ferdows et al., *The Internationalization of U.S. Manufacturing: Causes and Consequences* (Washington, D.C.: National Academy Press, 1990), pp. 23–24.

39. National trade policies are, of course, an enormous topic. For guidance, see, for example, Raymond Vernon and Louis T. Wells, *Manager in the International Economy* (Englewood Cliffs, N.J.: Prentice Hall, 1986), and Michael R. Czinkota, Pietra Rivoli, and Ilkka A. Ronkainen, *International Business* (Chicago: The Dryden Press, 1989).

40. Yves L. Doz, "Managing Manufacturing Rationalization Within Multinational Companies," *Columbia Journal of World Business*, Fall 1978, pp. 82–94.

41. This section is based on Ferdows, "Mapping International Networks."

42. Ferdows et al., *The Internationalization of U.S. Manufacturing*, p. 30.

43. Flaherty, "Coordinating International Manufacturing and Technology."

44. A survey study has found flexibility to be an increasingly important concern of Japanese manufacturers. See Arnoud de Meyer, Jinichiro Nakane, Jeffrey Miller, and Kasra Ferdows, "Flexibility: The Next Competitive Battle—The Manufacturing Futures Survey," *Strategic Management Journal*, Vol. 10, 1989, pp. 135–144.

45. For reviews of flexible manufacturing, see Joel D. Goldhar and Mariann Jelinek, "Computer Integrated Flexible Manufacturing: Organizational, Economic, and Strategic Implications," *Interfaces*, Vol. 15, May-June 1985, pp. 94–105, and Ramchandran Jaikumar, "Postindustrial Manufacturing," *Harvard Business Review*, November-December 1986, pp. 69–76.

46. James C. Abegglen and George Stalk, Jr., *Kaisha: The Japanese Corporation* (New York: Basic Books, 1985), pp. 89–90.

Chapter 6

Creating Global Marketing

Global marketing constitutes the fourth global strategy lever that companies can use to globalize their strategy. A worldwide business uses global marketing when it takes the same or similar approach or content for one or more elements of the marketing mix, that is, the same or similar brand names, advertising, and so on in different countries. Multinational companies increasingly use global marketing and have been highly successful— Nestlé with its common brand name applied to many products in all countries, Coca-Cola with its global advertising themes, and Xerox with its global leasing policies. But *global marketing is not about standardizing the marketing process.* Standardizing the way in which country subsidiaries analyze markets and develop marketing plans is merely good multinational practice—a way of transferring skills and setting high standards for the marketing function.[1]

Every element of the marketing mix—product design, product and brand positioning, brand name, packaging, pricing, advertising strategy, advertising execution, promotion and distribution—is a candidate for globalization. As with other global strategy levers, the use of global marketing can be flexible. A business can make some elements of the marketing mix more global and others less so. Within each element, some parts can be globally uniform and others not. For example, a "global" pack design may have a common logo and illustration in all countries, but a different background color in some countries. So both marketing as a whole and each individual marketing element can be global to a greater or lesser extent in its *content.2*

Global marketing can also vary in its geographic *coverage.* Few global marketing programs can realistically apply to all of the worldwide market. A marketing element can be global without being 100% uniform in content or coverage. Exhibit 6–1 illustrates a possibly typical pattern. In this hypothetical example, packaging is highly uniform in both content and coverage, pricing is highly uniform in a small number of countries, while the global promotion program has a great deal of local variation and is applied to a small number of countries only. The benefits of global marketing (and other global strategy levers) can be realized without total uniformity. A mostly uniform marketing approach that covers the major markets accounting for, say, 80% of revenues may be more than adequate. Indeed, there are probably diminishing returns to extreme uniformity as illustrated in Exhibit 6–2. The net benefits can rapidly decline if global marketing (and other global) programs are pushed to extremes of uniformity. The key in global strategy is to find the best balance between local adaptation and global standardization. *So global marketing is not a blind adherence to standardization of all marketing elements for its own sake, but a different, global approach to developing marketing strategy and programs that blends flexibility with uniformity.*

EXHIBIT 6–1   Example of Variation in Content and Coverage of Global Marketing

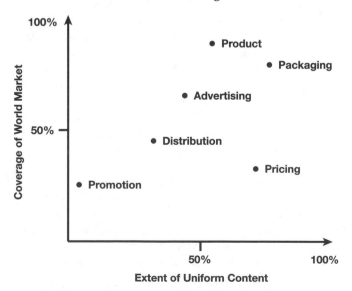

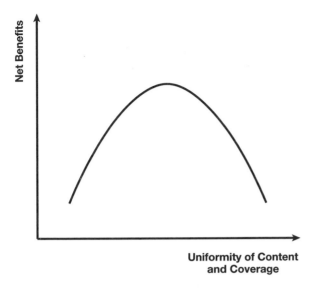

**Uniformity of Content
and Coverage**

EXHIBIT 6–2   Net Benefits Versus Degree of Uniformity

BENEFITS OF GLOBAL MARKETING

The conventional wisdom in international marketing has been that multinational companies should standardize marketing process rather than marketing content.[3] But worldwide businesses can use globally standardized marketing content to great effect. Like the other global strategy levers, global marketing can achieve one or more of four major categories of potential globalization benefits: cost reduction, improved quality of products and programs, enhanced customer preference, and increased competitive leverage.

Cost Reduction

In global marketing *cost reduction* arises from savings in both workforce and materials. Personnel outlays can be reduced when multiple national marketing functions are consolidated. In addition, personnel outlays are reduced when the use of global marketing eliminates duplication of activities so that national managers do not waste time reinventing each others' wheels. Materials costs are saved in producing global advertisements and commercials (which can represent up to 10% or more of the total advertising budget) and producing promotional materials and packaging print. (Savings from standardized packaging go well beyond the marketing sphere into that of inventory costs. Each packaging variant creates an additional stockkeeping unit. With typical inventory carrying costs at 20% of sales, any reduction in inventory can have dramatic effects on the profit margin.) As global and regional media—such as satellite television, multicountry programs, and international journals—increase in scope, global marketing can achieve additional cost savings by mounting multicountry campaigns through these vehicles. For example, EC Television, a subsidiary of the Interpublic Group (one of the largest multinational advertising agency concerns), has created a pan-European soap opera, action-adventure series, and variety show.

Cost savings can also translate into improved program effectiveness by allowing more money and resources to be put into a smaller number of programs. More lavish advertising executions can be afforded for a single global campaign than for multiple national ones. British Airways was able to afford very spectacular, and expensive, special effects for its highly memorable "Manhattan Landing" global television commercial (in which Manhattan skyscrapers were shown landing on an English village).

Enhanced Customer Preference

Global marketing helps build global recognition that can *enhance customer preference* through reinforcement. For many products and services, their buyers, whether consumers or members of organizations, travel, get transferred, or become exposed to multicountry media. So a uniform marketing message, whether communicated through the brand name, packaging, or advertising, reinforces their awareness, knowledge, and attitudes of the product or service. Anyone who has seen a billboard for a global product in a remote part of the world (such as a Coca-Cola billboard in Beijing) will know the feeling of reinforcement such an experience provides.

Improved Program Effectiveness

Much of the previous debate on global marketing has identified cost savings and increased recognition as the primary benefits and reduced program effectiveness as a major drawback. But a strong case can be made that *improved program effectiveness is often the greatest benefit of global marketing. Good ideas in marketing are scarce.* So a globalization program that overcomes local objections to allow the geographic spread of a good marketing idea can often raise the average effectiveness of programs around the world. Of course, objections are not couched as "not-invented-here" (often the real problem) but as "you-don't-understand-we-are-different" (the most common argument). In addition, globalization of some elements of the marketing mix, for example, the positioning strategy, would free up national managers' time to work on improving other elements, such as trade relations.

Exhibit 6–3 illustrates how global marketing can improve program effectiveness. Left on their own to develop, say, an advertising campaign, the businesses in different countries will achieve different levels of program effectiveness. So, as in Exhibit 6–3, there will be a wide range of effectiveness. But a global program can raise the average level of effectiveness. The two dashed lines in the exhibit show that the key in global marketing is to select a program that is *more* effective than the average of all the countries rather than to select one that is on average less effective. Exhibit 6–3 also shows that some loss in effectiveness is incurred even in the case of the successful global program—in countries G and H. In that case, why not let G and H opt out of the global program? First, the countries that will produce the better programs may not be known before the event, but only after letting each country duplicate the development effort. Second, allowing some countries to opt out may reduce the willingness of the others to use the global program.

Increased Competitive Leverage

Global marketing can *increase competitive leverage* in two ways. By focusing resources into a smaller number of programs, global marketing can magnify the competitive power of marketing efforts. While larger competitors may have the resources to develop different high-quality programs for each country, a smaller competitor may not. Using global marketing then allows the smaller competitor to lessen its disadvantage. But perhaps the

EXHIBIT 6–3   Gains and Losses of Global Marketing Programs

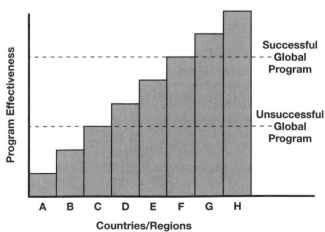

most important competitive benefit is that global marketing can get the entire organization behind one idea. Avis rental car created a global advertising and promotion campaign ("We're number two. We try harder.") that communicated in single-minded fashion not only to customers but to employees as well. As a result the entire organization pulled together to deliver on the global promise, not just in marketing but in all activities.

DRAWBACKS OF GLOBAL MARKETING

As with the other global strategy levers, global marketing can seem to run against the conventional wisdom of tailoring for local markets. The annals of international marketing overflow with horror stories arising from insufficient adaptation. For example, Pepsi-Cola once translated its advertising slogan "Come alive with the Pepsi generation" into Chinese for the Taiwan market. The selling pitch became "Pepsi brings your ancestors back to life"! In Japan, American Express's "Do you know me?" advertising slogan implies that its credit card should be used only one day a week (*doyo nomi* = "only on Sundays")! But amusing as such stories may be, they are mistakes of *international* marketing rather than of *global* marketing. These mistakes occur through poor or inadequate adaptation *after* a marketing program has been created for one country. But global marketing is not about forcing a domestic program onto the international subsidiaries. Instead, a global marketing program should be designed from the start with the needs of major target countries in mind. This last approach has its own dangers. In particular, programs designed for the global market run the risks of overaveraging or aiming for the lowest common denominator.[4] In addition, potential users of global marketing need to review the specific industry globalization drivers applying to their industry.

WHEN TO USE GLOBAL MARKETING

Industry globalization potential affects when to use global marketing. Market globalization drivers, not surprisingly, provide the strongest impetus for global marketing, while cost, government, and competitive globalization each have some effect as well.

Market Globalization Drivers for Global Marketing

All the individual market globalization drivers have major effects on the potential for using global marketing.

Common Customer Needs

The more common customer needs are across countries, the more opportunity there is for marketing to customers in the same way around the world. The same types of appeals and promises can be made. Some marketing-related determinants of common customer needs include the similarity of the stage of market development and market segmentation and the role of psychological appeals.

Global Customers and Channels

The presence of global customers requires a globally coordinated marketing effort, so that the business either makes the same claims, promises, or terms of trade around the world or knows when and why these differ.

Transferable Marketing

When marketing is globally transferable, it allows the use of the same marketing approaches and content around the world. A key determinant of marketing transferability is the extent to which usage of the product or service is rooted in national traditions. So, for example, the marketing of household cleaning products is rooted in traditional concepts of the role of homemaking. As these roles (or the concept of these roles) mostly differ from country to country, there is little transferability of those marketing elements, such as advertising, that depend most on these roles. In essence, there is not yet a concept of the "global homemaker"—almost a contradiction in terms. In contrast, products and services with little national culture attached to them tend to allow transferable marketing. Most industrial products and services fall in this category, as do many newer consumer products and services, such as fast food and credit cards.

Cost Globalization Drivers for Global Marketing

The more expensive it is to develop marketing programs and to produce them the greater the incentive to use global marketing that avoids national duplication. The cost of marketing programs and production (e.g., television commercials) is probably a function of both individual company approaches and of the industry as a whole—as lavish productions by one competitor spur others to match them. Not surprisingly, it is some of the most expensive-to-produce advertising that gets used globally—like Coca-Cola's hilltop group singing commercial of the 1970s and British Airways' "Manhattan Landing" commercial in the 1980s.

Government Globalization Drivers
for Global Marketing

Whether governments set *common marketing regulations* in an industry significantly affects the use of global marketing. Each element of the marketing mix can be subject to special regulation by a government in an important market. Advertising content is probably the most heavily and differently regulated marketing element. For example, comparative advertising is not allowed in several European countries, but may well be so allowed under new European Union rules.

Competitive Globalization Drivers
for Global Marketing

As with each of the other global strategy levers, it can be important to match or preempt competitors in their use of global marketing. Being the first to use global branding is probably one of the most effective ways to get a first-mover marketing advantage relative to competitors. Perrier's partial rebound in global markets, after its contamination problem in 1990, must be due in large part to the preeminent position it occupies as the first global mineral water brand.

HOW TO USE GLOBAL MARKETING

Having reviewed when to use global marketing, this next section discusses how to use global marketing for each element of the marketing mix. Each of the individual marketing elements has special considerations in globalization. These can be summarized as follows:

Marketing Element	Major Considerations in Globalization
Products	Commonality of customer needs and usage and of national technical standards
Positioning	Similarity of business's competitive position, purchase motivation (e.g., psychological appeals, ego involvement), and use/consumption patterns
Brand name	Global acceptance/prestige of home country of brand name; importance of having a name that means something; ease of pronunciation
Packaging design	Amount of information that needs to be communicated; similarity of distribution conditions (e.g., importance of display appeal); need for differentiation from local competitors; similarity of

usage patterns and measurement systems; acceptability of multilanguage labeling

Absolute pricing	Similarity of market price levels, laws, role of price, business's delivered cost position
Relative pricing	Similarity of business's competitive position, delivered costs, and market objectives
Advertising strategy	Similarity of business's competitive position and market objectives, stage of product life cycle, and buying motivation
Advertising execution	Universality of images, situations, and characters to be used; global recognizability of personalities; need for differentiation from local competitors
Advertising media	Availability of desired media; lack of restrictions on use
Sales promotion	Lack of legal and customary restrictions; similarity of incentive effect
Selling approach	Similarity of channel structure and customer buying methods and behavior
Sales personnel	Importance of technical expertise; acceptability of foreigners
Distribution	Similarity of distribution structure and business's relationship with channels
Customer service	Similarity of customer need and support infrastructure (e.g., toll-free phone service)

We have already considered global products in Chapter 4. But each of the other marketing elements needs discussion.

Global Positioning

Positioning is the act of designing the company's product and marketing mix to fit a given place in the customer's mind, usually with regard to competitive offerings.[5] A common global positioning can strengthen both the effectiveness of marketing programs and increase competitive leverage. It can strengthen program effectiveness by providing a positioning that is tried and tested in many countries and that provides the basis for commonality in other marketing elements. A common global positioning can increase competitive leverage by putting all the resources of the business behind developing assets and qualities (such as superior reliability in the case of Volkswagen cars or easy replacement in the case of American Express travelers' checks) to support that positioning. The head of global marketing

---

Volkswagen's Name Adaptations

Volkswagen has a model name series that denotes winds—Golf (Gulf wind), Scirocco (the hot wind from North Africa), and Passat (trade wind)—but made a highly successful switch of the Golf to Rabbit for the U.S. market, which made for a much better fit with the youthful segment that was the target in the United States. Similarly, in the 1980s Volkswagen renamed its Santana line as Quantum for the American market, perhaps to avoid connotations of the General Santa Anna who captured the Alamo. But Volkswagen tries to use the same model names around the world, because it views the car-buying public as very mobile.

---

in a major household products business considers brand positioning, rather than the brand name itself, to be the most important marketing element to be globalized. If a global brand positioning succeeded in several countries, then managers in other countries would "stop monkeying around" with the formula. In addition, more effort could be devoted to implementation. On the other hand, differences in the business's competitive position, purchase motivation (e.g., psychological appeals, ego involvement), and use/consumption patterns may argue for differing positions. For example, Volvo is positioned as a fairly unsophisticated automotive brand with high market share in Sweden, but it is positioned further upscale elsewhere in Europe. Many other automobile manufacturers, however, do position their marques, particularly luxury ones, the same way globally.

Companies that use a common positioning often find that they can make a large part of the marketing mix globally uniform. For example, M&M Mars was so confident of the similarities between the European and U.S. markets that it recently introduced two of its European brands, Bounty and Balisto, into the United States without any prior test marketing, based on the European positioning. The company uses the same packaging for the two brands, and advertising for the brands is similar. Packaging across markets is for the most part standardized. The company's slogan "melts in your mouth, not in your hands" is also used successfully across markets. The company used the same slogan to introduce M&M candies in Mexico.

Global Brand Names

Using a globally uniform brand name provides the easiest way of building global recognition. Around 1990 M&M Mars changed the name of its Marathon product, in the United Kingdom and other countries, to Snick-

---

Datsun's Switch to Nissan

Perhaps the biggest mistake in failing to use a global brand name comes, interestingly, from a Japanese company—Nissan. When Nissan first exported its automobiles, it used the name Datsun. After many years of establishing the name in the United States and elsewhere outside Japan, Nissan dropped the Datsun name in the early 1980s and went to the company name.[6] The goal of the worldwide name change, as stated by the Nissan Management Council, was to create a unified international image for the company. Before the change, Nissan had been the largest Japanese automobile importer into the United States. It now lags both Toyota and Honda in share of the U.S. market. In 1981, Nissan was the world's fourth largest manufacturer, with a 7.3% worldwide share. By 1986, it had fallen to fifth, with a 5.7% share. While a string of relatively weak Nissan products bears the brunt of the blame, the name change must also have played a major role in the decline.

---

ers, an American name. In the United Kingdom, M&M Mars went so far as to run a television commercial (featuring a frustrated Australian tourist) that explained the name change in terms of preventing confusion for traveling consumers. Furthermore, the possibility of combination names such as a globally standard umbrella name combined with a local product name provides flexibility.

The desirability of a global brand name depends in part on the global acceptance or prestige of the home country of the brand name, the importance of having a name that means something, and the ease of pronunciation. Its tongue-twisting (for Japanese) name caused Baskin-Robbins to use in Japan only the name "31 Ice Cream" in English with the same logo that it uses in the United States. Many companies have overcome company or brand names not designed for easy worldwide pronunciation (e.g., Nestlé, the latter being pronounced "NES-sull" by many in Britain), but few have designed a global brand name from scratch. Brand names that mean something may need to be translated in order to perform the positioning task for which they were designed. Thus, Unilever's Close Up toothpaste becomes Très Près (Very Close) in France, but retains its positioning (promotion of social confidence). In some cases companies adopt a foreign brand name that would never be used in its home country, witness the Nissan Cedric, which is sold in Japan, but certainly not in the United Kingdom or the United States. Similarly, "Soup-Career Woman" (branded in English not Japanese) may sell in Japan, but it would be too blatant for Western markets.

The World's Most Global Brands

While many companies use global brand names, few seem to have achieved the status of wide recognition as global brands. A 1990 study found only nineteen truly global brands in the sense of high worldwide awareness and esteem. The ranking of these brands was

1. Coca-Cola	11. Rolls-Royce
2. Sony	12. Honda
3. Mercedes-Benz	13. Panasonic
4. Kodak	14. Levi's
5. Disney	15. Kleenex
6. Nestlé	16. Ford
7. Toyota	17. Volkswagen
8. McDonald's	18. Kellogg's
9. IBM	19. Porsche
10. Pepsi-Cola	

(although this study seemed biased against some very well-known brands that may not have high esteem, e.g., Marlboro cigarettes, or that are more visual than verbal, e.g., the Shell logo).[7] This study surveyed consumers only. More specialized buyer groups would doubtless have identified other global brands that were relevant to them.

In many product and service categories the preeminence of producers from particular countries encourages customers to prefer brand names indicating origin from their countries. With the rapid rise in prestige of Japanese products, companies such as Toyota now use model names with Japanese rather than American connotations—like Celica, Corolla, and Camry.[8]

Companies, particularly in Europe, are now adapting their names to globalize them. The second-largest dairy cooperative in Europe, Mejeriselskabet Denmark, changed its name in the late 1980s to MD Foods and its packaging colors from red and white (as in the Danish flag) to green and yellow. The change was intended to underscore the international reach of its business and the fact that it sells much more than just dairy products. This changed image also helped make MD Foods much more attractive to job applicants. With a change in name and image came a change in organization design to coordinate production and marketing. Multiple subsidiaries in other countries were combined as a result. Interestingly, in another case, it was the marketers of an American product with purely domestic ambitions that created the fictitious but Scandinavian-sounding name, Häagen-Dazs.

Because of history, many companies, particularly in packaged goods, find themselves stuck with a wide variety of brand and product names that have little justification in real differences between countries. The brand management system encourages innovation, so that left to their own devices, national brand managers are liable to convert a "Boggo" brand into Bloggo, Bloxxo, and Bingo, making it far more difficult to use global packaging and advertising. A vice president of global marketing in a large American multinational consumer packaged goods business viewed ease of internal communication as an additional benefit of global brands. This company has a category of "federal charter brand" that is designated to be controlled by the center. Only very large and important brands are accorded this status.

Global Packaging

The ability to use global packaging depends on several factors:

- Amount of information that needs to be communicated; the similarity of distribution conditions (e.g., importance of display appeal)
- Need for differentiation from local competitors
- Similarity of usage patterns and measurement systems
- Acceptability of multilanguage labeling

The high proportion of camera film bought by travelers makes it imperative to use globally recognizable packaging, as Eastman Kodak has done so well with its ubiquitous bright yellow boxes and stylized "K" logo. Fuji Photo Film has copied this approach with its distinctive green boxes. Gillette has achieved highly uniform packaging for its shaving products by substituting visual graphics for most of the wording that would otherwise be there. Furthermore, Gillette's use of consistent color, logo, and graphics provides a powerful umbrella image that makes it easy to introduce changes and new products with minimal disruption.

Many companies have allowed unnecessary differences in their packaging. In the late 1980s a major New Zealand-based forest products company updated its corporate logo—a lion's head—that was printed on all its packaging, but in North America only! So customers, many of whom were global, saw a modern lion in North America and a traditional one elsewhere. Other companies simply fail to identify their products consistently. The management of a major manufacturer of textile tubes belatedly realized that many of its products lacked any corporate identification at all. The company had to make rapid efforts to correct that lapse. Many Japanese companies, particularly newly internationalizing ones, are now converting their corporate logos from Japanese *kanji* characters to more globally recog-

---

3M's Global Packaging

In the 1980s, 3M discovered that its segmented approach to the markets for magnetic tape products was inefficient. Because there were similar features in all markets, 3M decided to introduce a new global brand identity and packaging for the magnetic products line, developing a global marketing strategy. The new identity was designed to be used uniformly for all of the division's products and in all markets and all countries. 3M developed a global advertising program that emphasized the logo and took advantage of the global transferability of the packaging. The new global marketing program boosted volume and market share, and the uniform packaging and design reduced the cost of marketing. In addition, the uniform marketing package exposure achieved quick customer recognition of 3M products.

---

nizable versions. Fuji Bank, for example, now uses a stylized image of Mount Fuji for its logo and spells out its name in English.

But many customers seem to dislike packaging that signals foreign origin. Even multilanguage labeling has its potential pitfalls—companies selling in a particular country need to avoid adding the languages of those other countries that might trigger prejudice or connotations of poor quality—"If this is used in Country X then it can't be very good."

Differences in national culture have a surprising effect on labeling. In Germany and Japan, customers expect products to perform to high standards but do not expect performance beyond the stated level. So if a product is labeled as being able to bear 1,000 kilograms, it will do that and no more. In America standards can be lower, but customers also expect a lot more leeway in performance beyond standards.[9] So in the United States, labeling needs to allow for overloading or overdosage or else expect a lot of complaints and lawsuits. In Germany and Japan, the same policy would mean understating what the product can do, thus putting it at a competitive disadvantage.

Global Pricing

Global pricing can bring the benefits of consistency with global customers and distribution channels and the avoidance of "gray market" parallel importation or "transshipment." Multinational companies often find themselves charging different prices to global customers without good justification. An international vice president of sales and distribution found that his company sometimes quoted the same customer different prices and availability in different countries, while finding it very difficult to explain why. In contrast, General Electric sells its jet engines at U.S. dollar prices all over the world, although it takes into account local competitive considerations when negotiating contracts.

Charging the same absolute price can be very difficult because of inherent international differences in market price levels, laws, and the role of price, as well as differences in the business's market position and delivered costs. The creation of the single European market is rapidly eliminating any government sources of price differences, such as tariffs and taxes, within the European Union, as well as encouraging buyers to cross borders. So companies in the EU need to rapidly rationalize the wide price differences that many now have. To start with, headquarters managers need to know the prices in different countries. But surprisingly few companies have sufficient information about their worldwide pricing to make decisions on global strategy.

Another way to have global pricing is to charge the same prices *relative* to competitors in each market. Using uniform relative pricing helps provide a consistent positioning in the market. Its viability depends on the similarity of the business's competitive position, delivered costs, and market objectives. Most commonly, it seems to be luxury products that manage to have pricing consistency, probably because being expensive is an essential part of what they offer.

Global Advertising

Global advertising has received more attention and publicity than any other aspect of global marketing, probably because of its visibility. Essentially, global advertising can be used at three levels:

- *Same copy strategy*—the brand is positioned in the same way making the same claims. Colgate toothpaste has long used the globally common claim of protection against cavities. Using a common copy strategy depends on worldwide similarity of the business's competitive position and market objectives and similarity of the stage of market development and buying motivations.
- *Same script*—the advertising uses the same script in different countries, while the actual execution is different. Using a common script depends on the universality of the images chosen and of the situations and characters to be used, and also the need for differentiation from local competitors. Coca-Cola has often taken this second approach of a common script, as in its famous "little-boy-gives-Coke-to-sports-hero" campaign. In America, the first hero was Mean Joe Green of the Pittsburgh Steelers football team, and most recently Shaquille O'Neal of the Orlando Magic basketball team, in Latin America Diego Maradona, the Argentine soccer superstar, and in Thailand a local soccer star named Niwat. Rarely can the same personality be used, although IBM did this with its Charlie Chaplin campaign for its personal computers.
- *Identical advertisement*—where each country uses the same commercial or ad-

vertisement with only the voices or text translated. Coca-Cola used this approach very successfully in its Italian hilltop chorale commercial in which youngsters from around the globe stood together singing that they wanted to give the world a Coke.

As already mentioned, Saatchi & Saatchi's "Manhattan Landing" commercial for British Airways is probably the most famous piece of global advertising. But Benetton, the highly successful Italian clothing manufacturer, has probably produced the most courageous examples. Benetton has run a globally uniform "Colors of Benetton" advertising campaign that features interracial harmony as a central theme. Some of its global images backfired in the United States when American audiences saw racist stereotypes rather than harmonious integration (a black wrist and a white wrist handcuffed together and a white baby feeding at a black breast). Levi Strauss has used a mixture of all three levels of advertising uniformity. Its advertising strategy used a common positioning stressing the all-American heritage of its jeans. An Indonesian television commercial showed teenagers in Levis cruising around Dubuque, Iowa, in 1960s convertibles. In Japan, Levi's used James Dean, the 1950s American film star, as the centerpiece in virtually all its advertising. Some of Levi's advertising execution was uniform too—in most advertisements for Levi's 501 button-fly jeans the dialogue was in English.

Ironically, the one type of advertising that cannot be used worldwide is one that stresses the country of origin. By definition, such a claim usually has little benefit at home, unless the company is making patriotic as opposed to benefit claims. For example, Volkswagen boosted its advertising awareness in the U.S. market with its *Fahrvergnügen* (joy of driving) campaign that directly played on the image of German cars as having superior handling and drivability. Neither the claim nor the attention-grabbing German language headline would have worked at home. Similarly, British Airways' longtime use in U.S. advertising of an actor embodying the stereotypical Englishman would have done nothing for British audiences.

Being able to use the same advertising media worldwide depends on the availability of the desired media, and on the lack of restrictions on the content of the advertising. The existence of national media with global reach forces advertisers to be consistent. In many industrial and scientific fields, journals published in one country have very wide circulation. A U.S. manufacturer of chemical and process equipment advertises in industry journals that have worldwide circulation and had to stop its European subsidiaries from running in these journals advertisements that differed from the global positioning.

Taking a totally uniform advertising approach can limit competitive flexibility. So some companies increasingly use two campaigns—a globally uniform one setting out the main theme, and local campaigns for tactical purposes—while using local campaigns to address particular local communication needs.

Global Sales Promotion

The tactical and short-term nature of sales promotion makes it probably the least likely candidate for globalization. Globalizing promotion probably makes sense on an opportunistic basis only—encouraging other countries to adopt a campaign or device successful elsewhere. Even then, barriers may arise from legal and customary restrictions and differences in how buyers react to promotional incentives. Countries vary particularly in the kinds of promotion they allow. In Europe, Great Britain, Ireland, Spain, Portugal, and Greece permit virtually every type of promotion, while Germany, Norway, and Switzerland forbid or restrict most types.[10]

Trade shows provide an important exception to the desirability of globalizing promotions. In many industries they act as major communication and selling opportunities. More relevant to global strategy, they are often frequented by global customers. So it becomes important for a company to coordinate its trade show efforts around the world. Money can be saved by sharing trade show materials like booths and exhibits.

The extent to which headquarters should be involved in local promotion strategies depends in part on whether local, regional, or global brands are involved.[11] For a global brand the center should define an overall promotional strategy that has guidelines for the relative emphasis on sales promotion versus media activity, for the relative weight of consumer and trade promotions, and for the role of price deals versus value-added offers. This central coordination will then help protect the integrity of the brand across national markets, particularly important in the case of promotion, which can easily destroy a brand franchise if misused. For global brands, the center should also encourage the cross-fertilization of promotional ideas and facilitate information transfer, particularly about successes and failures in promotional activities. For regional brands, the objectives can be more modest. The target should be brand harmonization rather than standardization, and the center's optimum role may be to encourage cross-fertilization of ideas. Last, for local brands, the center's task should be that of information transfer only. But effective transfer will help to ensure that local managers benefit from the broader collective wisdom of the worldwide business.

Global Selling

Global selling can involve using a uniform selling approach, global account management, or a centralized sales force. Using a *uniform selling approach* can bring the usual multinational benefits of ensuring best practice and high standards of behavior. Doing so depends on the similarity of channel structure and customer buying methods and behavior. Successful selling approaches can often be easily globalized, as IBM did with its highly trained sales personnel and systematic methods and as Avon Products did with its use of part-timers calling on friends, neighbors, and work-colleagues. A uniform selling approach can be useful in industries where global customers or global channels are important.

Using global account management can provide a highly effective way of serving global customers. Global account managers can perform similar functions to those of national account managers, and companies need to be concerned with analogous issues, including how to select global accounts; how to manage them; how to develop, manage, and evaluate global account managers; how to organize a structure for global account management; and where to locate global account management in the organization.12 While national account managers typically control their accounts, the geographic scope of global account management makes such control much more difficult, and perhaps politically hazardous. A global account manager can probably be more effective by merely coordinating the selling efforts of national sales forces and acting as the one interface with the customer at its head office. So in almost all cases the global account manager should be located in the home country of the global customer.

One manager may be able to wear two hats—as a national sales executive and as a global account manager. The global account manager position is particularly vulnerable to turf battles and jealousy: National sales managers tend to resent interference with their local customers. If one manager becomes the global account manager, he or she may get little cooperation. But if several national sales managers are assigned global account responsibilities, then they all have to cooperate with each other. Global account management certainly brings the benefit of speaking to a customer with one voice and avoiding having subsidiaries compete with one another for a customer's business. But companies also need to recognize the risks involved in global account management. Customers may use the centralized contact to demand that the lowest national price become the global price (or, more generally, that the most favorable national terms of trade become the global terms). An effective global account manager will have good justification of international differences in prices and terms. In particular, this manager needs to know *all* the prices and terms being offered by his or her company in different countries. Advertising agencies also are beginning to appoint worldwide account directors. Agencies doing so include Lintas, Ogilvy & Mather, Saatchi & Saatchi, and Young & Rubicam.

Another way of globalizing selling is to use a *centralized sales force*, probably based at a number of regional head offices, rather than one global head office, because of the extensive travel required. In addition to the logistical issues, companies using global or regional selling need to worry

Citibank's Use of Global Account Management

Citibank has used a full-blown global management system for nearly 500 of its largest multinational customers since 1974.[13] Citibank grouped these accounts, representing about 20% of the bank's worldwide loan volume, into a new unit—the World Corporation Group (WCG). This global unit was given primary responsibility for all activities on these accounts around the world. For each of the companies assigned to the WCG, a parent account manager located in the company's home country was designated to handle relationships with the parent company. In each country where a WCG corporation had branches or subsidiaries, a field account manager handled the local relationship. The same individual might serve as a parent account manager for accounts in his or her own country and as a field account manager for one or more relationships with a company headquartered elsewhere. The establishment of the WCG as a unit with lone responsibility for its accounts constituted a significant change in approach for Citibank. Traditionally, the bank had placed strong emphasis on local autonomy for each country. With the WCG system, country managers had a reduced role for the global accounts: setting guidelines rather than making decisions. Similarly, all personnel who were part of the WCG were evaluated primarily by that unit and only secondarily by the manager of the country in which they worked. Citibank also added a global account management system that included global planning, budgeting, and performance measurement processes and a global profitability system that tracked total and country profitability quarterly.

This global account management system seemed to work well for Citibank. Between 1974 and 1977, profits on the global accounts increased 63%, and total borrowing increased 85%. But in 1980, Citibank eliminated the WCG as part of a corporatewide reorganization that had the objective of simplifying the organization structure. Although Citibank continued with the other aspects of the global account management system, such as the global planning and budgeting, the loss of a separate organization structure soon put the emphasis back on geographic management. Citibank has since renewed its use of global account management and now considers it to be one of its strongest sources of competitive advantage in servicing multinational customers.

about customer acceptance of foreign sales representatives. Sales specialists with technical expertise are usually quite acceptable, in contrast to foreign regular sales representatives responsible for the ongoing customer relationship. Customers would be much more willing to accept foreigners in the latter role.

WHERE TO USE GLOBAL MARKETING

A global marketing program need not be applied to every country. In general, a company can derive greater benefits by applying global marketing to larger countries, because all categories of benefits—cost reduction, improved program effectiveness, enhanced customer preference, and increased competitive leverage—will be larger. On the other hand, larger markets tend to be more demanding of local adaptation than smaller ones. Customers in smaller countries are more used to products and programs not being adapted for them and are typically subject to more cultural influence from larger neighbors. In contrast, customers in larger countries are somewhat spoiled by the importance of their market. Canadian customers are probably more willing to accept foreign products and programs than are American customers, Dutch customers more than German ones, Belgians more than the French, and Koreans more than the Japanese. So companies face a trade-off in terms of whether to globalize in larger on in smaller markets. One way to solve this dilemma is to design core global products and programs more for the needs of larger countries than of smaller ones.

A GLOBAL MARKETING SUCCESS STORY:
The Kuschelweich/Robijn/Bamseline/Cajoline/Coccolino/ Mimosin/Yumos/Snuggle/Fofo/Fafa/Pomi/Baubau/ Huggie Brand

Unilever's creation of a new worldwide fabric softener product provides an illuminating example of the flexible and successful use of global marketing.[14] Perhaps the most interesting aspect of this strategy is its use of globally standardized positioning, global advertising, and many other globally standardized marketing elements, but a different brand name in each country. In the early 1970s, Unilever trailed Procter & Gamble in the fabric conditioner category in most countries. In 1970, Sunlicht, Unilever's German household products subsidiary, introduced a new product that was targeted at the economy end of the fabric softener market. To offset the negative quality implications of its claims of economy, Sunlicht devised two elements to connote softness—the key benefit desired by users. These two elements were the name "Kuschelweich," which means enfolded in softness in German, and a picture of a teddy bear on the bottle. The bear was just a symbol of softness and had no active role in the advertising. Sunlicht's success with the new product encouraged Unilever in France to introduce a similar product. But the French company changed the name to Cajoline, which has connotations of softness in French, and adapted the advertising by bringing the teddy bear on the bottle to life in a television commercial, so that it became a more active symbol of quality and softness. Success in France then led to adoption by many other countries. In each case the local Unilever subsidiary kept the positioning of economy and softness, changed the brand name to something indicating softness in the local language, but used virtually the same advertising with little change except for redubbing the voiceover. In Taiwan and Korea a scientific-style magnified closeup of fabric strands was added in the commercials to appeal to the desire of customers in those countries for scientific proof. The bottle was kept virtually identical in all countries, except for a few in which the base color was changed to provide more contrast with local competition.

By 1990 Unilever marketed the teddy bear brand as Kuschelweich in Germany, Robijn in Belgium and The Netherlands, Bamseline in Denmark, Cajoline in France, Coccolino in Italy, Mimosin in Spain, Yumos in Turkey, Snuggle in the United States, Fofo in Brazil, Fafa in Japan, Pomi in South Korea, Baubau in Taiwan, and Huggie in Australia. But in every country, the same teddy bear provided the brand identity and positioning. Only in the United Kingdom where there was already a strong Unilever brand, Comfort, was the new product not launched. Unilever considers the product a great success. Its worldwide introduction has boosted Unilever's share of the category to the number one rank in many countries and second in many others.

Lintas, one of the major advertising agencies used worldwide by Unilever, played a key role in developing and adapting this global marketing effort. Lintas helped develop the positioning and advertising strategy as well as creating the actual advertising. Lintas set up a European account team coordinated through its Paris office and its international head office in London. Eventually creative work was also performed in New York, Tokyo, and Sydney. Unilever's use of Lintas for the product in almost all countries (except in South Korea, where a local agency accepted guidance from Lintas) made it much more possible to maintain and improve on the common marketing program. Lintas's coordination also saved a great deal of money in advertising production costs. Most of the television commercials in different countries used a large amount of common footage—helped greatly by the absence of human characters in the advertising.

This story has several lessons:

- Global companies need to seize on a big marketing idea—in this case, using a teddy bear to symbolize softness and to build brand identity in fabric care—and promote its widespread adoption.
- Such global marketing can be highly flexible. Only the marketing elements that can benefit from standardization should be standardized, and local adaptations to a core strategy can, and should, be allowed.
- Industry globalization drivers help to identify which elements should be standardized and which not. In particular, the fact that consumers do not buy fabric softener when away from home negated any need for a common name. So the company standardized the meaning of the brand name rather than the name itself.
- A highly successful program was developed by a number of countries building on each other's efforts.
- Encouragement from head office, the involvement of some lead countries, and the participation of a global advertising agency all contributed to the rapid and successful worldwide adoption of the program.

CONDUCTING GLOBAL MARKET RESEARCH

Global marketing presents a special difficulty in market research. Good marketing practice requires that most new marketing programs undergo some research to test their likely effectiveness. The potential pitfalls of translation (in its widest sense—linguistic, cultural, institutional, and so on) in international marketing make research doubly important. But global marketing also carries great dangers of doing too much research or doing the wrong kind of research.[15] In particular, testing a global program head-to-head against a best local program may result in the local programs winning many of the contests. But such market research cannot examine the strategic benefits of a unified global approach.

In essence, if there are good strategic reasons for global marketing, market research should be used to discover how to make a global program work better (and to avoid pitfalls in linguistic and cultural translation) rather than to pit it against each possible local program. If such head-to-head tests are conducted, the companywide benefits of global marketing mean that the global program need not achieve parity with the local alternatives in order to justify adoption. So executives might set some achievement benchmark such as the global program achieving 90% as much favorable purchase intention as the local program, in countries accounting for 80% of worldwide volume.

Using global marketing also allows managers to compare market research results from different countries. Provided the global marketing programs have a large enough common core, findings in one country can usefully be studied in other countries. Similarly, global market research can be

---

Marlboro's Avoidance of Too Much National Research

The potential danger of excessive research is illustrated dramatically by the experience of Marlboro cigarette's world-famous cowboy advertising campaign—probably one of the most widely recognized icons in the history of advertising. A senior executive at Philip Morris, the marketer of Marlboro, has commented that too much national research would have prevented the cowboy campaign from being adopted globally. National market research would probably have identified a boxer as the best symbol in Britain, a bullfighter in Spain, a cyclist in France, and a sumo wrestler in Japan. The power of the common global identity would then have never been achieved.

---

used in experiments to find the best core global programs. Conducting global market research has become more feasible as suppliers of marketing information like A. C. Nielsen and newer vendors themselves globalize— Nielsen added Hungary in 1991 to the countries in which it collects market information. More significant, Nielsen now offers a global information service that provides headquarters executives in multinational companies with a cross-country summary of the detailed data supplied to national subsidiaries. Another supplier, International Ratings Services, has begun to offer a subscription service that tracks the performance of specific U.S. television shows overseas. The service translates and standardizes ratings from over twenty countries and is aimed at movie studios and independent producers selling television shows abroad.

COLLECTING GLOBAL MARKETING INFORMATION

Collecting marketing information from most of the countries in which the business participates and might participate is essential for the ability to create global marketing programs. Such information is not the monthly sales and activity tracking data that the national companies collect for operating purposes. Instead this global marketing information should be strategically oriented and needs to be collected periodically only, probably once a year. The country subsidiaries should be asked to provide information on the business and the largest local competitors as well as all global competitors designated by headquarters management. These designated competitors should include all key actual and potential global competitors. All countries should report on these competitors, however small the latter may be locally. Without such a directive, a complete worldwide picture of such global competitors would not be built up. A 5% market share in a single country for a local or regional competitor is typically trivial but may mean much more for a global competitor. For example, the global competitor may be in the process of creating a base for further expansion into that, or neighboring markets. Similarly, tracking worldwide share changes over time for these global competitors will help to identify the direction of their efforts, and possible threats and opportunities. The information reported from each country for the business and its competitors should include

- Market share
- Products and sizes offered
- Brand names
- New product introductions
- Prices
- Advertising and promotion expenditures
- Advertising positioning and claims
- Product quality
- Customer satisfaction
- Distribution methods and penetration
- Delivered costs
- Estimated profitability

ORGANIZING FOR GLOBAL MARKETING

Global marketing raises some special issues for organization and management. In addition to global account managers, the other key organization element that can help implement global marketing is the use of global product or brand managers. Beginning in the 1980s Unilever, L'Oréal (the French cosmetics company), and Beiersdorf (a major German manufacturer of household products) all added European brand managers responsible for coordinating the strategy of brand groups that cut across countries.

As discussed in the fabric softener case history, advertising agencies can play a helpful role in helping companies implement global marketing. Most companies seem to use too many advertising agencies around the world to allow for easy coordination of global advertising. One survey, conducted in the late 1980s, found that only one-third of 85 U.S. multinational consumer goods brands were handled by one agency around the world.[16] As part of its globalization drive, Black & Decker consolidated its worldwide advertising in 1986. From the previous twenty or more advertising agencies around the world, Black & Decker selected two principal agencies to coordinate worldwide advertising. (Packaging and distribution were also harmonized around the world. B&D has similarly styled multilingual packages available at retail outlets.[17]) Saatchi & Saatchi played a major role in helping British Airways' corporate management convince its country sub-sidiaries to adopt the "Manhattan Landing" commercial, often reluctantly. The results seemed worthwhile. Tracking studies showed increases in un-aided awareness and recall of British Airways in almost all the twenty countries using the campaign, especially in the United States.[18] Clearly, only the larger agencies with wide global networks can perform such a function. But potential clients of such agencies need to look a bit closer to see how well the global network is integrated. In addition to experience with global accounts, factors affecting an agency's global integration capa-bility include the following:

- A network grown internally over time rather than put together from acquisition
- Fully owned subsidiaries rather than affiliates
- Frequent exchange of managers and staff between country subsidiaries

A rule of thumb that can help encourage the adoption of global mar-keting is to charge subsidiaries extra for products and programs that need to be different from the global standard or that require more than some minimum level of adaptation. When asked to pay a premium national man-agers often realize that perhaps they do not need that "essential" local ver-sion after all.

GUIDELINES FOR CREATING GLOBAL MARKETING

In many ways marketing is very difficult to globalize. Differences between countries are often greatest in the customer attitudes and behavior that marketers try to influence. Furthermore, many of the benefits of global mar-keting can be more subtle than for the other elements of global strategy. At the same time, using global marketing can integrate the worldwide efforts of an organization in a more visible and powerful way than any other. The following key guidelines should be considered:

- Marketing can be, and sometimes should be, uniform in its content as well as its process.
- Each element of the marketing mix has its own unique opportunities and limi-tations in global uniformity.
- Managers should seek to push the limits of their imagination in devising global marketing programs. They should not be constrained by conventional wisdom about national preferences and prejudices.
- Testing global marketing programs against national alternatives requires care to avoid both underestimating and overestimating nationalistic reactions.
- National marketing managers need to remember that they have been trained to look for local differences. Creating successful global marketing requires a reorientation to look for similarities.

DISCUSSION AND RESEARCH QUESTIONS

1. What is the difference between a multilocal and a global approach to marketing?
2. Select a company or business and describe which aspects of its marketing mix are local, and which global.
3. How should a company go about developing a global segmentation strategy?
4. Which elements of the marketing mix are the easiest to make global, and which the hardest?
5. When should a company use a global brand name and when should it use different local names?
6. Identify a global advertising campaign not described in this chapter. What makes this campaign effective, and why?

NOTES

1. Some researchers have focused on standardized marketing process as the key attribute of global marketing. See the discussion by Pradeep A. Rau and John F. Preble, "Standardization of Marketing Strategy by Multinationals," *International Marketing Review,* Autumn 1987, pp. 19–28.
2. Keegan (1989) identified five combinations of product and promotion adaptation—straight extension, communication adaptation, product adaptation, dual adaptation, and product invention—but there are many more combinations possible when each element of the marketing mix is considered. See Warren J. Keegan, *Multinational Marketing Management,* 4th ed. (Englewood Cliffs, N.J.: Prentice Hall, 1989), pp. 378–381.
3. See Ralph Z. Sorenson and Ulrich E. Wiechmann, "How Multinationals View Marketing Standardization," *Harvard Business Review,* May–June 1975, pp. 38–45, and Rau and Preble, "Standardization of Marketing Strategy by Multinationals."
4. For further discussion of the barriers to global marketing, see Robert D. Buzzell, "Can You Standardize Multinational Marketing?" *Harvard Business Review,* November–December 1968, pp. 102–113; Susan P. Douglas and Yoram Wind, "The Myth of Globalization," *Columbia Journal of World Business,* Vol. 22, No. 4, Winter 1987, pp. 19–29; and Kamran Kashani, "Beware the Pitfalls of Global Marketing," *Harvard Business Review,* September–October 1989, pp. 91–98. See also Subhash C. Jain, "Standardization of International Marketing Strategy: Some Research Hypotheses," *Journal of Marketing,* Vol. 53, January 1989, pp. 70–79, for a review of some of the conceptual research issues in global marketing and Susan P. Douglas and C. Samuel Craig, "Evolution of Global Marketing Strategy: Scale, Scope and Synergy," *Columbia Journal of World Business,* Fall 1989, pp. 47–57, for a review of the evolution of global marketing strategy.
5. From Philip Kotler, *Marketing Management,* 5th ed. (Englewood Cliffs, N.J.: Prentice Hall, 1984), p. 272.
6. In mid-1981, Nissan announced it would gradually phase out the Datsun brand in favor of the Nissan name worldwide. In the United States, the first model to bear the transition name (Datsun by Nissan) was the 1981 Maxima 810 (also the first export model to have a nonnumeric name). In 1982, the Nissan Stanza was introduced, and by 1985 all U.S. models and all U.S. dealers bore the Nissan name exclusively.
7. This study was conducted by Landor Associates, an image consulting concern based in San Francisco. Landor questioned 5,000 consumers in the United States, 3,000 in eight European countries, and 1,000 in Japan about 800 trademarks. See "Coke's Kudos," *The Economist,* September 15, 1990, p. 88, and "More Brand Names Gain Recognition

Around the World," *The Wall Street Journal,* September 13, 1990. See also Landor Associates, "The World's Most Powerful Brands" (San Francisco, 1990).

8. There is an extensive literature on country-of-origin effects. See, for example, Johny K. Johansson, "Determinants and Effects of the Use of 'Made in' Labels," *International Marketing Review,* Vol. 6, No. 1, 1989, pp. 47–58.

9. From Michael Czinkota and Ilkka Ronkainen, *International Marketing,* 2nd ed. (Chicago: The Dryden Press, 1990), p. 270.

10. From *Nielsen European Passport Survey* (Northbrook, Ill.: A. C. Nielsen, 1990).

11. This paragraph is based on Kamran Kashani and John A. Quelch, "Can Sales Promotion Go Global?" *Business Horizons,* Vol. 33, No. 3, May–June 1990, pp. 37–43.

12. This list is adapted from Kotler's (*Marketing Management,* p. 683) discussion of national account management.

13. This example is drawn from Robert D. Buzzell, "Citibank: Marketing to Multinational Customers," Case No. 9-584-016 (Boston: Harvard Business School, 1984, revised 1/85).

14. I thank Michael Bowman of Lintas: Worldwide for making the details of the Unilever teddy bear brand history available to me.

15. For a discussion of the problems in translating market survey instruments and a guide to conducting international market research, see Susan P. Douglas and C. Samuel Craig, *International Marketing Research* (Englewood Cliffs, N.J.: Prentice Hall, 1983), pp. 186–190.

16. Barry Nathan Rosen, Jean J. Boddewyn, and Ernst A. Louis, "Participation by U.S. Agencies in International Brand Advertising: An Empirical Study," *Journal of Advertising,* Vol. 17, No. 4, 1988, pp. 14–22.

17. Laurence J. Farley, "Going Global: Choices and Challenges," *Journal of Business Strategy,* Vol. 1, Winter 1986, pp. 67–70.

18. See John A. Quelch, "British Airways: Teaching Note," Case No. 5-587-016 (Boston: Harvard Business School, 1987).

Chapter 7

Making Global
Competitive Moves

Making globally integrated competitive moves constitutes the fifth and last set of global strategy levers that a company can use to globalize strategy. In many ways it is the most difficult of the five levers to use, because its consequences are less directly visible than globally standardized products or globally uniform advertising. At the same time, not making globally integrated competitive moves can undermine the competitive advantages built up in individual countries and weaken a business's worldwide position, as happened to Kodak.

KEY FEATURES OF GLOBAL COMPETITIVE MOVES

The Kodak–Fuji story illustrates how the last (and most often forgotten) global strategy lever, globally integrated competitive moves, can be highly effective. A global strategy approach to competitive moves means integrating competitive moves across countries rather than making moves one country at a time. Integrated competitive moves also affect all the other global strategy levers of global market participation, global products, global activity location, and global marketing, typically needing to be used in conjunction with one or more of them.

Kodak's Mistakes and Recovery in Japan[1]

In the 1980s, Eastman Kodak lost share in the U.S. and European markets for photographic film that it had long dominated. These losses resulted from a fierce global onslaught by a newly internationalized competitor, Japan's Fuji Photo Film. Kodak's response, which included drastic attempts to cut costs and prices, cost it dearly in margins and profitability. Kodak had seemed impregnable with a strong basis for competitive advantage—its high quality, worldwide name recognition, and distribution system—and had also globalized this strategy successfully. Kodak had widespread global market participation, a globally standardized product line, an efficient and concentrated activity chain, and memorable global marketing, including its highly distinctive and recognizable global packaging. But Kodak's global strategy had a number of potentially serious flaws. First, although its global market participation was widespread, it had neglected a globally strategic country—Japan, which was the home of a strong potential global competitor and the market for some of the world's most demanding customers. In this omission, *Kodak was making the same mistake that many other Western companies have done—avoiding Japan as unattractive on a stand-alone basis, while not seeing its global strategic importance.* So Kodak made little investment in Japan and relied on a Japanese trading company to act as its local distributor. As part of this neglect, Kodak did not adapt its core strategy sufficiently to meet Japanese needs—such as printing Japanese on its packaging (not until 1984) or offering the right kind of products. This ignoring of the Japanese market allowed Fuji to grow little challenged until it was powerful enough to take on Kodak outside Japan.

By the early 1980s, Fuji held 70% of a very large Japanese market, while Kodak held only a few percentage points. Then Kodak made a second mistake, in terms of the globally integrated competitive moves lever. Kodak defended against Fuji's challenge in the same countries in which it was attacked. With its larger sales base, any price cuts and special promotions that Kodak made wound up hurting itself more than Fuji. Eventually, around 1984, Kodak realized that it needed to use the fifth global strategy lever—the counterparry—as part of globally integrated competitive moves in conjunction with the first global strategy lever—increasing market participation in Japan. Kodak decided to counterattack its rival's home market by investing an estimated $500 million to revamp its distribution system (taking control by setting up a joint venture with its distributor), taking equity stakes in its suppliers, and investing heavily in promotion. This counterstrategy worked, squeezing Fuji's domestic margins, forcing it to recall some of its best executives from abroad, and generally weakening its global competitive capabilities. By 1990, Kodak had multiplied its share of the Japanese amateur photographer market to 15% *and* had started to turn back a severe global challenge.

Global competitive moves have several aspects:

- Cross-subsidization of countries within the same business
- Use of counterparries
- Globally coordinated sequence of moves
- Targeting of actual and potential global competitors
- Developing plans for each major country-competitor combination
- Preemptive use of global strategy

These types of moves can be described as follows:

Type of Move	Definition
Cross-country subsidization	Using profits from one country in which a business participates to subsidize competitive actions in another country
Counterparry	Defending against a competitive attack in one country by countering in another country
Globally coordinated sequence of moves	Simultaneous or planned sequence in which competitive moves are made in different countries in the same business
Targeting of global competitors	Identifying actual and potential global competitors and selecting an overall posture—attack, avoidance, cooperation, or acquisition—for each.
Developing country-competitor plans	Analyzing strengths and weaknesses, opportunities and threats for each global competitor in each major country, and developing a competitive plan of action for each country-competitor combination
Preemptive use of global strategy	Being the first competitor to make use of a particular element of global strategy—global market participation, global products, global activity location, and global marketing

Cross-Subsidization of Countries

Being willing and able to subsidize across countries within the same business is perhaps the key requirement of a global strategy. As described in the previous four chapters, the overall use of global strategy levers such as global products and global marketing can provide a worldwide platform of competitive advantage. But this advantage cannot be fully exploited unless global resources can be selectively focused on points of competitive pressure or opportunity. In other words, the worldwide business needs to practice cross-country subsidization. This cross-subsidization should not apply to the same countries all of the time but to different countries as needed.2 Global managers should view portfolio roles as long-term postures that may be modified to meet short-term competitive pressures and opportunities. A country designated for a maintenance role may need temporary extra spending, subsidized by the rest of the world, to fend off a competitive thrust.

Counterparry

The counterparry represents a special case of cross-subsidization in which an attack by a competitor in one country is countered by a response in another.3 Such a counterparry has the intention of retaliating where the competitor can be hurt most. In practice, the effectiveness of the counterparry depends both on cooperation among countries in the business using it and on the competitor receiving and understanding the signal.4 The counterparry is most easily understood when two home countries are involved—a business attacked in its home country retaliates in the home country of the attacker. So Kodak's response in Japan provided a classic example of a counterparry involving two home countries. To make a counterparry effective, a business typically needs to have a large enough presence in key countries, particularly the home countries of global competitors, to provide a base for counterattack.

Globally Coordinated Sequence of Moves

Globally integrated competitive strategy also requires that competitive moves such as price changes and the introduction of new products or programs be coordinated across countries in their timing. That does not necessarily mean that they take place at the same time, only that there be a planned sequence to the moves. Why does this matter? First, competitive moves use resources and also usually spur competitor responses that may require even more resources in counterresponse. So the timing of competitive moves in each country needs to be planned to make the best use of available resources. A business with a global strategy would usually find it difficult to sustain a price war in the United States, Germany, and Japan simultaneously, especially if the contest is with different competitors in each country. Second, *a major benefit of global strategy is being able to apply experi-*

ence from one country to another.[5] *The experience gained and transferred is most useful when the right countries make the first moves.* For example, entering markets in the right sequence can enhance the competitive advantages that build up with experience. Making a move on a tough market before the business is ready for it can damage long-term global prospects and not just performance in the specific market entered. Japanese companies have been particularly successful in sequencing perhaps this very important type of competitive move—market entry.

Targeting of Global Competitors

Actual and potential global competitors need to be identified and a worldwide competitive strategy developed for each one. A global competitor has significant market share on two or more continents and uses some elements of global strategy. So a potential global competitor for a business can either be a multinational company already competing in some of the same markets as the business that does not now use a global strategy but may do so; or a multinational that already uses a global strategy but is not yet competing in the same markets as the business. *Targeting one competitor in many countries is likely to bring greater long-term gains than is targeting several competitors in a few countries each, because opposition should be weaker in the former case.* But a multilocal approach to competitive strategy typically results in the latter pattern, because each local management selects its most troublesome local competitor. Similarly, the most dangerous global competitors may not receive the highest priority unless a global view is taken of them. For example, a competitor with a strong number two position in many markets may be globally more dangerous than other competitors with leading positions in a few markets only.

The strengths and weaknesses of each targeted competitor need to be analyzed. In addition, their current and potential use of global strategy needs to be evaluated. An overall posture needs to be decided on for each competitor. Key choices include

- Attack
- Avoid direct competition
- Cooperate
- Acquire

In *attacking a global competitor,* the business must develop a global plan rather than leave local management to develop separate plans. At the same time, local management must be involved in the formulation of the plans. Key decisions include which product lines and customers of the competitor to target, and the selection and timing of countries for offensive moves.

While a simultaneous attack on many fronts has more chance of overwhelming a competitor, it also makes it more likely that the competitor will recognize the severity of the threat and retaliate correspondingly. Instead, a sequential, but coordinated, plan of attack may lull the competitor into a pattern of country-by-country surrenders, none crucial in itself, but accumulating to an irreversible loss of position.

Avoiding direct competition with a global competitor can require as much planning and forethought as attack. Retreating into multilocal protected niches offers the simplest way to avoid confrontation with global competitors. But such a strategy depends on the long-term sustainability of the conditions, external or internal to the business, that allow protection from global competition. Furthermore, under this approach, headquarters management can do little to help the local businesses as the latter develop their own niches. A globally coordinated approach to avoiding competition may hold better hope of sustainability. To take such an approach requires predicting the likely expansion paths of global competitors in terms of products, customers, and geographic markets. It also requires prediction of how competitors will develop their sources of competitive advantage, such as in proprietary technology. Then the business needs to decide on which of these competitor expansion paths it can afford to get out of the way, and on which of these paths it has to dig in. For example, the business may be able to identify product lines, customers, and geographic markets that are less crucial than others, and be prepared to give ground there in order to defend better the remaining higher priority products, customers, and markets. Unfortunately, the track record of selective retreat has not been stellar in the face of determined global competitors. Both American and British motorcycle manufacturers retreated to larger engine models in the face of Japanese competition, only to find each engine size not defensible after all.

Cooperating with competitors via international joint ventures and alliances became highly popular in the 1980s. Several authors have provided very thorough frameworks for joint venture strategies, so none will be offered here.[6] A few aspects of joint ventures that are crucial in globally integrated strategy need to be highlighted. All joint ventures need to achieve some match between what each partner has to offer and what each partner will give up. In the specific context of global strategy, as opposed to corporate and competitive strategy in general, a key decision is the choice of which geographic markets will be made part of the joint venture. A joint venture can provide both defensive capabilities and offensive opportunities in the markets covered. But, at the same time, a joint venture can limit growth potential and, as argued in Chapter 3, reduces the degree to which the business can operate a truly integrated global strategy.

A worldwide business that operates as a self-contained globally integrated system rather than relying on joint venture partners will find it much easier to achieve the coordination and agreement needed to make a sequence of globally integrated competitive moves. In contrast, an open system that has outside organizations as partners will be much more difficult to manage for global strategy, particularly for this last lever. Making globally integrated competitive moves typically requires self-sacrifice and cross-subsidization by geographic entities. That is difficult enough to achieve among fully owned subsidiaries. With external partners, it becomes nearly impossible. Last, there is the argument that joint ventures serve as a crutch that discourages companies from developing their own capabilities.7

Acquiring competitors is the most effective means of eliminating competition. In the global context, acquisition can bring the added benefit of filling out geographic coverage. So in selecting acquisition candidates, managers should apply a global strategic perspective that seeks those companies that can strengthen the business's position in key countries, as well as the other, usual acquisition criteria. Other things being equal, acquirers should be willing to pay a higher premium for acquisitions that improve their geographic balance, improve their position in key countries, or strengthen other aspects of their global strategy.

Developing Country-Competitor Plans

The targets for individual global competitors can be further developed into plans for individual country-competitor combinations. To make these plans, it is first necessary to understand the strategic position of each global competitor in each country. To do so requires conducting the usual type of analysis of strengths, weaknesses, opportunities, and threats. Exhibit 7–1 provides an illustrative example of the summary output of such an analysis.

Following this analysis of country-competitor strategic positions, plans can then be developed for each country-competitor combination. In particular a target needs to be set for each combination. These overall targets can include several possibilities, for example,

- Attack
- Defend
- Avoid direct competition
- Stay out
- Preempt
- Cooperate
- Acquire

Exhibit 7–2 provides an illustrative example of a set of targets for one business. Presenting all country-competitor combinations together helps

Competitor	Region			
	N. America	**S. America**	**Europe**	**Far East**
Copeland, Inc.	Market leader	Weak products and distribution, slipping share	Increasing share, strong product line	Recent entrant, trying to build position
Westminster PLC	Market follower	Overpriced products	Market leader in some countries, but slipping share	Share is holding steady but not reinvesting much
Schumann AG	Market follower, some weak product lines	Market leader, building position further	Market leader in some countries, gaining share in others	Not yet present
Tokugawa K.K.	Small share but growing fast	Strong no. 2 in market	Strong no. 2 in most countries, share growing fast	Market leader with strong product lines and customer relationships

EXHIBIT 7–1   Situation Analysis for Country-Competitor Combinations: Illustrative Example

make it clear whether or not the business is being too ambitious. Exhibit 7–2 shows that the business has targeted one competitor, Westminster PLC, for all-out attack throughout the globe. For another competitor, Tokugawa K.K., the strategy is to hold defensively in all parts of the globe. Last, there

EXHIBIT 7–2   Strategies for Country-Competitor Combinations: Illustrative Example

Competitor	Region			
	N. America	**S. America**	**Europe**	**Far East**
Copeland, Inc.	Defend	Opportunistic attack	Avoid direct competition	All-out attack
Westminster PLC	All-out attack	All-out attack	All-out attack	All-out attack
Schumann AG	Opportunistic attack	Defend	Avoid direct competition	Preempt entry
Tokugawa K.K.	Defend	Defend	Defend	Defend

Japanese Strategy in VCRs

In the videocassette recorder industry, Japanese manufacturers such as Sony and Matsushita combined rapid coverage of all key markets, with offering the first global products, and an efficient production network based in the Far East, to secure adequate volume and a strong competitive position, including in the U.S. market. American competitors such as RCA, Zenith, or General Electric never had a chance to put up a fight, let alone take the battle to Japan. By the time these companies had set up their activity network with production and component purchasing in the Far East, the Japanese products were established and competing no longer on price but on recognized quality.[8]

---

is a selective strategy for Copeland, Inc., and Schumann AG that varies by region.

Preemptive Use of Global Strategy

Great advantages accrue for the first company in an industry that uses a global strategy. For global market participation, the first company to build a network of strong positions in all of the globally strategic countries gains a preemptive advantage, as well as boosting possible scale advantages. For global products, the first company to introduce a globally standardized product can reap the advantage of setting industry standards and customer expectations and preferences. For activity location, the first company to build a global network of optimally concentrated and located activities reaps early cost and quality advantages that competitors should find difficult to match. For global marketing, the first company to promote global brands and global advertising can build image and preference leads that are difficult to dislodge.

BENEFITS AND DRAWBACKS

The key benefit of globally integrated competitive moves lies in magnifying the resources available in any single country for competitive actions by leveraging the global resources of a business. So head office managers can design competitive strategies that involve the power of multiple moves, while local managers can call on help beyond that available in just their own countries. In addition, taking a globally integrated approach to competitive moves simply provides more options in attack and defense. Such an approach also helps managers to see country linkages so that they recognize the competitive interdependence of countries. That way the business can avoid the piecemeal, country-by-country, conquest that has been the fate of companies in many industries. Furthermore, managers taking a globally integrated approach to competitive moves are more likely to spot the preemptive actions that need to be taken—such as Becton Dickinson's moves to block Japanese expansion in Southeast Asia in the disposable syringe market.

On the other hand, integrating competitive moves can have drawbacks also. It can mean sacrificing revenues, profits, or competitive position in individual countries, particularly likely when the subsidiary in one country is asked to attack a global competitor in order to send a signal or to divert that competitor's resources from another country. The manager of the sacrificing subsidiary may be reluctant to perform such a selfless role. Overcoming such reluctance requires a performance evaluation and reward management system that encourages rather than discourages global cooperation.

GUIDELINES FOR MAKING GLOBAL
COMPETITIVE MOVES

Perhaps the ultimate test of a total global strategy is whether a worldwide business can make globally integrated competitive moves. Some guidelines help managers to perform this difficult task:

- Global competitive moves require coordination and agreement among national managers. In some cases it also requires national sacrifices for the sake of the worldwide business.
- Not making global competitive moves can be particularly damaging in the long term for a business's worldwide competitive position.
- It is critical for senior management to design and implement a system to both recognize the need for globally integrated competitive moves and to achieve cooperation among different countries.

DISCUSSION AND RESEARCH QUESTIONS

1. What is the difference between a multilocal and a global approach to making competitive moves?
2. Describe a competitive action or series of actions by a company that you think particularly exemplifies a global competitive move.
3. What should be the response of a company when a foreign competitor is dumping in that company's home market? Would your answer differ if the foreign competitor were (a) an exporter producing only in its home country or

(b) a multinational company with production and sales around the world? Would your answer differ by the nationality of the foreign competitor?

4. What organizational mechanisms are needed to allow a company to make effective global competitive moves?

NOTES

1. This example draws on "The Revenge of Big Yellow," *The Economist*, November 10, 1990, and "Kodak Chief Is Trying, for the Fourth Time, to Trim Firm's Costs," *The Wall Street Journal*, September 19, 1990, pp. A1, A18.

2. It is in the area of cross-subsidization, and also coordinated moves, the global strategy comes closest to military strategy. In the latter arena, concentration of forces at selected points to outnumber the enemy is perhaps the key maxim (or "get there fastest with the mostest" as one American general once said). For a more general discussion of analogies between business and military strategy, see Philip Kotler and Ravi Singh, "Marketing Warfare in the 1980s," *Journal of Business Strategy*, Vol. 1, No. 3, Winter 1981.

3. See Michael E. Porter, "Changing Patterns of International Competition," *California Management Review*, Vol. 28, No. 2, Winter 1986, pp. 9–40.

4. See Michael E. Porter, *Competitive Strategy: Techniques for Analyzing Industries and Competitors* (New York: The Free Press, 1980), Chapter 4, and A. Michael Spence, "Entry, Capacity, Investment and Oligopolistic Pricing," *Bell Journal of Economics*, Vol. 8, Autumn 1977, pp. 534–544, on the role of signaling in competitive strategy.

5. Sumantra Ghoshal, "Global Strategy: An Organizing Framework," *Strategic Management Journal*, Vol. 8, No. 5, September–October 1987, pp. 425–440, characterizes the ability to learn and adapt as one of the three key objectives in global strategy, the other two being achieving efficiency and managing risk. See also Christopher A. Bartlett and Sumantra Ghoshal, *Managing Across Borders: The Transnational Solution* (Boston: Harvard Business School Press, 1989), on how to organize for global learning.

6. See the works cited in note 16 in Chapter 3.

7. As argued by Michael E. Porter, *The Competitive Advantage of Nations* (New York: The Free Press, 1990).

8. This example is adapted from Herbert Henzler and Wilhelm Rall, "Facing Up To the Globalization Challenge," *The McKinsey Quarterly*, Winter 1986, pp. 52–68.

Chapter 8

Building the Global Organization

Organization factors form the third corner of the globalization triangle, along with industry globalization drivers and global strategy levers. They affect what the nature of global strategy should be as well as the effectiveness of its implementation. Here we focus on how the nature of the organization—its structure, management processes, people, and culture—affects the use of global strategy levers and the ability to implement global strategy. The chapter describes these organization factors in depth and discusses how to build a global organization.[1] Key issues in global organization include how to achieve balance between autonomy and integration. Subsidiaries need autonomy in order to adapt to their local environment. But the business as a whole needs integration to implement global strategy.[2] Global organizations need to achieve both integration and autonomy while fostering the increasingly important tasks of learning and knowledge transfer.[3] Being able to transfer knowledge from one country to another provides a key source of advantage for multinational companies.[4]

Many companies today are struggling to achieve a globally integrated organization that retains the capability for local flexibility and responsiveness. Virtually no company has achieved a totally satisfactory solution, but a few have created highly successful elements in the global organization and management puzzle. Black & Decker has already been described in ear-

---

ICI's Global Business Units

In the 1980s, ICI's management began the process of replacing its U.K. divisions and overseas national companies with global business units. These units have responsibility for overall global strategy, R&D, and resource allocation. Some are headquartered outside the United Kingdom—ICI's worldwide explosives business is managed out of Toronto. While ICI still uses a matrix structure that has product, geographic, and functional dimensions, it is now the product dimension that takes the lead. About half of ICI's activities are organized into globally integrated "international businesses" that have clear global strategies. The remaining businesses are localized within Europe but also export to the rest of the world.

---

lier chapters. Another company that seems to have developed effective global solutions is ICI in the United Kingdom, one of the world's largest chemical companies.

Organization provides the vehicle by which strategy can be formulated and implemented. The nature of the organization also affects the kind of strategy that can be developed. This is particularly true of global strategy. An organization of highly autonomous national business units, in which the managers from different countries seldom meet, with little transfer of personnel or information between countries, and with a nationalistic culture, is scarcely likely to be able to formulate a global strategy in the first place, let alone implement it. Such an organization may well believe that it does not need a global strategy—because it is not exposed to the information that might show otherwise.

Building the kind of company capable of formulating and implementing total global strategy is not easy. The task is achievable if managers break it down into digestible pieces and if they relate changes in organization to the specific changes needed in global strategy. A workable approach to global organization has two key requirements. First, it is no use announcing that the company needs a "global organization" without specifying the details of that organization. So managers need to view a global organization as comprising several factors and several elements within each factor. The second key requirement is to recognize that specific elements of global organization affect the ability to use specific elements of global strategy. For example, having a separate international division (an element of organization structure) makes it very difficult to design global products. So managers need to take an *elemental* approach to designing the global organization. The advantage of this elemental approach is that managers can make small changes that can build up over time[5] and can change one aspect of organization when blocked in another. Reorganizing the structure can be politically difficult, while less drastic changes in the management process may meet less resistance. Changes in some elements can reduce the barriers to more major changes.

Four factors and their individual elements determine the crucial organization forces that affect a company's ability to formulate and implement global strategy:

- *Organization structure* comprises the reporting relationships in a business—the "boxes and lines."
- *Management processes* comprise the activities such as planning and budgeting that make the business run.
- *People* comprise the human resources of the worldwide business and include both managers and all other employees.
- *Culture* comprises the values and unwritten rules that guide behavior in a corporation.

Each of these factors directly affects the others and the use of global strategy. Each operates powerfully in different ways. A common mistake, in implementing *any* strategy, is to ignore one or more of them, particularly the less tangible ones such as culture. A blockage in even one dimension of organization can severely cramp the ability to think and behave globally. Exhibit 8–1 lists the key factors and their key elements.

EXHIBIT 8–1   Elements of Global Organization

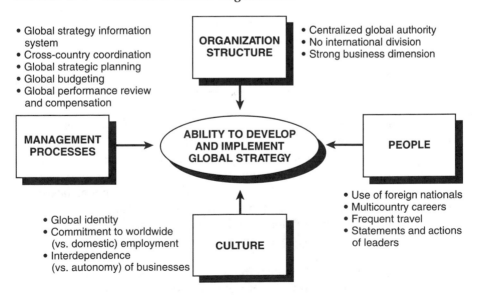

- Global strategy information system
- Cross-country coordination
- Global strategic planning
- Global budgeting
- Global performance review and compensation

ORGANIZATION STRUCTURE

- Centralized global authority
- No international division
- Strong business dimension

MANAGEMENT PROCESSES

ABILITY TO DEVELOP AND IMPLEMENT GLOBAL STRATEGY

PEOPLE

- Global identity
- Commitment to worldwide (vs. domestic) employment
- Interdependence (vs. autonomy) of businesses

CULTURE

- Use of foreign nationals
- Multicountry careers
- Frequent travel
- Statements and actions of leaders

Source: Adapted from Yip, Loewe, and Yoshino (1988).

Ford's European Strategy

Although on a continental rather than global scale, Ford of Europe, created in 1967, provides an excellent example of how organization changes have facilitated strategy changes.6 Ford of Europe was created to coordinate the company's activities in the region and to break down the barriers dividing Ford's country-based operations. The effects of this reorganization were far reaching over the next two decades. For example, the German divisions built special strengths in manufacturing while the British division excelled in product development and general enterprise management. Together they created cars for all of Europe (and eventually the world) and saved the rest of the company financially during the difficult 1979–1984 period. The change in organization culture that followed the creation of Ford of Europe helped to make Ford one of the most global automobile companies. Ford executives also believe that Ford's leading-edge aerodynamic designs, cost-cutting programs, and emphasis on quality all grew out of the new ways of working. The different country operations not only canceled out each other's weaknesses, but also set a higher base level for the quality of all operations. Good ideas and solutions to problems were sought throughout the company and flowed rapidly through the entire organization. The strengths of the European operation (exemplified in the Taurus and other European-styled cars) are now being imported to the United States. Another benefit of creating a central organization is that Ford of Europe has become much more attentive to what the Japanese are doing well and is able to act on the knowledge to keep pace. Furthermore, Ford is now seeking to apply the lessons it learned from Europeanization on a global scale.

Each organization factor and its elements have distinct effects on the use of each of the five global strategy levers. For example, having centralized global authority allows a more global approach to market participation—by allowing countries to be chosen more on the basis of global strategic importance and less on the basis of which regional manager has more political power. Centralized global authority also helps the development of global products, helps make global choices on the location of activities, and makes it easier to develop global marketing and to make global competitive moves.

The organization and management requirements of a global business can also be contrasted with those of a multilocal or export-based business. For these different businesses, each organization factor needs to stress different features. A *global* business needs some form of centralized global authority. But a *multilocal* business does better with dispersed national authority that allows each country to make its own decisions in adapting to local conditions. Last, an *export-based* business also needs centralized authority but one that takes the viewpoint of the home country business rather than that of the entire worldwide business. Exhibit 8–2 summarizes the desired organization features for each type of geographic strategy.

But, as with global strategy levers, companies need not adopt every global organization approach. Managers should select those global organization elements that seem the most helpful in achieving their global strat-

EXHIBIT 8–2   Desired Organization Features for Types of Geographic Businesses

Geographic Scope	Organization Structure	Management Processes	People	Culture
GLOBAL	Centralized global authority No domestic–international split Strong business dimension relative to geography and function	Extensive coordination processes Global sharing of technology Global strategy information system Global strategic planning, budgets, performance review, and compensation	Multicountry careers Foreign nationals in home and third countries Extensive travel	Global identity Interdependence
MULTILOCAL	Dispersed national authority No domestic–international split Strong geographic dimension relative to business and function	Transfer of technology from headquarters out National information systems National strategic planning, budgets, performance review, and compensation	Professional expatriates Nationals run local businesses Limited travel	Multinational identity Autonomy
EXPORT-BASED	Centralized home country control Separate domestic and international divisions May have strong functional dimension	Direction not coordination One-way information flow to headquarters No technology transfer Focus on sales targets	Home country nationals run local marketing subsidiaries	Home country culture

egy objectives. Furthermore, as change is usually necessary, managers should select those changes that they think their organization is capable of making. And, if the company cannot make the needed organization changes, it should not even try to have a global strategy. *Some companies are better off not trying to compete globally.* The CEO of a regional American manufacturer decided that his company had to go global to survive. He gave marching orders. And the organization marched on. The problem was they started marching right over a very big global cliff. The company set up a small operation in Brazil as management had targeted South America as part of the global strategy. But the executives appointed to run the operation had never been outside the United States before, and the company started losing money. When senior managers really analyzed the situation, they found that going global was just too unnatural to the company's cultural system and that a viable strategic alternative was to stay in the United States and play a niche strategy.[7]

ORGANIZATION STRUCTURE

The first organization factor, organization structure, has the most obvious and direct, although not necessarily the most important, effect on global strategy.[8] Changes in organization structure (and, therefore, lines of reporting) send the clearest signals, which can be good or bad. So such changes need to be used with caution. In some cases, changes in other, less direct, aspects of organization, such as management processes, may need to be made first to pave the way for changes in structure.

Centralization of Global Authority

One of the most effective ways to develop and implement a global strategy is to centralize authority so that all units of the same business around the world report to a common *global sector head.* Surprisingly few companies do this. Instead, they are tied for historical reasons to a strong country-based organization structure where the main line of authority runs by country rather than by business. Reorganizing along global lines, as General Electric began to do in the 1980s, makes fundamental changes in how resources are allocated. For example, the lighting business in GE Canada used to compete at GE's corporate headquarters with all other Canadian businesses for resources. But now the Canadian lighting business goes to the global lighting business head to seek funds. In some businesses, however, particularly vertically integrated ones in raw-material processing industries such as chemicals or pulp and paper, it can be very difficult to carve out stand-alone lines of business in each country. Each factory, for example, may serve several businesses both inside and outside the country in which the factory is located. In such cases an alternate structural, solution is to appoint *global business directors* who operate in matrix fashion across the functional and geographic organizations.

The roles and responsibilities for such global business directors can include the following:

- Taking profit accountability for individual lines of business
- Coordinating all functions affecting these lines
- Developing a strategic plan and financial budgets in cooperation with the functions and regions
- Working with the functions and regions to implement the strategic plan
- Contributing to the design, creation, and maintenance of global strategy, marketing, and financial information systems
- Contributing to performance evaluations for functional and regional managers
- Traveling frequently

Another way of centralizing global authority is to have *global heads of individual functions* or value-adding activities. These heads can have either direct line authority over the function or a stafflike coordination responsibility. Functional heads can be very effective. The corporate head of global marketing in a major American household products company viewed his role as partly to explain why ideas had failed in other countries. He would often say to a national manager: "You know more about your country than I do. I know more about the rest of the world. This strategy you propose has been tried in eight other countries. It failed in seven and here is why. Now let's examine your idea." But having real power can also be elusive. Companies sometimes delude themselves that they have created global authority by giving responsibility for global integration to an executive. The head of business planning in a large American computer equipment business commented that while his business had one global product head "on paper," the latter had no real control and, therefore, little effect on global strategy.

Absence of Domestic–International Split

A common structural barrier to global strategy is the presence of an organization split between a domestic and an international division.[9] Typically, the international division oversees a group of highly autonomous country subsidiaries, each of which manages several distinct businesses. A global strategy for any one of these businesses can then be fully coordinated only at the level of the CEO's office. This split is very common among U.S. firms, partly for historical reasons and partly because of the enormous size of the U.S. market. Ironically, some European multinationals with small domestic markets have separated out not their home market but the U.S. market. As a result they find it difficult to get their U.S. subsidiaries to cooperate in the development and implementation of global strategy. In one major European company, the heads of worldwide business sectors had to go "cap-in-hand to New York" to solicit support for their worldwide strategies. Recently, this company has strengthened the business sectors' direct authority over American operations.

Many, perhaps most, American companies have separate international and domestic divisions. There is a trend toward disbanding international divisions. A major financial service company has recently shifted to three regions for the whole world. Its business head viewed this eliminating of the U.S. divisions, and consequent breaking down of regional barriers, as one of the company's greatest successes in globalizing strategy. The benefits included better allocation of resources and the recognition that business lost in one country need not necessarily be replaced in the same country, but can be recouped elsewhere. The head of international sales and distribution for a leading U.S. industrial controls business views its domestic–international split as the biggest obstacle to global strategy. The head of another business complains that its heavily regional organization discourages global strategy by restricting the flow of information and technology. The head of marketing in the international division of a food and beverages business commented that the original advantage of having a separate international division was in building up a power base. But now, with a global brand fighting a global competitor, the business needs to use its U.S. profits to subsidize international efforts, and the current structure does not allow that.

Business Dimension Stronger than Geographic Dimension

Issues of central control affect the global strategy capability of a worldwide business. But most worldwide businesses are part of multinational companies that operate multiple businesses. The need to manage across both countries and businesses adds to the complexity of the challenge. Most multinational companies have evolved a matrix form of organization structure that combines business and geographic as well as functional dimensions.[10]

Unilever has long operated with a matrix system. Its global integration has been provided by a team of head office "coordinators" responsible for business sectors such as detergents and foods (the latter coordination being split at one time into Foods I, Foods II, and Foods III). These coordination executives have mostly held senior country and regional general management positions. Only recently has its archrival, Procter & Gamble, taken up a similar approach. In the 1980s P&G adopted a matrix type of structure, first in Europe and then worldwide. A brand manager now reports both to his or her country manager and to a category manager. P&G management believes this change has helped the company react more quickly to global competition.[11] At the same time some observers have criticized P&G's use of European product managers for slowing the European launch of its Pampers brand of disposable diapers. In particular, the change in reporting structure may have made national managers less interested in supporting Pampers. But, if true, that problem does not demonstrate the weakness of global organization or global marketing but of inadequate change in *all* the elements of global organization. P&G should also have changed the management evaluation and incentive process to support the new strategy. Dow Chemical has used a three-dimensional (function, business, and geography) matrix management since the 1960s to cope with its plants in over thirty countries and its 1,800 different products. After many changes, Dow has settled on a flexible approach in which, depending on the nature and needs of a business sector, one of the three dimensions of the matrix is chosen to carry more weight than the other two. Last, and perhaps most important, is that regardless of the organization structure, managers should think in matrix fashion.[12]

In a company pursuing a global strategy, the extent of integration within businesses needs to be very strong. At the same time, integration within each country is important in order to coordinate the activities of the different businesses and to be able to present a common front to host governments, suppliers, channels, customers, and community groups. In theory, strong integration along both business and country dimensions should be possible. In practice, the two efforts often conflict. Exhibit 8–3 illustrates some possible combinations of geographic and business integration. The situation in the top left box, "Fragmented Multilocal Strategies," illustrates the case of extreme global fragmentation, in which there is no organization structure integrating either businesses within a country or countries within a business. Senior executives in many large and small American multinational companies characterize (with embarrassment) their company that way.

The situation in the top right box, "Integrated Country Strategies," illustrates a historically very common form of multinational organization in which a country manager has great powers over all the businesses in his or her country. This form of integration was particularly popular in the early days of multinational expansion when communications and travel were far more difficult than today. European companies, with their heritage of colonial administration, probably developed the country manager role to its

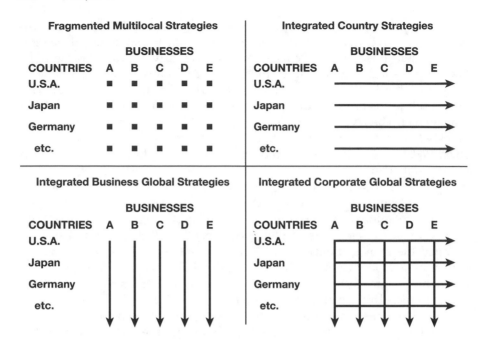

EXHIBIT 8–3   Different Corporate Approaches to Worldwide Strategy

highest degree of power. The country manager of India in a British multinational company used to "rule like a rajah." Many corporate executives have complained of national and regional "fiefdoms" run by these highly independent country managers. Even Roger Enrico, who persuaded Michael Jackson to sing and dance for Pepsi-Cola, could not control the head of Pepsico in Latin America.[13] But the need for global strategy, and improvement in communications, is causing many companies to reduce the role of the country manager. *In one sense, the country manager has been made obsolete by the fax machine.* In a major American financial service business the role of the country manager has changed a great deal—the country manager used to run the business in the country but is now more the titular head who represents the parent company in the country. It seems, however, that there will always be one role for the country manager. The Swiss chief financial officer of a European multinational said that his company would always need country managers, because "governments need one man to go after to put in jail"!

The bottom left box, "Integrated Business Global Strategies," illustrates the situation in which the organization structure provides strong global integration within each business across countries but provides little integration across businesses within each country. Only in the bottom right box, "Integrated Corporate Global Strategies," does the structure provide integration across both dimensions. When executives are asked which diagram best represents their corporation, few select this last box, but almost all say that their company is headed that way. Philips, the giant Dutch manufacturer of electrical products, provides an instructive example of a company that has long had a much more powerful geographic dimension than a business one but is now striving hard to "tilt the matrix" toward the business dimension. Because of the Dutch colonial heritage and because the head office was cut off from the subsidiaries during World War II, the latter grew to operate very independently. But under global attack from Japanese electronics manufacturers, and facing the integration of Europe, Philips is finding it needs a global rather than a multinational organization.[14] Last, companies need not adopt just one of the four models depicted in Exhibit 8–3. A mixture can be best, allowing some businesses (those in industries with low globalization potential) to be managed on a country-by-country basis, some countries (those with high barriers to trade) to operate independently with extensive control over the businesses in them, and other countries and businesses to be part of an integrated global matrix.

Designating Strategic Leaders

A less direct approach to globalization than changing the organization structure is to assign to a specific country the lead role in developing a product and to see to that product's spread into other countries and to its adaptation.[15] Thus some responsibilities are diverted from the other countries to the country acting as the strategic leader. One of the most effective ways of using this approach is to assign strategic leadership responsibility for different products to a number of different countries. In that way, each country has to cooperate with the others, and none is singled out.

Differences Among American, European, and Japanese Companies

Multinational companies from the three major business areas of the world—the United States, Western Europe, and Japan—tend to have differing organization structures and therefore face differing globalization challenges. Because of the small size of their home markets and because of their nations' overseas empires, European companies have typically been the most advanced in multinationalization whether measured by the percentage of their sales outside their home country or by their use of managers of different nationalities. More important, European multinationals, such as Unilever, Philips, and Nestlé, have probably given more autonomy to their foreign subsidiaries than have American or Japanese multinationals. Many

European multinationals face, therefore, a greater need to reduce multilocal autonomy and increase global integration.

Because of the huge size of their home market, American companies have been somewhat slower to go international than have comparable European and Japanese companies. Now there is increased pressure to internationalize because of increased foreign competition, slower growing domestic markets, and the new public recognition of America's trading problems. Although indirect, the last factor powerfully affects the attention paid to international business by corporate stakeholders (such as share owners, boards of directors, and employees) and, therefore, the attention of senior management. The size of the American domestic market has also created an issue that is more typical for American multinationals—the organizational and psychological division between the home country and other countries. Separate domestic and international organizations are common in American multinationals but rarer in European ones. As a result American companies pursuing global integration face the dual challenge of confronting not just local country autonomy but domestic–international divisions as well.

Most Japanese companies have until recently operated as exporters rather than as multinationals. Although they have typically used an international division, the export emphasis of their businesses has allowed very close links between their domestic and international businesses. Their rising domestic costs, plus the threat of protectionism in their foreign markets, have spurred an increasing relocation of their production activities to the countries of their markets. Japanese companies now face the task of learning how to operate as multinational companies and to build the needed organization structure. In terms of global strategy, they face a challenge opposite to that for American and European companies. Japanese companies have generally been highly effective in operating with an integrated global strategy. Now they face the task of retaining that global integration while allowing the local autonomy needed to operate as multinationals.

Potential for Cost Savings

Reorganizing along global rather than multilocal lines can produce major cost savings by reducing the extent to which activities are duplicated in multiple countries (as discussed in Chapter 5). The traditional way to cut costs in reorganization is to eliminate *horizontal* layers by cutting the number of levels in a company. Reorganization along global lines provides a *vertical* option for cost cutting, such as by eliminating nine out of twelve manufacturing sites in different countries. But companies need to beware of reorganizing globally just for the sake of cost savings. The reorganization must also make sense strategically, relative to industry globalization drivers and the type of global strategy needed.

MANAGEMENT PROCESSES

While organization structure has a very direct effect on management behavior, it is management processes that power the system. The appropriate processes and systems can even substitute to some extent for the appropriate structure. These processes and systems include the global strategy information system, cross-country coordination, global strategic planning, global budgeting, and global performance review and compensation.

Global Strategy Information System

Information systems comprise the data that are collected, analyzed, stored, and communicated as well as the methods for performing those activities. Information systems go beyond hardware and software. Having information about the world is a minimum requirement for being able to formulate and implement a global strategy. Information needs to be specified at a global level as well as at regional and national levels. So the system needs to contain information about *global* market share as well as national market share, and so on. A useful test for managers is to ask whether the system has information about the company's global share of a particular customer's business. The system also needs to collect strategic information regularly in a common format for easy comparison. Information needs to be communicated to headquarters in a manner that is as easy as possible for subsidiary managers. The information needs to be processed and analyzed for global strategy implications. *Perhaps most important, headquarters needs to disseminate its findings back to the countries so that they do not view the home country as a black hole, sucking in information but giving nothing in return.*

The term "system" needs to be interpreted loosely and need not be equated with computers. Many companies have foundered in their initial attempts at building global strategy information systems by getting sidetracked into developing complex computer-based data entry and retrieval systems that never became usable. They forgot that the more difficult task in global information is getting the data in the first place. A major chemical company has done quite well by keeping its information on paper, updating with notations as needed. The company has also found that subsidiary managers are much more willing to fax information in fairly casual formats than to enter data into a computer terminal. As an extreme example, one major international advertising agency used to collect global information by sending a senior executive traveling around the world. He would "beat the

---

3M's European Teams

3M uses "European Management Action Teams," one for each of its fifty product lines.[16] Each team has eight to fourteen members representing many functions and different countries and is chaired by a Brussels-based product manager. The teams help to translate global strategic plans into pan-European business plans, and then into action plans for the subsidiaries, and to make decisions about resource allocation, performance targets, and subsidiary investment.

---

information out of the national managers." The way in which information gets sent by the subsidiaries should be made as simple as possible. A medium-sized industrial equipment company has developed a one-page form on which national sales representatives can report competitive intelligence.

Cross-Country Coordination[17]

Creating cross-country coordination mechanisms provides a way to make up for the lack of direct reporting structure, although its use seems limited to date. The lack of coordination can bring drastic consequences. In defending an advertising claim, an American drug manufacturer (better left unnamed) argued to the U.S. Federal Drug Administration that the recommended dosage of *two* tablets for its full-strength analgesic product provided the maximum possible benefit. The regulatory agency accepted this argument until it discovered a television commercial by the same company in Canada recommending *three* tablets for severe symptoms. An industrial company frequently got into trouble with its global customers because businesses in different countries did not share its plans on pricing changes. In one instance, the business in France offered a temporary price reduction on a product line sold to a global customer that also bought from the United States. The customer then switched its purchases from the Untied States to France and shipped the product across the Atlantic—the price cut more than covering the additional transportation cost and duty.

Cross-country coordination mechanisms range from sharing of information—the least coercive—to setting direct requirements—the most coercive:

- Countries can *share information* about their strategic and operating plans. That alerts headquarters and other countries about opportunities and the possibility of conflicts.

- Countries can be required to *negotiate* their plans with headquarters and other countries that might be affected.
- Countries can be required to *clear* their plans with headquarters and other countries.
- Headquarters or some coordination group may *direct* countries to take certain actions. For example, all countries may be required to launch a particular new product. Giving direct orders verges on changing the organization structure to direct reporting. So management needs to be particularly cautious in heading down the path of directing countries' actions.

Exhibit 8–4 summarizes these different levels of coordination.

While informing, negotiating, clearing, and directing represent critical functions in cross-country coordination, their effectiveness is limited unless they are based on more than paper being shuffled around the globe. Processes directly involving managers can greatly enhance cross-country coordination. The least formal approach is to have regular *global meetings.* Holding global groups and forums allows exchange of information and building of relationships across countries. This, in turn, makes it easier for country nationals to gain an understanding of whether the differences they perceive between their home country and others are real or imagined. It also facilitates the development of common products, and the coordination of marketing approaches. While these meetings can be costly in travel time and expense, ways can be found to reduce such costs. For example, management training programs can be set up to double as global forums if participants are drawn from geographically mixed locations.

A more formal, and increasingly adopted, approach is to set up *global teams* (or regional, e.g., European, teams). These teams can take responsibil-

EXHIBIT 8–4   Levels of Cross-Country Coordination

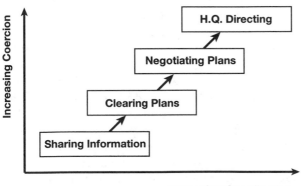

ity for specific programs or for all the global strategy. A French manufacturer of security devices uses councils of country managers, with different countries playing the lead role for different products. Although this approach is time consuming, the company has found that this reliance on line managers makes it easier for various countries to accept the input of other countries, and thus for global approaches to be pursued by all.[18]

In setting up the coordination process, top management needs to set a balance between doing too much and too little at the start. On the one hand, it is very tempting to appoint a powerful coordinator or even "czar." But such an appointment can immediately stimulate resistance from subsidiary managers who feel threatened by the new appointment. On the other hand, setting up a coordination committee with a weak leader where the real power lies with subsidiary managers can lead to little action.[19]

Going further, a business can appoint *global product managers* or *global account managers*. Although adding such managers might be viewed as a change in organization structure, their roles are typically more that of coordination. In both cases global product managers or global account managers perform similar roles on a global (or regional) scale to those performed by their national equivalents.

Armstrong World Industries, a leading U.S.-based manufacturer of flooring and other building materials, established in 1989 five cross-country planning and management teams for those businesses for which a global perspective is important. Team members are drawn from existing personnel of the parent company and its subsidiaries. These team members meet periodically to develop worldwide business plans that include the setting of strategic business choices, product development priorities, planning capital expenditures, and developing human resources.

Global Strategic Planning

Multinational companies and their subsidiaries are not quite skilled at developing *corporate* and *national* strategic plans.[20] But most have yet to develop *global* strategic plans that integrate the strategies of the same business in different countries, let alone that plus integrating strategies across multiple worldwide businesses. Too often, strategic plans are developed separately for each country and then summed to add up the numbers. But no real strategic integration has been planned. Failure to plan across countries makes it difficult to understand the business's competitive position worldwide and difficult to develop integrated strategic responses to competitors who do plan on a global basis.[21] This makes it difficult to design and implement global programs that need the cooperation of several countries. Ideally, there should be a global strategic planning process that involves the senior management from key countries and regions. Such a process would fit in with the corporate and national strategic planning cycles. Whether the global strategic planning process should precede or follow the national planning processes is less important than that it should be done at all. (Extensive research on formal strategic planning has shown that it needs to use a multilevel and multistage process. Agreement needs to be sought between levels—corporate, business, and function—at each of three stages—objective setting, program formulation, and budgeting—in contrast to a one-stage process in which the corporate level sets objectives and the business in turn responds with a complete plan that is a *fait accompli.*[22] For global strategic planning, a similar process can be used that involves corporate, global, and national levels.)

A key benefit of any strategic planning process is that it brings in the views of those who might not otherwise be heard. Such a benefit doubly applies in global strategic planning—it brings in the views of units that may be geographically distant but strategically critical. As the head of a multinational computer equipment business said, "Having a global strategic planning process helps give the 'outlanders' some say."

Having a formal global strategic plan provides a way to put teeth into cross-country coordination processes. Instead of coordinating with no particular end objective, managers in the different countries have to work together in producing the global plan. A global strategic plan needs to contain the usual plan information expressed at a global level. But, in addition, the global plan needs to contain strategies and programs that cut across countries and are, thus, inherently difficult to formulate without a cross-country planning effort.

Global Budgeting

Having global strategies and programs implies having global budgets to implement them. Adding up the country budgets into a global total for each product line provides a first step in global resource allocation.[23] Surprisingly few companies do this thoroughly. Many companies do not even know how much profit they make worldwide in a particular business. Typically, the profit contribution is spread across many national and regional accounts. Most alarming is that many managers believe that the global numbers are readily available only to find otherwise when asked to produce them.

Beyond knowing the global numbers, companies need to do three other, difficult, things:

- First, companies need to be able to transfer resources from one country to an-

---

Globalizing Rock Stars

Even as entrepreneurial a business as the music and recording industry has some need for global strategy. A leading multinational record company uses three different approaches for globalizing its programs. First, the company uses direction, by insisting on global adoption in the case of new albums by already established international recording stars. In the case of real superstars, the insistence is unspoken. National managers just know that they will get into serious trouble if they do not adopt the album. In other cases, a committee of regional heads agrees on artists and albums as global priorities, which all countries must then introduce. Unfortunately, getting agreement is seldom easy. Second, individual countries ("exporters") use flexible budgets to set up inducements for other countries ("importers") to adopt their national stars, by paying for such expenses as airfare and other tour and promotional expenses that would normally be the responsibility of the importers. Third, the company simply relies on voluntary adoption in other cases. This last approach has had its failures. When asked, each national manager was able to cite instances in which other countries incorrectly failed to adopt one of his or her artists or had waited too long, thereby missing the boat in this fast-changing business.

---

other in order to be able to subsidize across countries. Such strategic subsidization is a crucial requirement of global strategy. But the accounting system frequently interferes with such efforts. For example, many companies set transfer prices rigidly. So these companies cannot provide lower prices to countries that need them in order to strengthen their competitive position as part of the global strategy. If making a strategic move means incurring red ink, then many subsidiary managers will decline the invitation to participate in the global strategy. Some companies have found ways to have *flexible transfer pricing*—particularly where there is the opportunity to reduce taxes.[24] Flexible transfer pricing includes the use of different margins and allows for different rates at which capital equipment is amortized. [25] So why not be flexible for the sake of global competitiveness? *Companies should not allow their accounting systems to prevent them from having a global strategy.*

- The second difficult accounting task is to cost out these activities in a globally neutral way. For example, as one executive put it, the French subsidiary should not be charged a low price for raw materials just because the plant it buys from happens to be in France. Thus the global budgeting process needs to provide for *geographically neutral costs* as the base point. These prices can then be adjusted as strategically necessary.
- The third difficult accounting task is to have *global budgets* that are available only for global programs. Typically, budgets are controlled by national and

regional managers with limited amounts left to corporate. The drive against overhead has made large corporate budgets highly unpopular. But budgets for global programs do not provide for overhead. Instead, they can fund strategically vital activities, such as developing global products or subsidizing attacks on global competitors. Such activities are typically difficult for individual countries, or even regions, to undertake. Global budgets can provide a pot of money or "war chest" that managers with ideas for global activities can apply for. But protecting global budgets can be very difficult. Executives in one division of a diversified *Fortune* 500 company were worried that if they created a global budget for strategic contingencies, the money would be appropriated by corporate "the next day."

At its most extreme a global accounting system would charge companies the same cost for materials and products regardless of where they were shipped from. One of the largest companies in the world, a U.S.-based chemical company, is attempting to use such a transfer price approach. But the company has found its cost accounting system so inflexible that it has to make adjustments by hand in the business taking this approach. Executives at this company estimate that it will probably take them five to seven years to change the accounting system.

Global Performance Review and Compensation

The last and, in many ways, most important global management process involves the manner in which managers are evaluated and rewarded. Getting this process to support global strategy can go a long way to offsetting deficiencies in the other systems. If the financial reporting system cannot be changed, managers can still be motivated to undertake loss-incurring strategic actions if they are evaluated and rewarded appropriately. So rewards, especially bonuses, need to be set in a way that reinforces the company's global objectives. If not, the global strategy never takes off. For example, an electronics manufacturer decided to start penetrating the international market by introducing a new product through its strongest division. The division head's bonus was based on the current year's worldwide sales, with no distinction between domestic and international sales. Because increasing his domestic sales was a lot easier—and had a much quicker payoff—than did trying to open up new international markets, the division head did not worry much about his international sales. Predictably, the firm's market penetration strategy failed.

Most companies seem to have a long way to go. The head of international marketing and sales for an industrial controls business views the lack of global performance review as a major problem. To help remedy this defect, the company recently moved to basing a portion of incentive compensation for global team members on worldwide achievement. The head of business planning for a computer equipment company found that the difficulty of getting product managers to think globally was exacerbated by the lack of global reward systems. So it was all too common to not take the global job requirements as seriously as the domestic ones. Indeed, this executive believed that the product managers would like to be measured on a global basis and were willing to take their chances on that. In the same business, the director of international strategic planning also viewed the lack of global compensation as a major weak spot.

The last example shows the importance of rewarding those with global responsibility for global performance. Going further, companies also need to find ways to reward managers for performance in geographic areas *beyond their immediate control*, but that are influenced by their actions. Country managers need to be rewarded not just on the basis of their country's performance but on that of their region or the world. Thus, the French country manager needs to be given incentives to help and cooperate with the German country manager, and the German with the Italian. Performance review and compensation should depend not just on a manager's performance in his or her own region but on the performance of the rest of business globally, evaluations by global business managers, evaluations by managers of other regions, and the achievement of global objectives (e.g., the introduction of particular products into a region, implementation of a global program, or creation of an information system to report back to headquarters).

Getting Global Cooperation

Each of the methods just described has the common aim of getting global cooperation. Each company has to find what works best for a particular business at a particular time. Typically, using multiple methods reinforces the benefits.

PEOPLE

Global strategy can be implemented only by the people in the organization. Developing managers and other members of the organization to think and behave globally requires many of the policies used by successful multinational companies, but it also needs to go beyond that. In particular, the "United Nations" model of multinational management has favored having local nationals take over all positions in their countries. But in the extreme, such an approach reduces the benefit from executives having experience in many countries. The ideal human resource policy for global strategy provides a mix of different national backgrounds represented in the management of each country's business. And in further violation of the United Nations' spirit of equality, it is executives from globally strategic countries who should be favored for global careers. It is more important to spread their experience globally from these key countries than that of executives from strategically marginal countries. So while it might be easier to move a native of Liechtenstein around the world, it might help the global strategy more to move a Japanese.

Use of Foreign Nationals

High-potential foreign nationals need to gain experience not just in their home country but at headquarters and in other countries. This practice has three benefits. It broadens the pool of talent available for executive positions; it visibly shows the commitment of top management to internationalization; and it gives talented individuals an irreplaceable development opportunity. U.S. companies have been slow to do this, particularly at the most senior ranks. Promoting foreigners, and using staff from various countries, has often paid off. In 1972, an ailing NCR, the U.S. computer company now part of AT&T, vaulted the Scottish-Chinese head of its Asian business, William S. Anderson, to the top job. Anderson is widely credited with turning NCR around.

A French packaged-goods manufacturer undertook some years ago to move its European staff from country to country. Today, of fifteen staff working at headquarters, seven are French, three are English, three are German, and two are Italian. The company credits this practice, among others, for its remarkable turnaround. It can be particularly helpful to move national managers to headquarters early in their careers. The plastics division of a major U.S. chemical company has implemented a plan for moving foreign executives to headquarters early in their careers, placing them in market manager positions. These positions are ideal as they provide broad strategic exposure to the business in the home country but do not have direct selling responsibility, which typically poses the greatest cultural barriers. Companies should also use nonhome country nationals not just at headquarters but in other countries as well. Indeed, companies should ideally never use the term "foreign national" or even "home country." American companies could refer to "non-U.S. nationals," Japanese companies to "non-Japanese nationals" rather than to *gaijins,* and so on.

A global company also needs to have the courage and common sense to override local objections to foreigners. National managers are often nervous about bringing foreigners into their country. One of the more extreme examples concerns an American multinational professional services company. Its senior European managers recently held a meeting to select a new country manager for the Netherlands. When a Spanish manager was suggested, the Dutch executive present objected that Spain used to rule the Netherlands, so a Spaniard would not be welcomed. Surprised, an American executive asked when that rule was. The Dutchman replied: "About four hundred years ago, but the Spanish are still very much resented." This objection was overruled and the Spanish manager was appointed without subsequent problems.

Multicountry Careers

Making work experience in different countries a necessity for progression, rather than a hindrance, is another important step that helps a company become truly global. An electronics manufacturer decided to make a major push into Japan, but a middle-level executive offered a transfer there was loathe to take it. He was concerned whether there would be a job for him when he came back. As he put it, "the road to the executive suite lies through Chicago, not Osaka." In contrast, Jacques Maisonrouge, the former head of IBM World Trade (the company's international arm), initiated a policy that no executive could rise to a general manager position without having undertaken a foreign assignment beforehand. Using home country nationals overseas has been a very common practice. Increasing costs of relocation and the problems of moving dual-career couples have made this more difficult. But companies need to take a longer-term view of the benefits from such placements. Companies have to be willing to pay the cost of transferring executives around the world. A senior executive in a large American multinational company did not see the flaw in his company's position that it would pay American executives transferred overseas the higher of the American or local rate, but had trouble getting Swiss executives to come to the United States because of the lower American pay.

To encourage multicountry careers, companies may need to set tough rules such as the following:

- No advancement occurs beyond a certain level without two years outside the home country of the national.
- Transfers occur at an early stage of a manager's career.
- Target of all positions at a certain level and above being held by nonnationals is 10%.
- The best performers get transferred overseas.
- Transferees are guaranteed a position back home, but its level depends on performance overseas.

- Veterans of foreign assignments get job preference.

- Human resources department tracks and takes responsibility for the careers of overseas transferees.

Using foreign nationals and multicountry careers has the important additional benefit of gradually creating a group of subsidiary managers who are likely to be more sympathetic to global strategy. As managers gain multicountry experience, they are less likely to focus on the unique differences of the particular country in which they operate and more able to appreciate the benefits of also looking for global commonality. This greater sympathy for global strategy becomes more important as the role of subsidiary managers changes with globalization—from that of running their own show to that of integrating into a larger global effort.[26]

Frequent Travel

Senior managers must spend a large amount of time in foreign countries. The CEO of a large grocery products company spends half his time outside the United States—a visible demonstration of the importance and commitment of the company to its international operations. Also important, senior managers should spend more of their time in the strategically important countries rather than in countries with operational difficulties but that are not important in the global strategy. Such countries represent black holes for senior management time.

Statements and Actions of Leaders

The senior management of a company that wants to globalize its strategy needs to constantly restate that intention and to act in accordance with it. Otherwise, the rank and file will not believe that the globalization strategy is for real. One test among many is the prominence given to international operations in formal communications such as the chairman's letter in the annual report or statements to stock analysts.

CULTURE

Culture is the most subtle aspect of organization, but it can play a formidable role in helping or hindering a global strategy.

Global Identity

A strong national identity can hinder the willingness and ability to design global products and programs. It can also create a "them or us" split among employees. One firm was making a strong global push, and yet many of its corporate executives wore national flag pins! European companies are generally well in advance of both American and Japanese firms in adopting a global identity. Having multiple national identities—a different one in each country—is more international than having just the identity of the home country, but it is not global. Instead, a truly global culture would transcend the nationality of the home and other countries.27 At the same time, each national business still needs to be rooted in its local culture, or at least some of the executives, depending on their jobs, need such roots. Building a global identity is helped if nationalistic displays are avoided. Similarly, it helps if important meetings are not always held in the home country. Having foreign nationals on the corporate board also helps foster a global identity as well as bringing the substantive knowledge of these board members.

Partly to help foster a global identity, Procter & Gamble now seeks to instill a global perspective in all of its employees. P&G wants to establish the mind-set of seeing the world as the company's marketplace. To do so, P&G is cultivating two attitudes in its people. The first is to search for ideas that can be applied to its business around the world. The second is to find reapplications for good ideas that have already been developed. P&G also made a major commitment to globalization when in 1990 the company appointed as its new chief executive the head of its international division—jumping him over a more senior executive in the U.S. business.

Commitment to Worldwide not Domestic Employment

Many companies view their domestic employees as somehow more important than their foreign employees and are much more committed to preserving domestic employment than to developing employment regardless of location. This often leads them to decide to keep expensive manufacturing operations in the home country rather than relocate them in lower-cost countries—thereby putting them at a competitive cost disadvantage and threatening their overall competitive position. Of course, there may be good defensive reasons for maintaining higher-cost facilities in the home country. But cultural bias should not be one of them.

Interdependence of Businesses

A culture of local business autonomy, when carried too far, can also be a barrier to globalization. The culture needs to balance the celebration of autonomy with the recognition of interdependence. Achieving such a balance is not easy. Country managers are masters at ignoring directives from the head office. Like Admiral Nelson at the Battle of Copenhagen, they delight in putting the telescope to their blind eye. Top management can help foster a sense of country interdependence by educating staff in each country, particularly the home country, about achievements of operations in other countries.

Matching Culture to Globalization Needs

Companies pursuing global strategy need to develop not just a generally favorable culture but also specific cultural characteristics to support specific strategies. A large U.S. manufacturing company's culture included the following characteristics:

- A high degree of responsiveness to customers' requests for product tailoring
- A strong emphasis on letting every business and every country be highly autonomous
- A desire for 100% control over foreign operations
- A commitment to preserving domestic employment

Not surprisingly, the company found it very difficult to implement a global strategy. Senior management was able to understand its difficulties more clearly only after it spelled out the cultural change implications in global strategy. Specifically, the CEO came to realize that rapidly implementing a pure global strategy would require an organizational revolution. In contrast, a culturally less risky option would be to make a series of incremental changes in both strategy and organization, leading to a mixed strategy of globalization and national responsiveness. The CEO also considered an explicit rejection of globalization, which would require a conscious decision to build on the company's existing organizational and cultural characteristics to develop a pure national responsiveness strategy. Thinking through these cultural implications helped the company to make fundamental and realistic choices rather than assuming the unavoidable dominance of strategy over organization and of globalization over national responsiveness. Aided by this analysis, the company chose the second, mixed option of incremental change and has had satisfying results to date.

MINIMIZING THE DRAWBACKS OF GLOBAL ORGANIZATION

Globalization can have organizational as well as strategic drawbacks. Costs may rise because of increased coordination, reporting requirements, and even added staff. Globalization can also reduce management effectiveness in individual countries if overcentralization hurts local motivation and morale. But some approaches can minimize these problems. Costs can be held down if new global functions replace rather than add to national functions. When a manufacturer of chemical and refining process equipment reorganized its separate European businesses into one, the company was able to eliminate some of the general management and administrative support positions. Those savings more than paid for the positions related to the new office of the general manager for Europe.

Political infighting can be minimized if global responsibilities are shared by many executives, each of whom retains some national (or regional) roles. For example, the general manager of one country takes on the role of global marketing chief, while the general manager of another country becomes the global manufacturing chief. So each executive has to cooperate with the other. Resentment of headquarters can be assuaged if lead responsibilities get spread around the world. Thus different countries can be given the lead for different strategic thrusts.[28] Companies may even go so far as to relocate business headquarters out of the home country. IBM recently took this step, moving the management of its worldwide telecommunications business from the United States to Europe. Last, headquarters executives should try to be psychologically equidistant from any part of the world, making decisions on the basis of strategic advantage rather than emotional attachment.[29]

COMBINING STRATEGIC AND ORGANIZATIONAL ANALYSIS

In sum, the four organization factors—organization structure, management processes, people, and culture—play a key role in facilitating or hindering a company's move toward globalization. For example, take a company with a strong structural split between domestic and international activities, management processes that are country driven rather than business driven, people who work primarily in their home countries, and a parochial culture. Implementing global strategy in the company is likely to prove exceedingly difficult. If the analysis of industry globalization drivers has shown that such strategies are necessary for market, cost, or competitive reasons, top managers need to make a tough choice. Either they undertake a major change effort aimed at making the internal environment better adapted to the strategic moves the company needs to make, or they have to decide that the profound organizational changes needed to adopt a global strategy are too risky and that the company should avoid globalization and compete based on its existing organizational strengths.

I end this chapter with two examples of how to combine the analysis of all three elements in the globalization triangle: industry globalization drivers, global strategy levers, and global organization capability. The examples come from the experiences of two companies, both of them multi–billion-dollar multinationals. One company, disguised as TransElectronics, is a U.S.-based concern operating in many aspects of electronics. The other company, disguised as Persona, is a European-based manufacturer and marketer of consumer packaged goods. The two companies provide different views of the challenge of global strategy. TransElectronics is still developing as a fully multinational company and faces the challenge of accelerating that process to become a global competitor. Persona, on the other hand, has long been thoroughly multinational, with many highly autonomous companies operating around the world. Its challenge is to temper some aspects of that multinational autonomy in order to compete more effectively on a global basis.

Transforming TransElectronics

The communications sector of TransElectronics had one division, Electron, based in the United States, that sold what I will call "transcramblers" against fierce European and Japanese competition. A major market, Japan, closed until recently to foreign competition, was beginning to open through a combination of TransElectronics' efforts and U.S. government pressure on Japanese trade barriers. So developing a global strategy for transcramblers was a high priority for TransElectroncis. A complication was that Electron was not a stand-alone business unit—other units had related responsibilities. As will be described, this split of responsibilities was one of the major barriers to Electron's implementation of a global strategy.

Analyzing Industry Globalization Potential

Electron's managers were unsure as to how much potential for globalization there was in the transcrambler industry. A step-by-step analysis made this much clearer. First, *market* drivers pushed for globalization: there were few differences among countries in what they wanted from transcramblers. On the other hand, few global customers existed—national public sector telecommunications companies (PTTs) accounted for a large part of the market in each country. *Cost* drivers also strongly pushed for globalization: there were substantial scale economies and learning effects, sourcing efficiencies could be gained by consolidating manufacturing, and Electron's labor costs—a significant part of the product's total cost—were much lower in Puerto Rico and Taiwan than they were in the United States. *Government* drivers favored globalization: the privatization of some national PTTs was opening up previously closed markets, and products were becoming more standardized in Europe around a common format. An offsetting factor was local content requirements in many countries. Last, *competitive* forces were also pushing for globalization: Electron's major competitors (European and Japanese) took a global product approach with fewer price levels and with minimum product customization. The competitors had also largely centralized their manufacturing activities in just one or two countries each. In summary, strong external forces pushed the transcrambler industry to globalization. Not only was globalization already high, it was likely to continue increasing.

Evaluating Use of Global Strategy

The Electron managers next evaluated how much the business actually used global strategy. Electron was quite global in its *market participation*—its sales' split among countries closely matched that of the industry. Electron's *product line* was highly standardized—in fact, more than its executives realized. Electron's R&D and purchasing *activities* were specialized in the United States, but much of their manufacturing was dispersed across the United States, Puerto Rico, Taiwan, and Europe. *Marketing* was primarily done in the United States. Selling, distribution, and service were by necessity done locally, but were not at all coordinated across countries. Electron's competitors were all much more centralized and coordinated. The product positioning of transcramblers was consistent across countries, as was that of Electron's competitors. If anything, Trans-Electronics' marketing policies were too uniform, with a rigid pricing policy that did not allow Electron to adapt to the wide variations in price across countries. As a result, Electron did not use price as a strategic weapon. Last, Electron did not integrate its *competitive moves* across countries, but, fortunately, neither did its competitors.

From the previous analyses, the Electron managers concluded that their extent of globalization was significantly lower than the industry potential, and lower than that of their competitors. The industry potential for globalization was steadily increasing. It was clear that Electron had a strong need to develop a more global strategy than it had been pursuing in the past. The next issue was whether Electron would be able to implement such a strategy.

Evaluating Organizational Capability

Having understood the strategic changes needed, the Electron managers now had to understand the organization factors that might affect implementation. They diagnosed that TransElectronics' *organization structure* worked in two major ways against a global strategy. First, TransElectronics operated with a strong domestic–international split within each sector. Second, worldwide responsibilities for Electron's business were scattered throughout the organization. The Electron division itself had responsibility for some product development, some manufacturing, and some marketing. Other divisions in the United States and overseas shared these responsibilities. Selling was the responsibility of both local non-U.S. countries and in the United States of a totally separate distribution group for the entire communications sector. In effect, there was no manager below the sector head who had global authority over transcramblers.

Management processes did not help global strategy much. The budget process worked against a global approach in that the Electron division budgeted only a total number for overseas sales, without country targets. The International Group in the communications sector set country quotas for the entire sector, without product quotas or product-by-country quotas. The strategic planning process did not help either—the Electron Division and the International Group developed separate plans simultaneously. In terms of compensation, there were no international components in the bonus formula for domestic managers. In addition, Electron's strategic information systems provided only spotty coverage of key markets and key competitors.

TransElectronics' use of *people* worked against a global approach. There were few foreign nationals in the United States at either corporate or divisional levels. There were many foreign nationals overseas, but these were mostly in their home countries, and there was little movement between international and domestic jobs. In particular, the U.S. divisions were reluctant to give up people, and overseas assignments were not seen as being a desirable career track.

Last, TransElectronics' corporate *culture* worked against a global view in both obvious and subtle ways. At the obvious level, TransElectronics was very much an American company with a "them-and-us" mentality. Indeed, the CEO had made speeches calling for increased trade barriers against Japanese firms. More subtly, TransElectronics had a very strong culture of being responsive to customer requests for product tailoring, born of a heritage of selling exclusively to a very small number of automotive customers. This culture worked strongly against attempts to standardize globally.

So TransElectronics clearly had a very low organizational ability to develop a global strategy for transcramblers. It had certainly experienced many difficulties in its fitful attempts at doing so.

Changes Needed

The globalization analysis, just described, convinced the Electron managers that the most important business changes they had to make were to exploit more opportunities for product standardization and to specialize somewhat more as to where different activities (particularly manufacturing) were conducted. More widespread changes were needed in terms of management and organization. While many aspects of these needed to change, the most implementable change was in terms of management process. TransElectronics adopted for the transcrambler business a global strategic planning process and globally based evaluating and compensation. These relatively modest changes would pave the way for future acceptance of the more radical changes needed in organization structure, people, and culture.

Repositioning Persona

Persona had operating companies around the world that sold many kinds of personal care as well as other household products. The global strategy analysis was conducted for one particular product, "hairfloss," that was sold worldwide.

Analyzing Industry Globalization Potential

Persona's managers had always assumed that there were major differences in customer needs and trade practices across countries, such that the hairfloss category did not have much globalization potential. But the systematic globalization analysis revealed some surprises. *Market* drivers pushed strongly for globalization: market needs were very much the same around the world within income categories—higher income countries were earlier users of the new variants and ingredients that were introduced every few years. Brand names and advertising were also widely transferable—some competitors used just one major brand name around the world and essentially the same advertising campaign. *Cost* drivers were less important, given that product costs were only about 25% of total costs, economies of scale were low, and price was not a major basis of competition. Also the low value-to-weight ratio of hairfloss made it uneconomical to ship it far. Nonetheless, there was some centralized manufacturing on a multicountry regional basis, in parts of Western Europe, Southeast Asia, and Africa.

Government drivers did not particularly favor globalization. In Western Europe, however, the increasing importance of multicountry media, particularly satellite television with wide reception, and the increasing integration of the European Community, pushed for regional, if not global, approaches. It was *competitive* behavior that was the major force pushing the industry to globalization. Persona faced three major worldwide competitors, multinationals like itself. Two of these competitors took a much more standardized approach than Persona—they concentrated their resources behind the same one or two brands of hairfloss in each country. In contrast, Persona tended to market three of four brands in each country, and furthermore, these brands were different among major countries. Persona's competitors were also quick to transfer successful innovations from one country to the next, while Persona's brand fragmentation hindered its efforts. This global fragmentation seemed to be a major reason behind Persona's slipping share and profitability.

Persona concluded that there were strong external forces pushing the hairfloss industry toward globalization—at least to the extent of requiring coordinated regional operations—and this push toward globalization was likely to increase in the future.

Evaluating Use of Global Strategy

Although Persona had plenty of market and competitive information from virtually all the countries in which it operated, its managers did not make much use of that information to evaluate its global, as opposed to national, strategies. Using this information for global purposes revealed a new view of the worldwide hairfloss business. Persona's *global market participation* was very strong—it sold hairfloss in markets that accounted for almost 90% of worldwide category volume (excluding communist countries). Its largest competitor participated in almost 100%. Persona's hairfloss *product line* was quite highly standardized around half a dozen variants. Persona generally marketed a larger number of variants in wealthier countries, but the variants were still basically the same across countries. Like most consumer packaged-goods multinationals, Persona practiced very little specialization of *activities* by country—it fielded a full business operation in most countries. In terms of *global marketing,* Persona was severely lacking because of its multiple brands, multiple product positionings, and multiple advertising campaigns. Last, Persona did not do much to integrate its competitive moves across countries, although it had recently begun to experiment with such attempts. Overall, Persona's actual extent of globalization was somewhat lower than that of its competitors.

While Persona's worldwide hairfloss strategy was quite global in some respects, it was the lack of global marketing that was the biggest problem. The key variables that Persona could operate on were brand name and positioning. First, to increase local marketing muscle, Persona needed to reduce the number of brands in each country to two. Second, to achieve the benefits of global market uniformity, it had three broad alternatives:

1. A different brand but common positioning for each product variant in each country
2. A common regional brand and positioning
3. A common global brand and positioning

Because Persona already had strong brand names around the world that it did not want to abandon, and because a common positioning would achieve most of the benefits of uniformity, the company concluded that the second alternative was best. The next issue was whether Persona would be able to implement such a strategy.

Evaluating Organizational Capability

The Persona managers conducting the globalization analysis were the most discouraged by what they found about organizational capability. Persona's *organization structure* made it very difficult to develop and implement a global strategy. Persona operated with a strong geographic structure that was overlaid with a worldwide product direction function at corporate. This function, however, had advisory rather than direct authority over the individual country businesses. Furthermore, the direction function did not include the United States. *Management processes* were of limited help. The budget and compensation systems worked against global strategy—these were done on a strictly local basis, although aggregated geographically. But there was no mechanism to encourage local participation in a worldwide effort. A strategic plan was developed globally, but local acceptance was voluntary. Persona did, however, have an excellent strategic information system. Each year the subsidiaries provided detailed and accurate data for products, markets, and competitors. For example, Persona knew how much each global competitor spent on advertising on each product category in each country and even had fairly accurate estimates of each competitor's profitability in each country. Persona also scored highly on the global capability of its people. Managers were drawn from all over the world, and transfers both among countries and to and from corporate were common. Culture was really the biggest organization barrier. Persona had a very strong culture of giving autonomy to its local managers. Although corporate increasingly wanted to give direct orders on strategy, the firm was loath to risk the possible loss of local accountability and commitment. So, like TransElectronics, Persona had a low organizational capacity for global strategy, but for somewhat different reasons.

Changes Needed

As a result of the globalization analysis, Persona managers realized that the most important business changes they had to make in hairfloss were to reduce the number of brands in each country and develop a common brand by region and a common positioning for each major product variant. Organizationally, it was too huge a disruption to change the structure. What was needed was a greater willingness by corporate to push for countries to adopt a global approach. A first step was a directive that all countries should launch the new "high-gloss" variant within a six-month period. Persona hoped that a successful experience of common action would start moving the culture toward greater acceptance of global strategies.

GUIDELINES FOR BUILDING THE GLOBAL ORGANIZATION

In building the global organization, managers should keep in mind the following guidelines:

- A global strategy cannot succeed in the face of organization barriers and resistance.
- Different aspects of organization—whether organization structure, management processes, people, or culture—will be more difficult to globalize depending on the history and circumstances of the company. Managers may find it best to work on the most easily changed aspects first, in order to prepare the way for the more difficult changes.
- As with the elements of global strategy, different aspects of organization can have different levels of being global.
- But globalization will not work fully unless all aspects of organization complement each other to support the desired global strategy.
- Changing the organization, particularly toward globalization, can take a great deal of time. Senior management needs to instill a sense of urgency to drive toward the desired changes.

DISCUSSION AND RESEARCH QUESTIONS

1. What are the key elements of a global organization?
2. What are the ways in which organization structure can be used to implement global strategy?
3. What are the ways in which management processes can be used to implement global strategy?
4. What are the ways in which human resource policies can be used to implement global strategy?

5. What are the ways in which culture can be used to implement global strategy?

6. Select one company that has made significant changes in its organization in order to globalize. Describe and critique the changes that this company has made.

NOTES

1. This chapter is based in part on George S. Yip, Pierre M. Loewe, and Michael Y. Yoshino, "How to Take Your Company to the Global Market," *Columbia Journal of World Business,* Winter 1988, pp 37–48.

2. A stream of work has described and characterized this dilemma as the integration–responsiveness grid. See C. K. Prahalad, "The Strategic Process in a Multinational Corporation," unpublished doctoral dissertation, Harvard Business School, 1975; C. K. Prahalad and Yves L. Doz, "An Approach to Strategic Control on MNCs," *Sloan Management Review,* Summer 1981, pp. 5–13; and C. K. Prahalad and Yves L. Doz, *The Multinational Mission: Balancing Local Demands and Global Vision* (New York: The Free Press, 1987).

3. The importance of global learning has been particularly stressed by Sumantra Ghoshal, "Global Strategy: An Organizing Framework," *Strategic Management Journal,* Vol. 8, No. 5, September–October 1987, pp. 425–440, and Christopher A. Bartlett and Sumantra Ghoshal, *Managing Across Borders: The Transnational Solution* (Boston: Harvard Business School Press, 1989).

4. This view is particularly stressed in the literature on foreign direct investment, for example, John H. Dunning, "The Eclectic Paradigm of International Production: A Restatement and Some Possible Extensions," *Journal of International Business Studies,* Spring 1988, pp. 1–31, and on internationalization theory, for example, Peter J. Buckley and Mark Casson, *The Future of the Multinational Enterprise* (New York: Holmes and Meier, 1976); Alan M. Rugman, *International Diversification and the Multinational Enterprise* (Lexington, Mass.: Lexington Books, D. C. Heath, 1979); and Peter J. Buckley, *The Theory of the Multinational Enterprise, Acta Universitatis Upsaliensis, Studia Oeconomiae Negotiorum,* Vol. 26 (Uppsala, Sweden), 1987.

5. This incremental approach to strategic change has been advocated by many management theorists. See, for example, Charles E. Lindblom, *The Policy-Making Process* (Englewood Cliffs, N.J.: Prentice Hall, 1968); Henry Mintzberg, *The Nature of Managerial Work* (New York: Harper & Row, 1973); and James Brian Quinn, "Strategic Goals: Process and Politics," *Sloan Management Review,* Fall 1977, p. 22.

6. This example is based on Simon Caulkin, "Ford Tunes Up Europe," *Management Today,* July 1988, pp. 38–44.

7. This example comes from Yip, Loewe, and Yoshino, "How to Take Your Company to the Global Market."

8. Much early research on MNC management has confirmed the critical role of formal organization structure in influencing both parent and subsidiary strategy. Clee and de Scipio (1959) and Clee and Sachtjen (1964) were among the first to point out the shortcomings of the international structures adopted by multinational corporations and to recommend the implementation of global organization structures. See G. H. Clee and A. di Scipio, "Creating a World Enterprise," *Harvard Business Review,* November–December 1959, pp. 77–89, and G. H. Clee and W. M. Sachtjen, "Organizing a Worldwide Business," *Harvard Business Review,* November–December 1964, pp. 55–67. Fouraker and Stopford (1968), Stopford and Wells (1972), and Franko (1976) conducted a series of studies aimed at confirming Chandler's (1962) strategy-structure fit thesis with respect to international business, as did Egelhoff (1982, 1988) and Daniels, Pitts, and Tretter (1984). See Lawrence E. Fouraker and John M. Stopford, "Organization Structure and Multinational Strategy," *Administrative Science Quarterly,* Vol. 13, 1968, pp. 57–70; John M. Stopford and Louis T. Wells, Jr., *Managing the Multinational Enterprise* (New York: Basic Books, 1972); Larry G. Franko, *The European Multinationals* (Greenwich,

Conn.: Greylock Press, 1976); Alfred D. Chandler, Jr., *Strategy and Structure* (Cambridge, Mass.: The M.I.T. Press, 1962); William G. Egelhoff, "Strategy and Structure in Multinational Corporations: An Information Processing Approach," *Administrative Science Quarterly*, Vol. 27, 1982, pp. 435–458; William G. Egelhoff, "Strategy and Structure in Multinational Corporations: A Revision of the Stopford and Wells Model," *Strategic Management Journal*, Vol. 9, 1988, pp. 1–14; and J. D. Daniels, R. A. Pitts, and M. J. Tretter, "Strategy and Structure of U.S. Multinationals: An Exploratory Study," *Academy of Management Journal*, Vol. 27, 1984, pp. 292–307. But that stream of research focused on dimensions of international strategy (foreign product diversity and percentage of foreign sales) that do not relate directly to global strategy. More directly relevant to the latter, Davidson and Haspeslagh (1982) examined the role of global product and global matrix approaches and found that global product organizations had many disadvantages. See William H. Davidson and Philippe Haspeslagh, "Shaping a Global Product Organization," *Harvard Business Review*, July–August 1982, pp. 125–132.

Focusing on global strategy, Bartlett and Ghoshal (1987, 1989) argued for a network structure that facilitates global learning. See Christopher A. Bartlett and Sumantra Ghoshal, "Managing Across Borders: New Strategic Requirements," *Sloan Management Review*, Summer 1987, pp. 7–17, and Christopher A. Bartlett and Sumantra Ghoshal, *Managing Across Borders: The Transnational Solution* (Boston: Harvard Business School Press, 1989).

Ghoshal (1987) argued that the tendency of global strategy toward a centralized global authority, and the potential corresponding erosion of global learning benefits, is one of the "strategic trade-offs" associated with pursuing a global strategy. See Sumantra Ghoshal, "Global Strategy: An Organizing Framework," *Strategic Management Journal*, Vol. 8, No. 5, September–October 1987, pp. 425–440.

9. In a study of 180 leading U.S.-based multinationals, the Harvard Multinational Enterprise Project found that 163 initially created a separate international division to manage foreign operations. See William H. Davidson, *Global Strategic Management* (New York: John Wiley, 1982), p. 274. This study covered the period up to 1979.

10. According to the stages theory of multinational organization design, many firms evolve through either a product-dominated or geography-dominated structure toward some form of matrix organization (see Stopford and Wells, *Managing the Multinational Enterprise*).

11. "Perestroika in Soapland," *The Economist*, June 10, 1989, pp. 95–97.

12. Christopher A. Bartlett and Sumantra Ghoshal, "Matrix Management: Not a Structure, a Frame of Mind," *Harvard Business Review*, July–August 1990, pp. 138–145.

13. See Roger Enrico and Jesse Kornbluth, *The Other Guy Blinked: How Pepsi Won the Cola Wars* (New York: Bantam Books, 1986).

14. See Gerrit Jeelof, "Global Strategies of Philips," *European Management Journal*, Vol. 7, No. 1, 1989, pp. 84–91, and Francis J. Aguilar and Michael Y. Yoshino, "The Philips Group: 1987," Case No. 9-388-050 (Boston: Harvard Business School, 1988).

15. See also Roderick E. White and Thomas A. Poynter, "Strategies for Foreign-Owned Subsidiaries in Canada," *Business Quarterly*, Summer 1984, pp. 59–69, on the different strategic roles that national subsidiaries can play.

16. See Joseph M. Warren, "3M's European Management Action Teams: Managing Diversity in a Single European Market," *Journal of European Business*, July–August 1990, pp. 20–30.

17. For more on coordination between *businesses* in one company, see Michael E. Porter, *Competitive Advantage* (New York: The Free Press, 1985), Chapter 9.

18. I thank Pierre M. Loewe of The MAC Group, San Francisco, for this example.

19. See Yves L. Doz, "Managing Manufacturing Rationalization Within Multinational Companies," *Columbia Journal of World Business*, Fall 1978, pp. 82–94.

20. They have had plenty of help from both academics and consultants. For guides to strategic planning, see, for example, George A. Steiner, *Strategic Planning: What Every Manager Must Know* (New York: The Free Press, 1979); Peter Lorange, *Implementation of Strategic Planning* (Englewood Cliffs, N.J.: Prentice Hall, 1982); and Arnoldo C. Hax and

Nicolas S. Majluf, *Strategic Management: An Integrative Perspective* (Englewood Cliffs, N.J.: Prentice Hall, 1984).

21. C. K. Prahalad and Yves L. Doz, *The Multinational Mission: Balancing Local Demands and Global Vision* (New York: Free Press, 1987), have argued for using global strategic planning. For a discussion of different types of global strategic planning, see Balaji S. Chakravarthy and Howard V. Perlmutter, "Strategic Planning for a Global Business," *Columbia Journal of World Business,* Summer 1985, pp. 3–10, and David C. Shanks, "Strategic Planning for Global Competition," *Journal of Business Strategy,* Winter 1985, pp. 80–89.

22. See Richard F. Vancil and Peter Lorange, "Strategic Planning in Diversified Companies," *Harvard Business Review,* January–February 1975, and George S. Yip, "Who Needs Strategic Planning?" *The Journal of Business Strategy,* Vol. 6, No. 2, Fall 1985, pp. 30–42.

23. See the discussion of global management control in John J. Dyment, "Strategies and Management Controls for Global Corporations," *Journal of Business Strategy,* Spring 1987, pp. 20–26.

24. A survey of 52 *Fortune* 500 companies with international operations found that 29% sometimes, or more often, used case-by-case transfer pricing to benefit the overall corporation. In those cases, tax reduction was one of the primary motivations. See Penelope J. Yunker, "A Survey Study of Subsidiary Autonomy, Performance Evaluation and Transfer Pricing in Multinational Corporations," *Columbia Journal of World Business,* Fall 1983, pp. 51–64.

25. For an in-depth discussion, see Robert G. Eccles, *The Transfer Pricing Decision* (Lexington, Mass.: Lexington Books, 1985).

26. White and Poynter have written extensively on the role of subsidiary management. See Roderick E. White and Thomas E. Poynter, "Strategies for Foreign-Owned Subsidiaries in Canada," *Business Quarterly,* Summer 1984, pp. 59–69, and Roderick E. White and Thomas E. Poynter, "Organizing for Worldwide Advantage," in *Managing the Global Firm,* eds. Christopher A. Bartlett, Yves L. Doz, and Gunnar Hedlund (London: Routledge, 1990).

27. See Howard V. Perlmutter, "The Tortuous Evolution of the Multinational Corporation," *Columbia Journal of World Business,* January–February 1969, pp. 9–18, for the distinction among ethnocentric (national), polycentric (multinational), and geocentric (global) corporate cultures.

28. For example, Bartlett and Ghoshal, *Managing Across Borders,* p. 106, describe how Philips assigned responsibility for developing the teletext TV business to its U.K. subsidiary.

29. Kenichi Ohmae, *The Borderless World: Power and Strategy in the Interlinked Economy* (New York: Harper Business, 1990), p. 17.

Chapter 9

Measuring Industry Drivers and Strategy Levers

The previous chapters have discussed globalization concepts without specifically explaining how to measure them. Being able to measure industry globalization drivers and global strategy levers greatly increases the usefulness of these concepts. Usable measures allow management to compare the globalization potential of different industries at the same time, of one industry over time, of the extent of globalization of different businesses within a company, and of a business and its competitors. Measures also facilitate implementation by making it clearer what needs to be changed and by how much. Instead of deciding to "increase the extent of global products," which is a very vague goal, it is far better to be able to decide to "increase the proportion of revenues in global products from 60% to 80%."

Good measures encourage implementation by exploiting the familiar idea that executives manage what is measured. So this chapter provides a series of practical measures of globalization. These measures have been developed and tested on over fifty American, European, and Japanese businesses and their executives in both research and consulting settings. Those who wish to undertake the step-by-step global strategy analysis described in the next chapter should use the measures described in this chapter. Users should also feel free to adapt the measures suggested here and to develop their own. The important thing is to make some measurement.

Geographic Basis for Measurement

Measures can be made at both global and subglobal (e.g., regional) levels. Often, a global measure may be less useful than separate regional measures. For example, in measuring common customer needs, there may be significant commonality within regions (Europe, North America, etc.) but major differences among regions. So the commonality of customer needs should be measured at both levels—between countries within a region and between regions. Also, the definition of the world varies. The definition should usually exclude markets that are effectively closed to Western (and other market economy) multinational companies.

Who Should Do the Measuring?

Because the measures of industry globalization and business global strategy cut across countries, it is important to get input from representatives of the major regions or countries in a business. While one manager (or team) should be responsible for assembling and updating the measurements, he or she should involve managers from different geographic locations, as well as different functions, in developing and checking the measures. Chapter 10 will describe further how to assemble a global team to diagnose globalization potential and to develop global strategy.

MEASURING INDUSTRY GLOBALIZATION DRIVERS

As each of the four types of industry globalization drivers—market, cost, government, and competitive—differ in their nature, measures for them vary. Many, but not all, of the measures can be quantified.

Summary of Globalization Measures

Driver	*Measure*
Market Drivers	
Common customer needs	Extent to which customer needs are common around the world
	Percentage (by cost) of components of a global product or service that can be common worldwide
National global customers	Share of worldwide market sales to customers who search the world for vendors

Multinational global customers	Share of worldwide volume accounted for by customers who purchase or select centrally
Global channels	Share of worldwide volume accounted for by channels that purchase centrally
Transferable marketing	For each element, share of world market accounted for by countries where foreign element is acceptable
Lead countries	Number of countries that account for the most important product innovations

Cost Drivers

Global scale economies	Percentage of world market needed for minimum efficient scale production or service operation
Steep experience effects	Percentage decrease in unit production costs with each doubling of accumulated capacity
Sourcing efficiencies	Potential percentage savings in purchase expenditures from making all purchases centrally
Favorable logistics	Transportation cost over a standard intercontinental route, excluding customs and duties, as a percentage of the selling price
Differences in country costs	Ratio of lowest to highest cost countries in the industry for (1) fully loaded hourly cost of the most common form of production labor and (2) total unit production cost
High product development costs	Total cost of developing (but not marketing) a major new product or service, as a percentage of the expected lifetime sales of the product or service
Fast-changing technology	Market life of typical new product

Government Drivers

Tariffs	Percentage of the pretariff selling price, averaged globally
Subsidies	Percentage of the presubsidy selling price, averaged globally Net percentage effect on selling prices of subsidized competitors
Nontariff barriers	Percentage of the world market that is blocked from imports
Compatible technical standards	Percentage, in cost, of the typical product that is in components that are technically compatible worldwide
Common marketing regulations	Proportion of the industry's worldwide marketing expenditures that are in activities allowed in every country
Government-owned competitors	Combined global market share of all government-owned competitors

Government-owned customers	Combined share of global industry purchases made by government-owned customers

Competitive Drivers

Exports	Exports as a percentage of the world market
Imports	Imports as a percentage of the world market
Competitors from different continents	Number of continents that are the home of global competitors
Interdependent countries	Amount of volume sold in each country that is dependent on production facilities that supply more than one country, averaged across competitors
Competitors globalized	Extent to which competitors use global strategy levers (discussed shortly)

Market Globalization Drivers

Measuring market globalization drivers requires making some qualitative judgments in addition to quantitative estimates.

Common Customer Needs Driver

Common customer needs represent perhaps the most difficult driver to measure, because customer need in a product or service category is actually a bundle of different needs. For example, in a passenger automobile, safety is one kind of need and comfort is another kind. The only common yardstick is to measure the proportion of total cost accounted for, in a typical product, by the product or service components that satisfy each individual need. In an automobile, components such as brakes and caging provide safety, while components such as seating and shock absorbers provide comfort. If these safety and comfort components account for about 10% of the total cost of a typical vehicle, and if safety and comfort needs are the only ones to vary by country, then needs are 90% common. Of course, what customers consider a comfort need in one country may be considered a safety need in others (for example, rust on automobiles is viewed as a safety hazard in Germany).[1] But such differences do not matter. What matters is the sum of the costs for all components that need to differ between countries.

An important consideration is to distinguish between changeable and unchangeable differences in country needs. Changeable needs arise from differences in customer tastes and preferences. For automobiles these changeable needs include styling and comfort. Unchangeable needs arise from legal, technical, or physical differences. For automobiles, unchangeable needs include the side the steering wheel is placed, emission control systems, heavy-duty batteries in cold countries, and air conditioning in hot ones. A manufacturer has to adapt its products to meet unchangeable needs but may be able to alter or offset changeable needs through marketing. Volkswagen used innovative advertising in the late 1960s and early 1970s in changing some American consumers' previous preference for large automobiles. Clearly, there are gray areas that fall somewhere between changeable and unchangeable needs. For example, the size of vehicles is affected by both preferences (a changeable factor) and by road and traffic conditions in a country (an unchangeable factor).

Managers using the type of measure just described usually find that customer needs are much more common than they might have seemed before applying the measure. Managers, particularly those with single-country responsibilities tend to focus on the differences between countries, because it is the differences that require effort in adaptation. But when taking a global view, it is helpful to use this measure to get a better understanding of the extent of commonality.

The measures can also be applied to separate product categories where there is more than one, and to separate features of an individual product. In the latter case the ratings of the separate features can be summed into a composite for the entire product.[2]

Global Customers and Channels

There are two types of global customers: national and multinational. For industries that sell to organizations, the extent to which there are *national* global customers can be measured by the share of worldwide market sales to customers who search the world for vendors. The extent to which there are *multinational* global customers can be measured by the extent to which these customers buy or select centrally for global use. These multinational global customers may do all of the buying at one or a small number of central points or may make centrally major decisions such as the selection of vendors. An analogous measure is for regional customers. For industries that sell to consumers or individuals, the measure applies to purchases made outside the home country.

The extent to which there are *global channels* can be measured by the share of worldwide sales through channels of distribution that buy or select centrally. An analogous measure is for regional channels.

For both global customers and global channels, it may be worth repeating that mere multinationality does not qualify—the customers and channels have to make central purchase or selection decisions. Only then does the selling business need to respond with global programs for selling to and servicing these customers and channels. On the other hand, the selling business may be able to help convert a multilocal customer into a global customer.

Transferable Marketing

Marketing transferability can be measured by analyzing the extent to which customers around the world accept or would accept a foreign element of the marketing mix (e.g., a foreign brand name or sales representative). This measure should be applied to all elements of the marketing mix—company name, brand name, packaging, advertising, promotion, and sales representatives. For company and brand names, being foreign means having a name that is generally recognized as being from another country, for example, McDonald's in non–English-speaking countries or Louis Vuitton in non–French-speaking countries. For packaging, being foreign means using a nonlocal language for the pack copy, including multilanguage packs. For advertising, being foreign means not just using a foreign language (which is usually, but not always, undesirable) but also using recognizably foreign situations, scenery, or characters. To be more precise, transferable marketing can be measured for each marketing element by the share of the world market accounted for by countries where a foreign element is acceptable.

Lead Countries

Lead countries can be easily identified as those in which the most important product or process innovations occur. The measure can be made more precise by identifying the countries that accounted for the last ten major innovations in the industry. In some industries the last ten major innovations will have occurred over a short time span, such as one year or less. In other, slow-changing industries the time span may cover decades.

Cost Globalization Drivers

Cost globalization drivers are probably both the easiest and the most difficult to measure. They should be the easiest because they can be quantified. They can be the most difficult because most companies seem to collect little cost information that applies on a global basis. Yet understanding the fundamental cost economics of a global business is critical for efforts to improve its global strategy.

Global Economies of Scale and Scope

Managers can measure global economies of scale by the share of the worldwide market needed to support a minimum efficient scale production or service operation. The extent of global economies of scope is usually more difficult to measure. It is indicated by the minimum global market share needed for a viable worldwide business. Global economies of scale or scope are typically significant when a global market share of 5% or more is needed to achieve the minimum efficient scale. In the passenger automobile business, the fifth and sixth largest global competitors, Nissan and Chrysler, had global market shares of only just over 5% in 1990. It can also be important to measure where in the value chain these scale economies occur.[3] In many industries, such as pharmaceuticals and electronics, it is in R&D rather than in manufacturing that world-scale economies occur.

Steep Experience Effects

The extent to which there are learning and experience effects is measured by the percentage decrease in unit production costs for each doubling of accumulated experience. This is the standard measure of the experience effect popularized by the Boston Consulting Group.[4]

Sourcing Efficiencies

Managers should keep in mind that the extent of sourcing efficiencies is more easily measured for an individual competitor within an industry than for the industry as a whole. The measure is the potential percentage savings in purchase expenditures from making all purchases centrally.

Favorable Logistics

The extent to which there are favorable logistics can be measured by the transportation cost over a standard intercontinental route in the particular industry, such as Tokyo to Chicago, or Chicago to Frankfurt, excluding customs and duties, as a percentage of the selling price. Transportation costs below 10% of the manufacturer selling price seem to be generally favorable for globalization. On the other hand, managers need to keep in mind that transportation, other logistical costs, and tariffs need to be related to margins and to the competitive price range. In general, the total transportation and tariff cost as a percentage of price needs to be at most half that of the competitive price range in most countries; that is, if the competitive price range is from 90 to 110 as an index, for a spread of 20%, transportation and tariff costs need to be no more than about 10%. For example, gourmet foods are globally competitive while basic foods are not, because the former's transportation cost is low relative to their price and the competitive price range. In addition, the availability of local products and trade barriers has the major influence on whether final products are shipped between countries.

Differences in Country Costs

The extent to which there are differences in country costs is measured in two ways. Each involves a comparison between the highest-cost country and the lowest-cost country in which there is production in the industry. In addition, managers may find it necessary to include countries that are potential producers. One measure of the differences in country costs is to compare fully loaded hourly cost of the most common form of production labor in the industry. The other measure is more complete but also more difficult and may require making hypothetical estimates. It is to compare the total unit cost of production between the highest- and lowest-cost countries.

High Product Development Costs

The extent to which product development costs affect industry globalization potential is measured by the total cost of developing (but not marketing) a major new product or service, as a percentage of the expected lifetime sales of the product or service. Both parts of this measure are difficult to estimate. Managers will need to make intelligent projections from past experience in most cases.

Fast-Changing Technology

The rate of change of technology can be measured by the market life of typical new products. It can be particularly helpful to measure this over time to see if the pace of technology change is accelerating (as Philips did for the telecommunications industry—described in Chapter 2).

Government Globalization Drivers

Measuring government globalization drivers requires a good understanding of the worldwide trade and other government policies and practices that affect a particular industry.

Favorable Trade Policies

Managers can use several different measures of the extent to which trade policies are favorable to industry globalization:

Tariffs. The importance of tariffs is measured by their charge as a percentage of the pretariff selling price. Usually it is just the individual country tariffs that matter when making decisions about single country-markets. But when taking a global view managers will find it helpful to calculate a single global number that represents the average worldwide extent of tariffs in a particular industry. A global average can be calculated by averaging tariffs across all countries, weighted by the share of the worldwide market accounted for by each country and adjusted for the universality of the tariff (i.e., a tariff may be levied against imports from some countries and not others). The latter adjustment can be made for each tariff-imposing country by weighting by the share of imports. For example, if France imposes a 10% tariff on electronics products from countries outside the European union, and these countries account for 70% of electronics imports into France, the weighted tariff for France is 10% × 70% = 7%.

Subsidies. The level of government subsidies is measured by their effect as a percentage of the selling price (including the full terms of sale such as financing and warranties). This effect is what matters to competitors rather than the effect on profitability. Estimating the effect on the selling price can be complicated, as subsidies are often in the form of a flat amount. It is their effect on the selling price that matters, not the total amount of the subsidy. For example, Airbus Industrie, the European aircraft consortium, is estimated to have received over $10 billion in subsidies from its start in 1970 to mid-1989, but to have delivered only 500 units over that period. If the full amount of the subsidy were allocated, the per aircraft amount would be $20 million, equivalent to about 50% of the average selling price. Even Boeing and McDonnell-Douglas, vociferous complainers about the Airbus subsidies, would not claim that their rival underprices by that amount. More relevant is the much smaller percentage price discount, of the order of 10% to 20%, that Airbus Industrie has in effect offered to customers. As in the case of tariffs, it is useful to be able to calculate one global number. A global average can be calculated by averaging subsidies across all competitors weighted by their global market share.

Nontariff Barriers. The strength of quotas and other nontariff barriers is measured by the share of a country's market that is blocked from imports. For example, France's nontariff restrictions on Japanese automotive imports has restricted the latter's share to less than 5%. Without these restrictions Japan's share of the French automotive market might be closer to 20% (the level in the United Kingdom). The effect is, therefore, 15%. Local content requirements can be accounted for by using an analogous procedure to estimate the market value of the foreign content that is kept out. To calculate an overall global number, the national estimates should be summed and weighted by each country's market size as a percentage of the world total.

Compatible Technical Standards

Whether technical standards are globally compatible is measured by the percentage, in cost, of the typical product that is in components that are technically compatible worldwide. For example, in a television receiver, a large percentage of the product cost is in components that need to meet different technical specifications in different countries.

Common Marketing Regulations

The degree to which there are common marketing regulations cannot be easily quantified. One approach is to estimate the proportion of the industry's worldwide marketing expenditures that are in activities allowed in every country. For example, in the cigarette industry, television advertising is banned in many, but not all, countries. So worldwide TV advertising as a proportion of industry marketing expenditures accounted for by advertising in *any* medium is the measure of marketing regulations not being common.

Government-Owned Competitors and Customers

The extent of government-owned competitors or customers can simply be measured by their combined global market share.

Competitive Globalization Drivers

Measuring competitive globalization drivers requires an effective global competitive intelligence system.

High Exports and Imports

The level of exports and imports is simply measured by the sum of world exports and imports as a percentage of the world market size.

Competitors from Different Continents

The extent to which there are competitors from different continents is measured by counting the number of continents that are the home of multinational competitors.

Interdependent Countries

Whether countries are competitively interdependent can be measured by the degree to which individual competitors share activities within a global network. The key activity is production. For each competitor the extent of sharing is measured by the amount of volume sold in each country that is dependent on production facilities that supply more than one country. For example, an American business may have 50% of its U.S. volume supplied from Taiwan and 30% of its volume in Italy also supplied from Taiwan. Summing up the total volume dependent on shared facilities and dividing by the competitor's global volume yields that competitor's country interdependence. For the industry as a whole, interdependence of countries is simply calculated by averaging across all competitors weighting by their global market share.

Globalized Competitors

Managers can measure the globalization of competitors by first estimating the extent of globalization for each individual competitor, using the measures described later in this chapter for global strategy levers. To get the industry average, weight by each competitor's global market share.

MEASURING GLOBAL STRATEGY LEVERS

In addition to measuring the globalization potential of the industry in which a business participates, its managers also need to measure where the business is in terms of the use of global strategy levers. Only then can the managers know whether they are adequately exploiting the industry's globalization potential. In addition, it helps to make three kinds of comparisons:

- Comparative measurement over time helps to identify the speed and direction of change in the business's globalization strategy.
- Measurement of competitors' strategies helps to provide both a guide to what might be done in this business and an indication of competitive opportunities and threats.
- Comparing measurements for multiple businesses in the same company helps to set benchmarks for what each business should target in the use of global strategy levers.

Summary of Measures of Global Strategy Levers

Lever	Measure
Global Market Participation	
Global market share	Business's global volume (units or revenues) divided by the total volume of the worldwide market
Globally strategic market share	Business's volume in globally strategic country-markets only divided by the total volume in those markets
Global share balance	Index of the worldwide business's geographic split of revenues compared with that of the worldwide market
Market presence Number of selling countries	Number of countries in which the worldwide business sells
Global coverage	Share of global volume accounted for by the countries in which the worldwide business sells
Global Products and Services	
Mix standardization	Percentage of worldwide revenues in a common product or service mix
Content standardization	Percentage of cost of product or service that is in components that are standardized
Global Location of Activities	
Concentration of individual activity	(1) Share of global spending on activity in the country with the most of that activity (2) Index of concentration across all countries
Concentration of entire value chain	Weighted average of the concentration indices of individual value activities
Global Marketing	
Comparative marketing intensity	Standard deviation of marketing intensity by country, for advertising, promotion, and selling
Marketing element uniformity	(1) Share of the business's worldwide revenues accounted for by the countries that have a uniform approach (2) Degree of similarity of each country's marketing element to that in a base country
Overall marketing uniformity	Score on each element weighted by each country's share of the business's worldwide revenues and by each element's importance

Global Competitive Moves	
Multicountry competitive moves	Moves that involve three or more major countries
Counterparry moves	Response to a competitive attack in one country with a move in a different country; number out of last ten responses

Global Market Participation

Global market participation can be measured in several ways. Each measure provides a different perspective on its extent.

Global Market Share

Global market share is measured by the worldwide business's global volume (units or revenues) divided by the total volume of the worldwide market. Managers should also consider an important variant—*globally strategic market share*—measured by the worldwide business's volume in globally strategic country-markets only divided by the total volume in those markets. *Globally strategic countries* can be identified simply by reviewing the key characteristics discussed earlier:

- Large source of revenues or profits
- Home market of global customers
- Home market of global competitors
- Significant market of global competitors
- Major source of industry innovation

Global Share Balance

Global share balance can be measured by managers in a number of ways. The simplest approach is to compare the percentage split of the worldwide business's revenues accounted for in each country with the percentage split of the world market accounted for in each country. A business with a "perfect" global share balance would have its percentages match the market's exactly. For example, if 30% of the world market were in the United States, 20% in Japan, and 50% in Europe, the business would have its revenues distributed the same way.

To calculate the global share balance, count the business's split in each country only to the extent that it does not exceed the market's split in that country. Using the previously mentioned market split, if the business's split is 60% in the United States, 10% in Japan, and 30% in Europe, its global share balance would be 0.7 (30% United States + 10% Japan + 30% Europe). One way to think about this balance is that it represents the portion of the business's revenues that are in the right countries relative to the location of the worldwide market. An index value of 1.0 indicates that the worldwide business's sales are in perfect balance with the market's. An index value of 0 indicates the limiting case where 100% of the worldwide business's volume is in a country that accounts for 0% of the world market volume.[5]

Market Presence

The extent of *market presence* can be measured by the *number of selling countries* (the number of countries in which the worldwide business sells) and by *global coverage.* The latter is the share of global volume (units or revenues) accounted for by the countries in which the worldwide business sells. This is not the same measure as the business's global market share.

Global Products and Services

Managers can measure the use of global products and services by examining the level of standardization across countries. This standardization needs to be measured at two levels: mix standardization and content standardization.

Mix Standardization

A business may sell a different mix of product types or models in different countries. For example, Volvo does not sell its smaller automobiles in the United States. If these smaller models account for 30% of Volvo's worldwide automotive revenues, only 70% of its mix is global. Within this global mix, the products themselves have varying levels of standardization. So a complete measure of product or service standardization would read as follows: "This business sells a product (or service) mix that is 80% globally common. Of that common mix, products are 70% standardized in countries that account for 90% of world market volume."

Content Standardization

Managers will find that measuring the extent of content standardization is complex because of the multidimensional nature of a product. Cost is the most common denominator, and is, therefore, the best basis for measurement. Content standardization is measured by the percentage of the product's cost in components that are the same in each country. If the worldwide business sells more than one product, a composite measure can be used weighted by the worldwide sales volume of each product. An electronics business, part of an American multinational company, had a product line that was highly standardized—in fact, more than its executives realized. They initially thought that their product was not standard across countries, because 40% of the product cost was in a decoder that was different in each country. But digging deeper, however, they discovered that within the decoder, only the software was unique. Furthermore, the software was embodied in purchased parts (masked ROMs). Therefore, there was no difference in the manufacturing process, only in the inventory to be kept. Also, the cost of developing the unique software was amortized over a large sales base. As a result, what initially appeared to be 40% nonstandard turned out to be only 3% nonstandard.

The foregoing measure may need to be adjusted for major countries only, or particular groups of countries. This adjustment is particularly necessary if the worldwide business sells a highly standardized product in some but not all countries. With the geographic adjustment the measure has two numbers, as follows: "The worldwide business sells products that are X% standardized in countries that account for Y% of world market volume." The product XY (X times Y) can be used if a single statistic is desired.

The measure cannot adequately handle all possibilities. For example, the statistic XY would be the same for a worldwide business with 90% standardization in countries accounting for 55% of worldwide volume and no standardization in the remaining countries, and for another worldwide business that also has a different standardized product for the remaining countries.

Global Location of Activities

As with the other global strategy levers, companies need to have an idea of where they are in their use of global activity location before they can decide whether and how to change it. Some useful measures include the following:

Concentration of Individual Activity. Each activity should be analyzed in terms of how the geographic share of expenditure on that activity compares with the geographic share of the worldwide business's revenues. This can be done visually via comparative bar charts, numerically by comparing the percentage of the activity in key countries with the percentage of the world market or of the business's revenues in the same countries, or via concentration indices.[6] These comparisons then provide some of the basis for deciding whether the pattern of location is out of line with what it should be.

Concentration of Entire Value Chain. One measure can be developed for the concentration of the entire value-adding chain by using the weighted average of the concentration indices of individual value activities.

Production Location Matrix. Managers can better understand their global strategy for production location by creating a matrix of where products are produced versus where they are sold. Such a matrix helps to identify the flow of products and also shows the extent of reliance on local manufacture. Exhibit 10–4 in Chapter 10 provides an example.

Global Marketing

Much of marketing is qualitative so that precise quantification of the extent of globalization will be difficult. But a number of measures can be applied to global marketing. These measures include the following:

Comparative Marketing Intensity. This measures the degree to which spending on each element of the marketing mix, such as advertising, promotion, and selling, varies by country. It is measured by the standard deviation of the expenditure-to-sales ratios in each country for each marketing element.

Marketing Element Uniformity. This can be measured in two ways: (1) by the share of the business's worldwide revenues accounted for by the countries that have a uniform approach and (2) by the degree of similarity of each country's marketing element to that in a base country.

Overall Marketing Uniformity. Last, an overall measure of global marketing can be created by the similarity score on each element weighted by each country's share of the business's worldwide revenues and by each element's importance.

Global Competitive Moves

Chapter 7 described six key types of global competitive moves:

- Cross-subsidization of countries within the same business
- Use of counterparries
- Globally coordinated sequence of moves

- Targeting of actual and potential global competitors
- Developing plans for each major country-competitor combination
- Preemptive use of global strategy

Each of these six key moves can be used to measure how much this global strategy lever is used by a business or by its competitors. But two of these features are more easily quantified than the others: the use of counterparries and the use of a globally coordinated sequence of moves. The use of counterparries can be measured by how often a business responds to a competitive attack in one country with a move in a different country. The use of a globally coordinated sequence of moves can be measured by the number of countries involved in each sequence of moves.

MEASURING GLOBAL ORGANIZATION

Measuring the extent to which management and organization help global strategy involves more subjectivity than measuring industry globalization potential and the use of global strategy levers. Because the effects of organization are so specific to individual companies, corporate managers might find it particularly helpful to measure global organization in their different worldwide businesses. They are likely to find that some elements are common across businesses, while others differ. Then they can investigate if these differences have helped or hurt the globalization efforts of each business. These measures are as follows:

Organization Element	*Measure*
Organization Structure	
One global head	Whether there is one person whose primary job it is to be head of the worldwide business
International division	Whether there is an international division that dces not contain the domestic business
Functional line heads	Whether there is a single head with line authority for each function
Functional staff heads	Whether there is a single staff coordinator for each function
Strength of business dimension	In a matrix structure, the strength of the business dimension relative to the geographic and functional dimensions

*Management
Processes*

Global strategic information system	Extent to which the business collects strategic information, such as market share and competitor data, from around the world in a consistent format on a regular basis
Cross-country coordination	Extent to which the business has processes for coordinating strategy across countries—*sharing information, negotiating plans, clearing plans with headquarters* and *direction by headquarters*
	Frequency of *global meetings*
	Use of *global teams*
	Number of *global product managers* or *global account managers*
Global strategic planning	Extent to which the business uses an effective strategic planning process that integrates across countries rather than just adding up the national plans
Global budgeting	Extent to which the business has global budgets that are used for global programs, as opposed to national budgets for national programs
Global performance review and compensation	Extent to which senior managers are evaluated and compensated on the basis of global and not just regional or national performance; percentage of compensation tied to global performance

People

Foreign nationals in home country	Percentage of senior managers in home country who are foreign nationals
Home country nationals in other countries	Percentage of senior managers in other countries who are home country nationals
Foreign nationals in other countries	Percentage of senior managers in other countries who are non–home country foreign nationals

Culture

Global culture	Extent to which corporate or business culture is global rather than national
Interdependent culture	Extent to which culture favors interdependence rather than autonomy

DISCUSSION AND RESEARCH QUESTIONS

1. What are the benefits of measuring globalization and global strategy?
2. Which industry globalization drivers are the easiest to measure, and which the most difficult and why?
3. How often should measures of globalization and global strategy be made? and by whom?
4. Select one company and its product line. Describe how you would measure that product line's extent of global standardization. Also, how would you get the necessary information?

NOTES

1. I thank Ed Davis, University of Virginia, for this example.
2. The composite can be derived by weighting the individual features according to their share of product cost, as follows:

$$H_i = \Sigma\, S_j C_j$$

   where
   H_i = the homogeneity index of product i
   S_j = the similarity score for feature j
   C_j = the percentage of product i's cost accounted for by feature j
3. See Michael E. Porter, *Competitive Advantage: Creating and Sustaining Superior Performance* (New York: The Free Press, 1985).
4. See Arnoldo C. Hax and Nicolas S. Majluf, *Strategic Management: An Integrative Perspective* (Englewood Cliffs, N.J.: Prentice Hall, 1984), Chapter 6.
5. This measure of global share balance can be somewhat tedious to calculate if there are a large number of countries. The same index can be developed more easily by applying a computer spreadsheet program to the following formula:

$$\text{Index} = 1 - \frac{\Sigma(|BS_i - MS_i|)}{200}$$

   where
   BS_i = the percentage share of the worldwide business's volume in country i
   MS_i = the percentage share of the worldwide market's volume in country i
   The index will range from 0 to 1.0 in value.
6. The following index for activity concentration can be used:

$$\text{Index} = \sqrt[2]{\Sigma_i S_i^2}\,,$$

   where S_i is the ith country's share of global expenditure on the activity.

Chapter 10

Conducting a Global Strategy Analysis

This last chapter provides a guide to the more practical aspects of applying the global strategy framework and conducting the necessary analyses. It also provides a number of forms that have proven useful in guiding executives through the analysis. One of the greatest challenges for the would-be global manager is acquiring the information that is needed both to formulate and to implement a global strategy. Surprisingly few companies have complete and readily accessible information about the products and services they offer worldwide. Often, complete information by country exists only at the country level. Some companies even get trapped in a circular dilemma—they cannot collect information about a particular country because they do not participate in it, and they do not participate there because they do not have any information about the country.

WORKSTEPS

A global strategy analysis can range in effort from a one-day brainstorming exercise to a multimonth study. The analysis can also cover an entire business, or even the entire company, or be restricted to a narrow range of issues, such as developing a global pack design or a global purchasing policy.

The following list (depicted in Exhibit 10–1) sets out the steps for a comprehensive effort:

A. Assembling the global team
B. Defining the business
C. Identifying key markets
D. Identifying key competitors
E. Checking the core strategy
F. Checking country selection
G. Diagnosing industry globalization potential
H. Evaluating current and potential use of global strategy levers
I. Evaluating organization capability
J. Developing global programs

Also, as shown in Exhibit 10–1, feedback should be provided at each step to earlier steps. For example, discovering an opportunity to use global strategy at step H may generate a need to reconsider the core strategy checked earlier in step E.

A. ASSEMBLING THE GLOBAL TEAM

Involvement of managers from different functions and locations is absolutely crucial to the success of a global strategy. So selecting the team to participate in the global analysis is a key decision. The team needs to be selected from the following:

- Head of the worldwide business, if there is one
- Senior representatives from related businesses (that share facilities or staff)
- Senior corporate executive
- Heads of major regions/countries
- Heads of key functions

Ideally, the team should consist of no more than six to eight regular members. If choices have to be made, full geographic representation should be favored over full functional representation. In addition, the team needs support staff, such as from the planning function, or staff from the organization of the individual members. The invitation to join the global team should come from the highest possible level, ideally from the CEO. The inviter needs to stress the importance and relevance of the effort and indicate the hoped for outcome. The team should have a leader, who should be the head of the worldwide business or the nearest equivalent.

Although perhaps obvious, the most difficult practical problem is often setting up a meeting schedule. So that should be done at the first

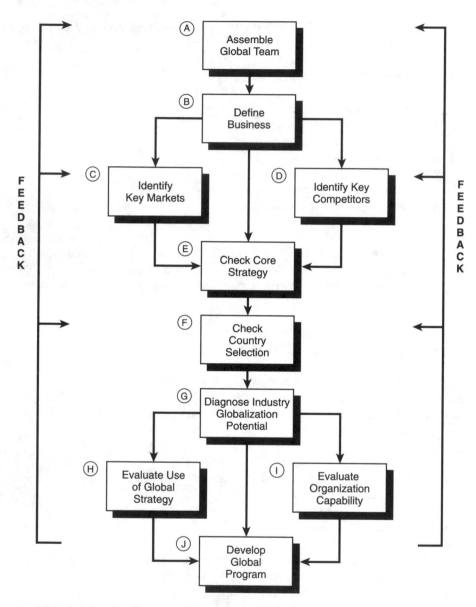

EXHIBIT 10–1   Steps in Global Strategy Analysis

meeting. Because each of the executives is extremely busy, it is better to establish a set schedule even though the work may not fit exactly. At least
three meetings should be set up, between one and two months apart, perhaps piggybacking onto other events such as corporate planning meetings.
It is also very helpful to move the location of the meeting around the

world—anything to avoid the appearance of a head office/home country-driven project helps. In addition, rotating the location helps the team members undertake the travel needed in a global business and allows local staff to participate.

The schedule should also allow enough time between meetings to collect and analyze information and to develop strategies and reports. Having new input greatly enhances what can be achieved in each meeting.

B. DEFINING THE BUSINESS

The leader of the global team needs to have a good idea of what business will be analyzed before he or she can assemble the global team, but developing a complete definition needs the input of the team. *Business definition is an important issue, because a global strategy analysis is often more effective by starting out with a piece of the business rather than with the entire business.* Experience with analyzing this part of the business can then be transferred to subsequent expanded efforts. Perhaps as important, the first global analysis needs to achieve usable results within a short time span, say, six months at the most. Classically, business definition has focused on the three dimensions of product (or service) function, technology employed, and customer groups served.[1] In the context of global strategy, the fourth dimension of geography must, of course, be added. Taking account of the geographic dimension will make it clearer which businesses face broader global issues and, therefore, have a greater need for global strategy. In addition, the team may wish to restrict the analysis to just one region, such as Europe. So, for example, a manufacturer of medical equipment may have several options in defining the business to study:

- The entire medical equipment division (and the industries in which it participates)
- The worldwide hospital equipment business
- The worldwide hospital radiography equipment business
- The European hospital radiography equipment business

Another concern is to define the business sufficiently broadly to encompass competition from actual and potential substitutes.

C. IDENTIFYING KEY MARKETS

The global team cannot collect and analyze information about every country in which the business operates or might operate, because of both the time and effort needed for collection and the resulting information overload. One approach is to split the analysis into two levels, first by region and then by country within each region. The choice of regions is usually easy—North America, South America, Europe, Far East, or Pacific Rim being the most common. Matching the region definitions to the way in which the company is organized may not be the purest approach, but it is usually the most practical for data gathering and for subsequent implementation. Some companies use unusual regional groupings. Gillette has organized a North Atlantic region, because of the similarity in income levels and lifestyle among the United States, Canada, and Western Europe. Sterling Drug has used a JCAP region, combining Japan, Canada, and other Pacific Rim countries, managed out of New York. Citibank also has an unusual grouping for its global finance business—JENA, an acronym for Japan, Europe, North America, Australia, and New Zealand, in short, most of the developed world. When selecting countries within regions, the definition of a country is flexible, as described in Chapter 1. For example, a "country" can be Benelux or Scandinavia. As with regions, only the most important countries should be chosen. Criteria for country selection should include the largest country-markets, the countries in which the company has the largest businesses, and globally strategic countries.

Splitting the analysis into two levels—global and regional—reduces the number of geographic entities that need to be considered at one time. *It is surprisingly important to be able to view all key markets spread across one exhibit as a comparative chart.* Executives are able to generate new understanding and insight when they can compare and contrast across regions and countries. Furthermore, when the members of the global team view these comparative charts *together*, they stimulate each other in developing ideas. So a total of no more than ten geographic entities plus "all other" and "total world (region)" columns should be used. At the country level, markets should be selected for analysis using the criteria in Chapter 3 on global market participation. The list should include the six or so largest markets in which the business participates, any other country-markets among the largest six in the world even if the business is not there, any other markets that are strategically important, and any other markets in which the worldwide business has its largest country-businesses. This combination will usually result in a list of eight to ten countries. In deciding on the "all other" category, the team needs to define the world. As stated in Chapter 1, the world market includes only country-markets that are accessible to multinational companies. Such accessible countries vary from industry to industry and also change over time. Until the changes of regime in 1989, most countries in Eastern Europe might have been excluded. Similarly, the ongoing reconstruction of the former Soviet bloc may add new countries to the list of accessible markets. In some industries, it may be useful to add a column combining the countries that are not accessible to the business. Having such a column will give a better perspective on the total market and may help the global team avoid being blindsided by developments coming out of in-accessible countries.

The global team should then use the list of countries as the basis on which most of the information will be collected and displayed.

Information to Be Collected for Each Region/Country

In conducting analysis of individual countries in order to make an entry decision, for example, a large amount of information needs to be collected (some of which will be identified later in step F). But for this step of identifying key markets, much less information is needed. The following basic set of information needs to be known for each country-market:

- Market size in units and revenues
- Stage of product life cycle
- Number of global competitors
- Number of regionwide competitors
- Number of national or local competitors
- Percentage of country production (in the industry) exported
- Percentage of country consumption imported
- Local content requirement
- Labor cost
- Government share of customer purchases
- Tax rate for local and for foreign companies
- Percentage foreign ownership allowed

Coping with Exchange Rates

Currency exchange rates obviously have a very crucial role in globalization decisions. To make data collection simple and to ease subsequent analysis, all data should be reported in the currency of the headquarters country at historical exchange rates, that is, using the same exchange rates that were applied by the local businesses when they reported to headquarters in each time period in the past. Typically, that means the annual average exchange rate for revenue and profit items and year-end exchange rates for balance sheet items. The key reason for converting to the home currency is that most owners or shareholders care about the worldwide business's contribution to revenues and profits in their home currency. Similarly, the key reason for using historical exchange rates is that for a globalization analysis, the need is to know how each country-business contributed to the total business. So a depreciating local currency, for example, needs to be recognized for its impact on the role that the local business can play. (In contrast, evaluating the performance of local managers should generally be done using figures in their local currency.)

D. IDENTIFYING KEY COMPETITORS

Just as every country cannot be analyzed, neither can every competitor. So the global team needs to select the most important competitors to study. Competitors that need to be analyzed include the following:

- All global competitors, as defined by all competitors that have significant market presence in North America, Europe, and Asia and have at least 5% global market share. (This definition may need to be adapted in industries where the key continents are different from those listed.)
- The largest competitors based in each lead country and major region, even if they are not global.
- Potential global competitors.

If possible, the list of all competitors should be kept to ten or fewer.

The list of key competitors combines with the list of key markets to make a very powerful organizing framework for displaying and analyzing information. Exhibit 10–2 illustrates the different kinds of data matrices that are useful to develop for this market-competitor combination—such as global and European matrices for competitors' market share, relative prices, relative costs, and relative quality.[2]

E. CHECKING THE CORE STRATEGY

In conducting a global strategy analysis, it is common for the members of the global team to either not know what the business's core strategy is or, more commonly, to hold differing views on what it is. So the global team will find it very helpful to check its core business strategy early in the process. The best way to conduct this check is to have executives from both headquarters and from each major region or country write down the core strategy. Doing so has two benefits. First, if the core business strategy is not already specified in some document, this procedure helps make explicit what may have been implicit. In addition, many statements of business strategy are typically less detailed than they should be and often consist of what Americans like to call "motherhood and apple pie" statements, such as "this business will profitably offer the highest quality products and provide the best value to our customers." Such statements can be very helpful in motivating organization members and reassuring shareholders but provide little strategic guidance. The essence of a strategy is that it makes

Example:

MARKETS COMPETITORS	N. America	S. America	Europe	Asia	All others	TOTAL
Our company						
Competitor A						
Competitor B		Market share %				
Competitor C		• 3 years ago				
Competitor D		• this year				
Competitor E		• 3 years in future				
All others						
TOTAL						

MARKETS COMPETITORS	Germany	France	U.K.	Italy	All others	TOTAL
Our company						
Competitor A						
Competitor B		Market share %				
Competitor C		• 3 years ago				
Competitor D		• this year				
Competitor E		• 3 years in future				
All others						
TOTAL						

Create also for | Relative Prices | | Relative Costs | | Relative Quality |

EXHIBIT 10–2 Data Matrices for Analyzing Competitors

choices, something that the previous example does not. After all, who would choose the opposite: "This business will unprofitably offer the poorest quality products and provide the worst value to our customers"? Andrall E. Pearson, then president of Pepsico, very succinctly captured the importance of strategic choice when he said, "A strategy is something that someone else would not be stupid not to choose."[3] So managers should write out their core business strategy in some detail and in a format that makes choices explicit.

The statement of core strategy should include

- Business definition
- Strategic thrust
- Financial targets
- Sources of competitive advantage
- Strategy elements
- Value-adding activities
- Competitive strategy

Exhibit A–1 in the appendix provides forms that are useful for specifying the core strategy.

The second benefit of having each major region or country specify its view of the core business strategy is that differences among the regions and countries can then be identified. Identifying these differences is facilitated by summarizing and combining the strategy statements into comparative charts such as those in Exhibit A–2 in the appendix.

F. CHECKING COUNTRY SELECTION

Country selection is one of the most important elements in both internationalization and globalization. It is also a decision for which analytical techniques can be particularly helpful. Traditional analytical approaches to selecting countries for entry have focused entirely on stand-alone attractiveness.[4] But managers need to consider the global strategic importance of a country. Of additional relevance is the potential for synergy between the business under consideration and sister businesses in each country. For example, a leading American forest products company finds that a key factor in deciding whether or not to expand a particular business into a new country is that business's potential for absorbing paper production capacity already in place in the country. So three sets of overall factors should determine country selection:

- Stand-alone attractiveness
- Global strategic importance
- Synergy

The global team should evaluate country selection using the following steps:

1. Identify countries/regions for analysis
2. Develop a list of subfactors for each of the three sets of overall factors
3. Assign weights to each subfactor

4. Rate each country/region on each subfactor
5. Combine the weights and ratings to arrive at a total score for each country or region
6. Adjust the total score for country risk

1. Identify Countries/Regions

The global team should identify all countries or regions in which the business already participates or might do so. Existing countries should be analyzed in order to help determine the level of effort that should be devoted to them and to provide a benchmark for evaluating new countries. It is particularly important to include countries that may be difficult to enter but that are globally strategic or potentially so.

2. Develop List of Subfactors

The global team should develop its own list of subfactors to assess each of the sets of factors. Such a list might include the following:

Stand-Alone Attractiveness of Country/Region

- Size of market
- Growth rate of market
- Barriers to entry
- Competitive situation
- Price levels
- Tax rates
- Macroeconomic conditions
- Political risk
- Cost of adaptation

Global Strategic Importance of Country/Region

- Home market of global customers
- Home market of global competitors
- Significant market of global competitors
- Major source of industry innovation
- Home of most demanding customers

Synergy with Other Businesses in Country/Region

- Sharing activities with other company businesses
- Using upstream (e.g., raw material production) capacity
- Using downstream capacity (e.g., final assembly or distribution) capacity
- Having proximity to other markets

For countries in which the business is not already present, *potential* synergy is what should be evaluated.

3. Assign Weights to Each Subfactor

The global team should next assign a weighting to each subfactor such that the total for all subfactors sums to 100 points. One approach is first to split the 100 points among the three overall factors of stand-alone attractiveness, global strategic importance, and synergy with other businesses. For example, these three overall factors might be assigned 40, 40, and 20 points, respectively. Then the points for each overall factor can be split among the individual subfactors.

4. Rate Each Country/Region on Each Subfactor

The global team should then rate each country or region on each individual subfactor on a scale from 0 to 10. A practical way to do this is to set benchmarks by giving a rating of 10 to the country or countries with the strongest showing on each particular factor. For example, on the market size subfactor, the largest market can be assigned a score of 10 and all other countries scaled in proportion. In some other cases no country may qualify for the maximum score, so the global team needs to consider what would rate a maximum score, and scale the countries accordingly. The exact approach used is not as important as the end result of differentiating among the countries on the various subfactors.

5. Combine the Weights and Country Ratings

To arrive at a total rating for each country, the weights and ratings should be multiplied together and summed (and divided by 10 to get a total country rating that is out of 100).

6. Adjust for Country Risk

Finally, the total country ratings should be adjusted for country risks such as political instability, the risk of expropriation, and the risk of currency devaluation. Traditionally, country risk has been included with other factors in evaluating stand-alone attractiveness rather than being considered separately as done here.[5] This separate approach is preferable for three reasons. First, it separates the business factors from the political ones. For example, both Brazil and Japan are large markets that may be highly attractive in particular industries. But the level of country risk has been much higher in Brazil than in Japan. Mixing the two types of factors makes it difficult to recognize two fundamentally different sources of uncertainty that need to be managed in different ways. Second, risk can be viewed as a discount factor applied to expected returns from participating in a country. Third, country risk changes much more quickly than business attractiveness, as it did for China in June 1989, the Middle East in August 1990, and the Soviet Union in August 1991. Various services such as Political Risk Services (formerly the Frost & Sullivan Political Risk Letter) provide relatively low cost and comprehensive ratings of country risk.[6] The ratings provided by these services should be converted into a risk adjustment factor scored from 0 as hopelessly risky to 1.0 as no risk at all.

Using the Ratings

The resulting ratings should be used as one input to the decision on country selection and should not be used in a mechanistic way. The global team should solicit the input of mangers familiar with the individual countries as well as use their own individual judgment. Although a lot of work, this kind of comprehensive analytical process can be helpful in dispelling myths or clearing up ignorance about the attractiveness of particular countries. The process can also force companies to recognize the importance of entering countries that have been avoided for their difficulty. In summary, the benefits of this technique include identifying relevant data, reducing complexity, encouraging a systematic approach, providing quantitative measurement, and complementing intuition. At the same time, users have to be cautious of its weaknesses, which include oversimplifying, requiring subjective evaluations, and needing modification for each application. Most important, this technique must not be used blindly.

G. DIAGNOSING INDUSTRY GLOBALIZATION POTENTIAL

Diagnosing industry globalization potential can best be done in two stages.[7] In the first stage, the global team can make preliminary assessments through group discussion at one of its meetings, using the measures summarized in Chapter 9. These assessments should be written up so that they can be verified by country managers and staff in a second stage. A typical assessment might be as follows:

> The globalization driver of global customers rates a moderate score today and is increasing in strength. Global customers now account for about 20% of the market, up about 5 percentage points from three years ago, and regionwide customers a further 35%, up about 10 points from three years ago. We expect

both global and regionwide customers to increase their share of purchases. Showa K.K. behaves the most globally as a customer. In its last request for proposal, it required a bid with standard prices for each country. Duvall & Cie. is starting to behave as a global customer and now requires all products to be approved in Paris even though its local subsidiaries make their own purchase decisions. We are not sure what Schmidt AG is doing and want each country manager to report back with an assessment.

Next, the global team should identify how industry globalization drivers give rise to opportunities to use global strategy levers. For example, what does the diagnosis on global customers indicate for the use of global marketing such as global account management?

H. EVALUATING CURRENT AND POTENTIAL USE OF GLOBAL STRATEGY LEVERS

Identifying changes to be made in the use of global strategy levers requires a diagnosis of both their current and their potential use. There are three major sources of ideas for diagnosing the potential use of global strategy levers:

- Analysis of the potential benefits from using global strategy
- Analysis of the industry globalization drivers
- Analysis of what competitors are doing

Various analytical and display techniques can help diagnose the individual global strategy levers, as explained next.

Global Market Participation

A key aspect of a global approach to market participation is the extent to which the business's revenues are in geographic balance with those of the market as a whole. It can be very helpful to depict graphically the global share balance to compare where the business has its revenues with the overall global market. A comparative bar chart might show, for example, that a business has far too much of its revenues concentrated in the United States and not nearly enough in Japan, and that this imbalance will worsen in the next five years.

Global Products and Services

The key analysis needed for product standardization decisions is the calculation of potential cost savings. Potential cost savings from product standardization can be small for individual factors but can add up significantly. Exhibit 10–3 illustrates the type of analysis needed.

Reducing the number of products worldwide by 33% would save	
	% of Sales
Manufacturing	3% to 4%
Inventory (14% of sales times 20% carrying cost)	2.8%
Out-of-stock and orders not pushed from fear of out-of-stocks (10% of sales times 40% gross margin)	4.0%
Total	10% to 11%

These potential savings can be compared with a pretax margin of 8% and a media budget of 12%.

EXHIBIT 10–3   Calculation of Potential Savings from Product Standardization

Global Activity Location

As with market participation, the analysis of activity location can be enhanced through the use of visual display. Working with an industrial supplies company, I found one such display helped to highlight the dominance of Germany in R&D and manufacturing relative to its share of the business's global revenues. The implications depend, of course, on the specific situation of the business. In this example, the business's high level of concentration helped to achieve economies of scale in R&D and manufacturing. But the business also suffered from a lack of R&D facilities in two of the most innovative markets—the United States and Japan.

The location of manufacturing is typically the most difficult issue in global strategy. It helps to start with a good understanding of where products are produced and where they are shipped. Exhibit 10–4 provides an example of a *production location matrix* that helps managers understand their current production location strategy. In Exhibit 10–4 the shaded boxes indicate units that are sold in the country of production. So in this example, 51% of production is for local sale, which in most cases is probably greater than it should be under a globally integrated strategy.

Having evaluated each value-adding activity, the team should summarize the actual and target location of each activity in terms of whether it is, or should be, mostly local or mostly central. In addition, the team should decide on the nature of headquarters coordination and control needed for each activity.

Global Marketing

As with value-adding activities, it can be useful to summarize the actual and target use of global marketing. Exhibit 10–5 provides a format for summarizing conclusions on which marketing element to globalize and to

Units in Millions

SOLD IN / PRODUCED IN	United States	Germany	France	United Kingdom	Japan	Brazil	Others	TOTAL UNITS PRO-DUCED
United States	1,320						230	1,550
France		380	250	210			130	970
Brazil						140		140
Taiwan					470		220	690
TOTAL UNITS SOLD	1,320	380	250	210	470	140	580	3,350

■ = produced and sold in same country

51% of production is for local sale (United States, France, and Brazil = 1,710 million units out of 3,350 million total)

EXHIBIT 10–4   Production Location Matrix

what extent. It can provide a helpful focus on the end objective of the analyses of industry globalization drivers, potential benefits of global strategy levers, and competitors' approaches.

The global team can also use a *relative price map* to deal with the one marketing element that is easy to quantify—pricing. Such a map shows the business's pricing in each country indexed relative to the home country (or any one reference country). This index can be constructed in a number of ways. The easiest way is if there exists a typical product that is sold in every country or region being analyzed. If no one product meets this criterion or if different products have different patterns of international pricing (e.g., one major product may be priced in Europe above the company's home country price, while another major product may be below the home country price), then the global team needs to create either a number of different charts or a single weighted composite.

Global Competitive Moves

Most companies have very poor information about their competitors' moves. If the information exists, it is usually scattered around the company with different people and in different countries. Historical information about competitors' moves is even scarcer. *But collecting and maintaining such*

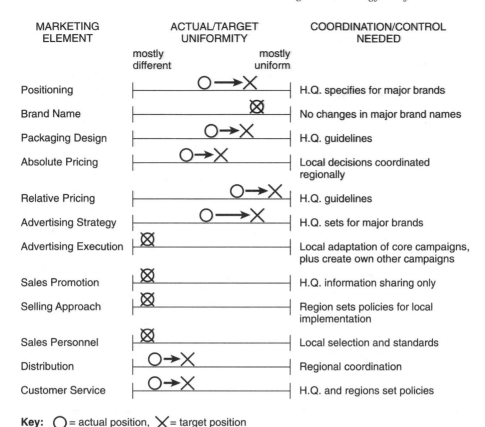

MARKETING ELEMENT	ACTUAL/TARGET UNIFORMITY	COORDINATION/CONTROL NEEDED
Positioning		H.Q. specifies for major brands
Brand Name		No changes in major brand names
Packaging Design		H.Q. guidelines
Absolute Pricing		Local decisions coordinated regionally
Relative Pricing		H.Q. guidelines
Advertising Strategy		H.Q. sets for major brands
Advertising Execution		Local adaptation of core campaigns, plus create own other campaigns
Sales Promotion		H.Q. information sharing only
Selling Approach		Region sets policies for local implementation
Sales Personnel		Local selection and standards
Distribution		Regional coordination
Customer Service		H.Q. and regions set policies

Key: ◯ = actual position, ✕ = target position

EXHIBIT 10–5   Summary of Global Marketing Strategy

information is crucial for understanding and predicting the pattern of competitors' global moves.[8] For example, mapping the history of each major competitor's moves, as in Exhibit 10–6, helps to identify the extent to which they globally integrate their competitive moves. In the example in Exhibit 10–6, Haneda K.K. seems to make its price and product moves in North America first, closely followed by the other regions. In contrast, new advertising campaigns seem to start in Asia. It is also helpful to map the history of competitors' global responses to your business's moves.

Summary of Business and Competitors

Having evaluated the use of each individual global strategy lever and its elements, it is helpful to summarize the total use of global strategy by the business and its major competitors. The example in Exhibit 10–7 illus-

Example:

COMPETITOR: Haneda K.K.

PERIOD / MARKET	N. America	S. America	Europe	Asia	Other
1988 Q1	▲ Raised price on T29 model				
1988 Q2			▲ Raised price on T29 model		
1988 Q3				▲ Raised price on T29 model	
1988 Q4					
1989 Q1		▲ Raised price on T29 model			▲ Raised price on T29 model
1989 Q2				● New ad campaign	
1989 Q3	■ Introduced S32 line		■ Introduced S32 line		
1989 Q4			● New ad campaign		
1990 Q1				■ Introduced S32 line	
1990 Q2	● New ad campaign				
1990 Q3	▲ Raised price on S32 line				■ Introduced S32 line
1990 Q4			▲ Raised price on S32 line		

Key: ▲ = pricing move   ● = product move   ■ = advertising move

EXHIBIT 10–6   Map of a Competitor's Moves

trates the position of the business and its three major competitors in terms of their use of each of the five global strategy levers.

I. EVALUATING ORGANIZATION CAPABILITY

Organization and management factors make a crucial difference in how well global strategy can be developed and implemented. So it is also essential to evaluate the organization's capability for global strategy and to diag-

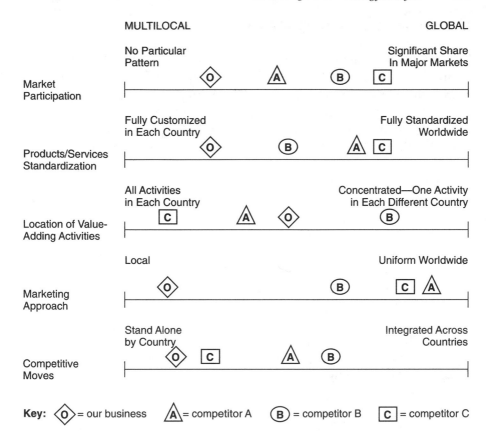

EXHIBIT 10–7 Summary of Competitors' Use of Global Strategy

nose the necessary changes. Chapter 8 discussed each of the sets of factors and their individual elements to determine together the organization's capability for global strategy. The global team should systematically evaluate each of these factors and elements using the measures described in Chapter 9. Typically, the methodology for this step should include getting the views of both headquarters and subsidiary managers through interviews, group discussions, and surveys. In this data gathering process, the global team should not just collect information about problems (which managers are usually happy to talk about) but also find out about possible solutions, as well as test for reactions to solutions devised by the team. To help find the best solutions, the global team should try to discover how other effective companies in the same industry or comparable industries organize and manage for global strategy.

J. DEVELOPING GLOBAL PROGRAMS

The last task in a global strategy analysis is to specify plans for global programs in sufficient detail that they can take on a life of their own. In other words, this last step ensures the transition to implementation. The previous analyses will typically have identified a large number of global programs. For example, one company that conducted a global strategy analysis concluded with the following programs that needed to be implemented:

- Global Products
- Global Technology Management
- Global Materials Procurement
- Global Marketing Management
- Global Account Management
- Global Pricing
- Global Identification
- Global Trade Show Coordination
- Global Market Intelligence

To move to implementation, the company developed plans for each program. The following summary illustrates the plan for the global products program:

GLOBAL PRODUCTS PROGRAM

Product and process are so interlinked that we need to treat them together. Our ability to develop highly customized products for fundamental customers is a key competitive advantage. At the same time, global customers expect to be able to purchase consistent/uniform products wherever they operate sophisticated equipment. But consistent products require a consistent manufacturing process, which we do not have. There is now wide variation from region to region in our manufacturing approach, arising from a combination of raw material availability, equipment, customers' expectations, and local economic conditions. The result is that products are not as standardized as they could or should be.

Objective

Maintain and augment our competitive advantage of being able to provide consistent/uniform products around the world to those customers who require consistency. In addition, cut costs.

Overall Strategy

Increase standardization across countries by individual characteristics at tighter specifications that provide added value to customers. We will standardize only when the additional cost is low or is recoverable from customers.

Potential Benefits

- *Cost savings for the company*
- *Improved quality or performance for the customer*
- *Increased barriers to competition*
- *Improved trust of the company by customer management*
- *Training efficiencies*

Potential Disadvantages

- *Possibly easier for competitors to copy*
- *May be too expensive in many cases*
- *Impact on upstream product profitability and availability*
- *Customer perception of reduced flexibility*

Implementation

1. *Use the strategic account management programs in the various regions to develop an information base on the types of products required by key accounts throughout the world: type of equipment, product specifications, performance criteria, quality, and so on. This activity will be managed by the global marketing manager.*
2. *Develop a complete database on our manufacturing capabilities for sophisticated textile tubes worldwide. This activity will be managed by the global technical manager. An attachment shows a partial and preliminary analysis for the XYZ product and lists the key variations across countries.*
3. *Decide on which products and characteristics to standardize, and develop a cost–benefit analysis to justify each recommendation. This will be done jointly by the global marketing and technical managers.*

Next Steps: Complete analysis of worldwide capabilities for all high-end products
Responsibility: John Poulenc and Maria Suzuki
Timing: By end of June 1995

FURTHER STEPS

The global strategy analysis described in this chapter provides four concrete outputs:

- An assessment of how global an industry is today and is likely to become in the future
- An understanding of how global a company's approach is today, and how it compares to its competitors and to the industry potential for further globalization
- An identification of the organizational factors that will facilitate or hinder a move toward globalization
- A broad action plan, specifying strategic and organizational change priorities

The analysis in and of itself does not provide the details of a global competitive strategy. If its output has shown that adopting some form of global strategy is indeed desirable, the analysis needs to be followed by another effort aimed at developing a detailed total global and competitive strategy. Among the decisions that will need to be made are the definition of a competitive posture in various countries (i.e., in what part of the world should we compete on our own and in what part should we form alliances?), the articulation of specific functional strategies (manufacturing, marketing, financial, etc.), and the adoption of organizational mechanisms aimed at reinforcing the strategic objectives sought.

SOME GUIDING IDEAS FOR IMPLEMENTING A TOTAL GLOBAL STRATEGY

In conducting a global strategy analysis and then globalizing a business's strategy, the reader may wish to keep in mind a number of guiding ideas that summarize the concepts in this book:

1. Do not assume that "it cannot happen here." Almost any industry has the potential for globalization and global competition.
2. Global industries are not born but are created by global companies. The rewards of globalization go to the first movers.
3. Globalization requires a clear vision of the firm as a global competitor. It also requires a long-term time horizon and a commitment from top management.
4. Globalization is not all or nothing. A business can be global in some elements of its strategy and not in others.
5. Shift the burden of proof from assuming that strategy should be local unless proven otherwise to assuming that the strategy should be global unless proven otherwise. So in deciding on product and program adaptation, search for what is really necessary rather than assuming that the local managers know best.
6. Be careful to match strategy changes with the necessary organization and management changes.
7. Globalization should not be a religion but a philosophy.[9]
8. The slogan "think global, act local" is wrong. It should read, instead, "think and act global and local."

DISCUSSION AND RESEARCH QUESTION

1. Using the framework in this chapter, select a company and one of its world-wide businesses and conduct a complete global strategy analysis.

NOTES

1. See Derek F. Abell, *Defining the Business: The Starting Point of Strategic Planning* (Englewood Cliffs, N.J.: Prentice Hall, 1980).

2. Evaluating relative quality is a very difficult task. The PIMS program has developed some useful techniques. See Robert D. Buzzell and Bradley T. Gale, *The PIMS Principles: Linking Strategy to Performance* (New York: The Free Press, 1987), Chapter 6.

3. He made this statement at a presentation at the Harvard Business School in 1982. See also George S. Yip, "Planning at Pepsi (B)," Case No. 9-583-051 (Boston: Harvard Business School, 1983).

4. For example, Franklin R. Root, *Entry Strategies for International Markets* (Lexington, Mass.: D. C. Heath, 1987), provides a thorough method for scoring country attractiveness.

5. See ibid. for a discussion of country risk.

6. Some observers have commented that the level of political risk varies by company. Companies with good ties to local power groups (such as via the prime minister's brother-in-law's cousin) face less risk of expropriation and other forms of risk affected by government actions.

7. For an example of an industry analysis, see George S. Yip and George A. Coundouriotis, "Diagnosing Global Strategy Potential: The World Chocolate Confectionary Industry," *Planning Review*, January/February 1991, pp. 4–14.

8. There are now many guides on how to collect competitive intelligence. See, for example, Leonard Fuld, *Competitor Intelligence: How to Get It—How to Use It* (New York: John Wiley, 1985).

9. A religion involves adoption and application of dogma in all situations, while a philosophy means an adherence to a set of principles that are used as guidelines for decision making. I thank Trevor Pardoe, Managing Director—United Kingdom, and manufacturing coordinator—Europe, Glitsch International, division of Foster-Wheeler, Inc., for this idea and the definitions.

Appendix

Worksheets for Evaluating Core Strategy

EXHIBIT A–1   Specification of Core Business Strategy

BUSINESS_____

REGION/COUNTRY_____

Date Completed_____

1. BUSINESS DEFINITION

The essence of both business definition and strategy formulation is choice. By defining your business in a certain way, you are choosing to do some things and not others. Similarly a strategy involves selecting certain customer groups and not others, offering some types of products and not others, and so on. MENTION ANY CHANGES THAT YOU PLAN TO MAKE IN YOUR BUSINESS DEFINITION, for example, shift from one type of customer to another type.

Customer Needs Addressed:

_____

Technologies Used:

_____

_____

Customer Segments Served:

_____

_____

_____

Products Offered:

_____

_____

_____

Geographic Scope

_____

2. STRATEGIC THRUST

State whether you are trying to grow, maintain, or shrink the size of this business and at what rate.

State your short-term performance priorities in terms of market share, revenues, and profitability.

Direction:

Rate:

Performance Priorities:

1st _____

2nd _____

3rd _____

3. FINANCIAL TARGETS

4. SOURCES OF COMPETITIVE ADVANTAGE

State your major sources of competitive advantage. These sources both must be important to customers and must give you a significant advantage over competitors. The following list provides categories of advantage—you need to add more detail to the ones you specify:

- Patents
- Research capability
- Development capability
- Product or service quality
- Alignment of offerings with critical needs of customers
- Breadth of product line
- Customer relationships
- Access to lower cost or more effective factors of production
- Location of manufacturing near customers or sources of supply
- Unique manufacturing technology
- Vertical integration
- Operating efficiency
- Access to distribution channels
- Physical distribution capability
- Marketing skills
- Reputation of company
- Strength of brand name
- Sales force effectiveness
- Technical support strength
- Customer service
- Government support or protection
- Size of business
- Superior financial resources
- Lower-cost finance
- Cross-business synergy
- Corporate support

Describe in order of importance your most important sources of competitive advantage:

_____

_____

_____

_____

_____

5. STRATEGY ELEMENTS

For each strategy element, specify the nature of your strategy.

Technology:

_____

_____

Manufacturing:

_____

_____

Product Line:

_____

_____

Pricing:

_____

_____

Selling Approach:

_____

_____

Marketing Communications:

_____

_____

Distribution:

_____

_____

Customer Service:

_____

_____

6. VALUE-ADDING ACTIVITIES

Specify the location of each value-adding activity in your business. Examples of value-adding activities include

- Research
- Development
- Procurement
- Raw material processing
- Intermediate production/subassembly
- Final production/final assembly
- Marketing
- Selling
- Distribution
- Customer service

Activity   Location

_____   _____

_____   _____

_____   _____

_____   _____

_____   _____

_____   _____

7. COMPETITIVE STRATEGY

Identify your major competitors and specify your strategy versus each of them. Examples of competitive strategy are

- To keep competitor A as the second choice vendor by maintaining closer relationships with our customers
- To be a fast follower of innovations by competitor B
- To avoid head-to-head price competition with competitor C
- To restrict competitor D to its current segment of customers
- To gain 5 points of share in the next three years from competitor E

Competitor	Strategy vs. Competitor
_____	_____
_____	_____
_____	_____
_____	_____
_____	_____
_____	_____
_____	_____
_____	_____
_____	_____

STRATEGY / MARKETS	Region A	Region B	Region C	Region D	Region E
1. BUSINESS DEFINITION					
Customer Needs					
Technology					
Segments					
Products					
Geographic Scope					
2. BUSINESS STRATEGIC THRUST					
Direction					
Rate					
Priorities					
3. FINANCIAL TARGETS					
4. SOURCES OF COMPETITVE ADVANTAGE					
5. STRATEGY ELEMENTS					
Technology					
Manufacturing					
Marketing					
Other					

EXHIBIT A–2   Chart for Comparing Core Strategies

STRATEGY \ MARKETS	Region A	Region B	Region C	Region D	Region E
6. VALUE-ADDING ACTIVITIES					
Research					
Development					
Procurement					
Raw Material Processing*					
Intermediate Production*					
Final Production*					
Marketing					
Selling					
Distribution*					
Customer Service*					
7. COMPETITIVE STRATEGY					
Competitor A					
Competitor B					
Competitor C					
Competitor D					

* For service businesses use Production Operations, Support Operations, and Delivery Operations instead.

EXHIBIT A–2 continued   Chart for Comparing Core Strategies

Bibliography

Abegglen, James C., and George Stalk, Jr., *Kaisha: The Japanese Corporation.* New York: Basic Books, 1985.

Abell, Derek F., *Defining the Business: The Starting Point of Strategic Planning.* Englewood Cliffs, N.J.: Prentice Hall, 1980.

Advertising Age, various issues.

Aguilar, Francis J., and Michael Y. Yoshino, "The Philips Group: 1987," Case No. 9-388-050. Boston: Harvard Business School, 1988.

Baden Fuller, C., C. P. Nicolaides, and J. M. Stopford, "National or Global? The Study of Company Strategies and the European Market for Major Appliances," *London Business School Centre for Business Strategy,* Working Paper Series, No. 28, 1987.

Baldwin, Carliss Y., "The Capital Factor: Competing for Capital in a Global Environment," in *Competition in Global Industries,* ed. Michael E. Porter. Boston: Harvard Business School Press, 1986.

Bartlett, Christopher A., and Sumantra Ghoshal, "Matrix Management: Not a Structure, a Frame of Mind," *Harvard Business Review,* July–August 1990, pp. 138–145.

Bartlett, Christopher A., and Sumantra Ghoshal, *Managing Across Borders: The Transnational Solution.* Boston: Harvard Business School Press, 1989.

Bartlett, Christopher A., and Sumantra Ghoshal, "Managing Across Borders: New Strategic Requirements," *Sloan Management Review,* Summer 1987, pp. 7–17.

Bartlett, Christopher A., Yves L. Doz, and Gunnar Hedlund, eds., *Managing the Global Firm*. London: Routledge, 1990.

Beamish, Paul W., J. Peter Killing, Donald J. Lecraw, and Harold Crookell, *International Management: Text and Cases*. Homewood, Ill.: Richard D. Irwin, 1991.

Behrman, Jack N., and William A. Fischer, "Transnational Corporations: Market Orientations and R&D Abroad," *Columbia Journal of World Business*, Fall 1980, pp. 55–60.

Boddewyn, Jean J., Robin Soehl, and Jacques Picard, "Standardization in International Marketing: Is Ted Levitt in Fact Right?" *Business Horizons*, Vol. 29, November–December 1986, pp. 69–75.

Buckley, Peter J., "The Theory of the Multinational Enterprise," *Acta Universitatis Upsaliensis, Studia Oeconomiae Negotiorum* 26 (Uppsala, Sweden), 1987.

Buckley, Peter J., and Mark Casson, *The Future of the Multinational Enterprise*. New York: Holmes and Meier, 1976.

Burggraeve, Chris C., "Meeting Product Standards in the Single Market," *The Journal of European Business*, May–June 1990, pp. 22–26.

Business Asia, various issues.

Business International, various issues.

Business Month, various issues.

Business Week, various issues.

Buzzell, Robert D., "Citibank: Marketing to Multinational Customers," Case No. 9–584–016. Boston: Harvard Business School, 1984, revised 1/85.

Buzzell, Robert D., "Can You Standardize Multinational Marketing?" *Harvard Business Review*, November–December 1968, pp. 102–113.

Buzzell, Robert D., and Bradley T. Gale, *The PIMS Principles: Linking Strategy to Performance*. New York: The Free Press, 1987.

Buzzell, Robert D., Bradley T. Gale, and R. G. M. Sultan, "Market Share—A Key to Profitability," *Harvard Business Review*, January–February 1975, pp. 97–106.

Cecchini, Paolo, *The European Challenge: 1992, The Benefits of a Single Market*. London, England: Wildwood House, 1988.

Chakravarthy, Balaji S., and Howard V. Perlmutter, "Strategic Planning for a Global Business," *Columbia Journal of World Business*, Summer 1985, pp. 3–10.

Chandler, Alfred D., Jr., *Strategy and Structure*. Cambridge, Mass.: The M.I.T. Press, 1962.

Clee, G. H., and A. di Scipio, "Creating a World Enterprise," *Harvard Business Review*, November–December 1959, pp. 77–89.

Clee, G. H., and W. M. Sachtjen, "Organizing a Worldwide Business," *Harvard Business Review*, November–December 1964, pp. 55–67.

Collis, David J., "Saatchi and Saatchi Company, PLC," Case No. 1-387-170. Boston: Harvard Business School, 1986.

Contractor, Farok J., and Peter Lorange, *Cooperative Strategies in International Business*. Lexington, Mass.: Lexington Books, 1988.

Cvar, Marquise R., "Case Studies in Global Competition: Patterns of Success and Failure," in *Competition in Global Industries*, ed. Michael E. Porter. Boston: Harvard Business School Press, 1986, pp. 483–516.

Czinkota, Michael R., Pietra Rivoli, and Ilkka A. Ronkainen, *International Business*. Chicago: The Dryden Press, 1989.

Daniels, J. D., R. A. Pitts, and M. J. Tretter, "Strategy and Structure of U.S. Multinationals: An Exploratory Study," *Academy of Management Journal*, Vol. 27, 1984, pp. 292–307.

Davidson, William H., *Global Strategic Management*. New York: John Wiley, 1982.

Davidson, William H., and José de la Torre, *Managing the Global Corporation: Case Studies in Strategy and Management*. New York: McGraw-Hill, 1989.

Davidson, William H., and Philippe Haspeslagh, "Shaping a Global Product Organization," *Harvard Business Review*, July–August 1982, pp. 125–132.

de Meyer, Arnold, Jinichiro Nakane, Jeffrey Miller, and Kasra Ferdows, "Flexibility: The Next Competitive Battle—The Manufacturing Futures Survey," *Strategic Management Journal*, Vol. 10, 1989, pp. 135–144.

Dess, G., and P. Davis, "Porter's (1980) Generic Strategies as Determinants of Strategic Group Membership and Organizational Performance," *Academy of Management Journal*, Vol. 27, 1984, pp. 467–488.

Dicken, Peter, *Global Shift: Industrial Change in a Turbulent World*. London: Harper & Row, 1986.

Dornbush, Rudiger, Stanley Fisher, and Paul A. Samuelson, "Comparative Advantage, Trade and Payments in a Ricardian Model with a Continuum of Goods," *American Economic Review*, Vol. 67, December 1977, pp. 823–839.

Douglas, Susan P., and C. Samuel Craig, "Evolution of Global Marketing Strategy: Scale, Scope and Synergy," *Columbia Journal of World Business*, Fall 1989, pp. 47–57.

Douglas, Susan P., and C. Samuel Craig, "Examining Performance of U.S. Multinationals in Foreign Markets," *Journal of International Business Studies*, Winter 1983, pp. 51–57.

Douglas, Susan P., and C. Samuel Craig, *International Marketing Research*. Englewood Cliffs, N.J.: Prentice Hall, 1983.

Douglas, Susan P., and Yoram Wind, "The Myth of Globalization," *Columbia Journal of World Business*, Vol. 22, No. 4, Winter 1987, pp. 19–29.

Doz, Yves L., *Government Control and Multinational Management*. New York: Praeger, 1979.

Doz, Yves L., "Managing Manufacturing Rationalization Within Multinational Companies," *Columbia Journal of World Business*, Fall 1978, pp. 82–94.

Dunn, S. W. "Effect of National Identity on Multinational Promotional Strategy in Europe," *Journal of Marketing*, October 1976, pp. 50–57.

Dunning, John H., "The Eclectic Paradigm of International Production: A Restatement and Some Possible Extensions," *Journal of International Business Studies*, Spring 1988, pp. 1–31.

Dyment, John J. "Strategies and Management Controls for Global Corporations," *Journal of Business Strategy*, Spring 1987, pp. 20–26.

Eccles, Robert G., *The Transfer Pricing Decision*. Lexington, Mass.: Lexington Books, 1985.

Egelhoff, William G., "Strategy and Structure in Multinational Corporations: A Revision of the Stopford and Wells Model," *Strategic Management Journal*, Vol. 9, 1988, pp. 1–14.

Egelhoff, William G., "Patterns of Control in U.S., U.K. and European Multinational Corporations," *Journal of International Business Studies*, Fall 1984, pp. 73–83.

Egelhoff, William G., "Strategy and Structure in Multinational Corporations: An Information Processing Approach," *Administrative Science Quarterly*, Vol. 27, 1982, pp. 435–458.

Enrico, Roger, and Jesse Kornbluth, *The Other Guy Blinked: How Pepsi Won the Cola Wars*. New York: Bantam Books, 1986.

Farley, Laurence J. "Going Global: Choices and Challenges," *Journal of Business Strategy*, Vol. 1, Winter 1986, pp. 67–70.

Ferdows, Kasra, "Mapping International Factory Networks," in *Managing International Manufacturing*, ed. Kasra Ferdows. Amsterdam: Elsevier Science (North Holland), 1989.

Ferdows, Kasra, et al., *The Internationalization of U.S. Manufacturing: Causes and Consequences*. Washington, D.C.: National Academy Press, 1990.

Flaherty, M. Therese, "Coordinating International Manufacturing and Technology," in *Competition in Global Industries*, ed. Michael E. Porter. Boston: Harvard Business School Press, 1986.

Forbes, various issues.

Fortune, various issues.

Fouraker, Lawrence E., and John M. Stopford, "Organization Structure and Multinational Strategy," *Administrative Science Quarterly*, Vol. 13, 1968, pp. 57–70.

Franko, Larry G., "Organizational Structures and Multinational Strategies of Continental European Enterprises," in *European Research in International Business*, eds. M. Ghertman and J. Leontiades. Amsterdam: North Holland, 1978.

Franko, Larry G., *The European Multinationals*. Greenwich, Conn.: Greylock Press, 1976.

Fuld, Leonard, *Competitor Intelligence: How to Get It—How to Use It*. New York: John Wiley, 1985.

George, Abraham M., and C. William Schroth, "Managing Foreign Exchange for Competitive Advantage," *Sloan Management Review*, Winter 1991, pp. 105–116.

Ghemawat, Pankaj, *Commitment: The Dynamic of Strategy*. Boston: Harvard Business School Press, 1991.

Ghoshal, Sumantra, "Global Strategy: An Organizing Framework," *Strategic Management Journal*, Vol. 8, No. 5, September–October 1987, pp. 425–440.

Goldhar, Joel D., and Mariann Jelinek, "Computer Integrated Flexible Manufacturing: Organizational, Economic, and Strategic Implications," *Interfaces*, Vol. 15, May–June 1985, pp. 94–105.

Hamel, Gary, and C. K. Prahalad, "Do You Really Have a Global Strategy?" *Harvard Business Review*, July–August 1985, pp. 139–148.

Hamermesh, Richard G., *Making Strategy Work: How Senior Managers Produce Results*. New York: John Wiley, 1986.

Harrigan, Kathryn R. *Managing for Joint Venture Success*. Lexington Mass.: Lexington Books, 1986.

Haspeslagh, Philippe, "Portfolio Planning: Uses and Limits," *Harvard Business Review*, January–February 1982, pp. 58–73.

Hatsopoulos, George N., "High Cost of Capital: Handicap of American Industry," report sponsored by the American Business Conference and Thermo-Electron Corporation, April 1983.

Hax, Arnoldo C., and Nicolas S. Majluf, *Strategic Management: An Integrative Perspective*. Englewood Cliffs, N.J.: Prentice Hall, 1984.

Henzler, Herbert, and Wilhelm Rall, "Facing Up to the Globalization Challenge," *The McKinsey Quarterly*, Winter 1986, pp. 52–68.

Hill, J. S., and R. R. Still, "Adapting Products to LDC Tastes," *Harvard Business Review*, March–April 1984, pp. 92–101.

Hirschey, Robert C., and Richard E. Caves, "Research and Transfer of Technology by Multinational Enterprises," *Oxford Bulletin of Economics and Statistics*, Vol. 43, No. 2, May 1981, pp. 115–130.

Hofstede, Geert, *Culture's Consequences: International Differences in Work-Related Values*. Beverly Hills, Calif.: Sage Publications, 1984.

Hout, Thomas, Michael E. Porter, and Eileen Rudden, "How Global Companies Win Out." *Harvard Business Review*, September–October 1982, pp. 98–108.

Jaikumar, Ramchandran, "Postindustrial Manufacturing," *Harvard Business Review*, November–December 1986, pp. 69–76.

Jain, Subhash C., "Standardization of International Marketing Strategy: Some Research Hypotheses," *Journal of Marketing*, Vol. 53, January 1989, pp. 70–79.

Japan Times, various issues.

Jeelof, Gerrit, "Global Strategies of Philips," *European Management Journal*, Vol. 7, No. 1, 1989, pp. 84–91.

Johansson, Johny K., "Determinants and Effects of 'Made in' Labels," *International Marketing Review*, Vol. 6, No. 1, Spring 1989, pp. 47–58.

Kacker, M. P. "Patterns of Marketing Adaptation in International Business," *Management International Review*, Vol. 12, issues 4–5, 1972, pp. 111–118.

Kacker, M. P. "Export Oriented Product Adaptation," *Management International Review*, Vol. 6, 1975, pp. 61–70.

Kashani, Kamran, "Beware the Pitfalls of Global Marketing," *Harvard Business Review*, September–October 1989, pp. 91–98.

Kashani, Kamran, and John A. Quelch, "Can Sales Promotion Go Global?" *Business Horizons*, Vol. 33, No. 3, May–June 1990, pp. 37–43.

Keegan, Warren J., *Multinational Marketing Management*, 4th ed. Englewood Cliffs, N.J.: Prentice Hall, 1989.

Kester, W. Carl, and Timothy A. Luehrman, "Are We Feeling More Competitive Yet? The Exchange Rate Gambit," *Sloan Management Review*, Winter 1989, pp. 19–28.

Kogut, Bruce, "Joint Ventures: Theoretical and Empirical Perspectives," *Strategic Management Journal*, Vol. 9, No. 4, July–August 1988, pp. 319–332.

Kogut, Bruce, "Designing Global Strategies: Comparative and Competitive Value-Added Chains," *Sloan Management Review*, Summer 1985, pp. 27–38. (a)

Kogut, Bruce, "Designing Global Strategies: Profiting from Operational Flexibility," *Sloan Management Review*, Fall 1985, pp. 27–38. (b)

Kotabe, Masaaki, and Glenn S. Omura, "Sourcing Strategies of European and Japanese Multinationals: A Comparison," *Journal of International Business Studies*, Vol. 20, No. 1, Spring 1989, pp. 113–130.

Kotler, Philip, *Marketing Management*. Englewood Cliffs, N.J.: Prentice Hall, 1984.

Kotler, Philip, Liam Fahey, and S. Jatusripitak, *The New Competition*. Englewood Cliffs, N.J.: Prentice Hall, 1985.

Kotler, Philip, and Ravi Singh, "Marketing Warfare in the 1980s," *Journal of Business Strategy*, Vol. 1, No. 3, Winter 1981.

Lessard, Donald R., "Finance and Global Competition: Exploiting Financial Scope and Coping with Volatile Exchange Rates," in *Competition in Global Industries*, ed. Michael Porter. Boston: Harvard Business School Press, 1986.

Levitt, Theodore, "The Globalization of Markets," *Harvard Business Review*, May–June 1983, pp. 92–102.

Lewis, Geoff, "Carlton & United Breweries," in *Cases in Australian Management*, eds. Geoff Lewis and Peter Fitzroy. Sidney: Prentice Hall, 1991.

Lindblom, Charles E., *The Policy-Making Process*. Englewood Cliffs, N.J.: Prentice Hall, 1968.

Lorange, Peter, *Implementation of Strategic Planning*. Englewood Cliffs, N.J.: Prentice Hall, 1982.

Management Analysis Center, *Implementing Strategy*, ed. Paul J. Stonich. Cambridge, Mass.: Ballinger, 1982.

Management Europe, various issues.

Management Today, various issues.

Markides, Constantinos C., and Norman Berg, "Manufacturing Offshore Is Bad Business," *Harvard Business Review*, September–October 1988, pp. 113–120.

Martinez, Jon I., and J. Carlos Jarillo, "The Evolution of Research on Coordination Mechanisms in Multinational Corporations," *Journal of International Business Studies*, Vol. 20, No. 3, Fall 1989, pp. 489–514.

McCormick, Janice, and Nan Stone, "From National Champion to Global Competitor: An Interview with Thomson's Alain Gomez," *Harvard Business Review*, May–June 1990, pp. 127–135.

McGee, John F., "1992: Moves Americans Must Make," *Harvard Business Review*, May–June 1989, pp. 78–84.

Mintzberg, Henry, *The Nature of Managerial Work*. New York: Harper & Row, 1973.

Morrison, Allen J., *Strategies in Global Industries: How U.S. Businesses Compete*. Westport, Conn.: Quorum Books, 1990.

New York Times, various issues.

Ohmae, Kenichi, *The Borderless World: Power and Strategy in the Interlinked Economy*. New York: Harper Business, 1990.

Ohmae, Kenichi, *Triad Power: The Coming Shape of Global Competition*. New York: The Free Press, 1985.

Ohmae, Kenichi, *The Mind of the Strategist*. New York: McGraw-Hill, 1982.

Ouchi, William G., *Theory Z: How American Business Can Meet the Japanese Challenge*. Reading, Mass.: Addison-Wesley, 1981.

Pascale, Richard Tanner, and Anthony G. Athos, *The Art of Japanese Management: Applications for American Executives*. New York: Simon & Schuster, 1981.

Perlmutter, Howard V., "The Tortuous Evolution of the Multinational Corporation," *Columbia Journal of World Business*, January–February 1969, pp. 9–18.

Pierson, Robert M., "R&D by Multi-Nationals for Overseas Markets," *Research Management*, July 1978, pp. 19–22.

Porter, Michael E., *The Competitive Advantage of Nations*. New York: The Free Press, 1990.

Porter, Michael E., "Changing Patterns of International Competition," *California Management Review*, Vol. 28, No. 2, Winter 1986, pp. 9–40.

Porter, Michael E., "Competition in Global Industries: A Conceptual Framework," in *Competition in Global Industries*, ed. Michael E. Porter. Boston: Harvard Business School Press, 1986.

Porter, Michael E., *Competitive Advantage: Creating and Sustaining Superior Performance*. New York: The Free Press, 1985.

Porter, Michael E., *Competitive Strategy: Techniques for Analyzing Industries and Competitors*. New York: The Free Press, 1980.

Prahalad, C. K., "The Strategic Process in a Multinational Corporation," unpublished doctoral dissertation. Cambridge, Mass.: Harvard Business School, 1975.

Prahalad, C. K., and Yves L. Doz, *The Multinational Mission: Balancing Local Demands and Global Vision*. New York: The Free Press, 1987.

Prahalad, C. K., and Yves L. Doz, "An Approach to Strategic Control on MNCs," *Sloan Management Review*, Summer 1981, pp. 5–13.

Prestowitz, Clyde V., Jr., *Trading Places*. New York: Basic Books, 1988.

Quelch, John A., "British Airways: Teaching Note," No. 5-587-016. Boston: Harvard Business School, 1987.

Quelch, John A., Robert D. Buzzell, and Eric R. Salama, *The Marketing Challenge of 1992*. Reading, Mass.: Addison-Wesley, 1990.

Quelch, John A., and Edward J. Hoff, "Customizing Global Marketing," *Harvard Business Review*, May–June 1986, pp. 59–68.

Quinn, James Brian, "Strategic Goals: Process and Politics," *Sloan Management Review*, Fall 1977, p. 22

Rau, Pradeep A., and John F. Preble, "Standardization of Marketing Strategy by Multinationals," *International Marketing Review*, Autumn 1987, pp. 18–28.

Ronstadt, Robert, and Robert J. Kramer, "Getting the Most Out of Innovation Abroad," *Harvard Business Review*, March–April 1982, pp. 94–99.

Root, Franklin R., *Entry Strategies for International Markets*. Lexington, Mass.: D. C. Heath, 1987.

Rosen, Barry Nathan, Jean J. Boddewyn, and Ernst A. Louis, "Participation by U.S. Agencies in International Brand Advertising: An Empirical Study," *Journal of Advertising*, Vol. 17, No. 4, 1988, pp. 14–22.

Roth, Kendall, and Allen J. Morrison, "An Empirical Analysis of the Integration-Responsiveness Framework in Global Industries," *Journal of International Business Studies*, Vol. 21, No. 4, Fourth Quarter 1990, pp. 541–564.

Rugman, Alan M., *International Diversification and the Multinational Enterprise*, Lexington, Mass.: Lexington Books, D. C. Heath, 1979.

Rugman, Alan M., "The Corporate Performance of U.S. and European Multinational Enterprises, 1970–79," *Management International Review*, Vol. 23, No. 2, 1983, pp. 4–14.

Rumelt, Richard P., and Robin Wensley, "In Search of the Market Share Effect," *Proceedings*, Academy of Management Annual Meeting, 1981, pp. 2–6.

Segal-Horn, Susan, and John McGee, "Strategies to Cope with Retailer Buying Power," in *Retail and Marketing Channels*, eds. Luca Pellegrini and Arinivas K. Reddy. London: Routledge, 1989.

Shanks, David C., "Strategic Planning for Global Competition," *Journal of Business Strategy*, Winter 1985, pp. 80–89.

Skinner, Wickham, *Manufacturing: The Formidable Weapon.* New York: John Wiley, 1985.

Sorenson, Ralph Z., and Ulrich E. Wiechmann, "How Multinationals View Marketing Standardization," *Harvard Business Review,* May–June 1975, pp. 38–167.

Spence, A. Michael, "Industrial Organization and Competitive Advantage in Multinational Industries," *American Economic Review,* Vol. 74, No. 2, May 1984, pp. 356–360.

Spence, A. Michael, "Entry, Capacity, Investment and Oligopolistic Pricing," *Bell Journal of Economics,* Vol. 8, Autumn 1977, pp. 534–544.

Steiner, George A., *Strategic Planning: What Every Manager Must Know.* New York: The Free Press, 1979.

Stopford, John M., and Louis T. Wells, Jr., *Managing the Multinational Enterprise.* New York: Basic Books, 1972.

Takeuchi, Hirotaka, and Michael E. Porter, "Three Roles of International Marketing in Global Strategy," in *Competition in Global Industries,* ed. Michael E. Porter. Boston: Harvard Business School Press, 1986.

The Economist, various issues.

Vancil, Richard F., and Peter Lorange, "Strategic Planning in Diversified Companies," *Harvard Business Review,* January–February 1975.

Vernon, Raymond, *Storm over the Multinationals.* Cambridge, Mass.: Harvard University Press, 1977.

Vernon, Raymond, and Louis T. Wells, *Manager in the International Economy.* Englewood Cliffs, N.J.: Prentice Hall, 1986.

The Wall Street Journal, various issues.

Walters, Peter G. P., "International Marketing Policy: A Discussion of the Standardization Construct and Its Relevance for Corporate Policy," *Journal of International Business Studies,* Summer 1986, pp. 55–69.

White, Roderick E., "Generic Business Strategies, Organizational Context and Performance: An Empirical Investigation," *Strategic Management Journal,* Vol. 7, 1986, pp. 217–231.

White, Roderick E., and Thomas A. Poynter, "Strategies for Foreign-Owned Subsidiaries in Canada," *Business Quarterly,* Summer 1984, pp. 59–69.

White, Roderick E., and Thomas A. Poynter, "Organizing for Worldwide Advantage," in *Managing the Global Firm,* eds. Christopher A. Bartlett, Yves L. Doz, and Gunnar Hedlund. London: Routledge, 1990.

Woo, Carolyn Y., and Karel Cool, "Porter's (1980) Generic Strategies: A Test of Performance and Functional Strategy Attributes," Working Paper, Purdue University, 1983.

Yip, George S., "A Performance Comparison of Continental and National Businesses in Europe," *International Marketing Review,* Vol. 8, No. 2, 1991, pp. 31–39.

Yip, George S., "Do American Businesses Use Global Strategy?" Working Paper No. 91-101. Cambridge, Mass.: Marketing Science Institute, January 1991.

Yip, George S., "Global Strategy . . . In a World of Nations?" *Sloan Management Review,* Vol. 31, No. 1, Fall 1989, pp. 29–41.

Yip, George S., "An Integrated Approach to Global Competitive Strategy," in *Frontiers of Management Research and Practice,* ed. Roger Mansfield. London: Routledge, 1989.

Yip, George S., "Who Needs Strategic Planning?" *The Journal of Business Strategy*, Vol. 6, No. 2, Fall 1985, pp. 30–42.

Yip, George S., "Planning at Pepsi (B)," Case No. 9-583-051. Boston: Harvard Business School, 1983.

Yip, George S., "Gateways to Entry," *Harvard Business Review*, September–October 1982, pp. 85–92.

Yip, George S., and George A. Coundouriotis, "Diagnosing Global Strategy Potential: The World Chocolate Confectionery Industry," *Planning Review*, January–February 1991, pp. 4–14.

Yip, George S., Pierre M. Loewe, and Michael Y. Yoshino, "How to Take Your Company to the Global Market," *Columbia Journal of World Business*, Winter 1988, pp. 37–48.

Yoffie, David B., and Helen V. Milner, "An Alternative to Free Trade or Protectionism: Why Corporations Seek Strategic Trade Policy," *California Management Review*, Summer 1989, pp. 111–131.

Yoshino, M. Y., "Global Competition in a Salient Industry: The Case of Civil Aircraft," in *Competition in Global Industries*, ed. Michael E. Porter. Boston: Harvard Business School Press, 1986, pp. 517–538.

Yunker, Penelope J., "A Survey Study of Subsidiary Autonomy, Performance Evaluation and Transfer Pricing in Multinational Corporations," *Columbia Journal of World Business*, Fall 1983, pp. 51–64.

Index